# The Soul of Discernment

# The Soul of Discernment

## A Spiritual Practice
## for Communities and Institutions

Elizabeth Liebert, SNJM

WESTMINSTER
JOHN KNOX PRESS
LOUISVILLE · KENTUCKY

© 2015 Elizabeth Liebert

*First Edition*
Published by Westminster John Knox Press
Louisville, Kentucky

15 16 17 18 19 20 21 22 23 24—10 9 8 7 6 5 4 3 2 1

*Book design by Sharon Adams*
*Cover design by Mark Abrams*
*Cover illustration © Svilen Milev/www.efffective.com*

**Library of Congress Cataloging-in-Publication Data**
Liebert, Elizabeth, 1944–
  The soul of discernment : a spiritual practice for communities and institutions / Elizabeth Liebert, SNJM. — First edition.
    pages cm
  Includes bibliographical references.
  ISBN 978-0-664-23967-1 (alk. paper)
  1. Discernment (Christian theology) 2. Decision making—Social aspects.
3. Decision making—Religious aspects—Christianity. I. Title.
  BV4509.5.L536 2015
  261—dc23

                                              2014049522

∞ The paper used in this publication meets the minimum requirements
of the American National Standard for Information Sciences—Permanence
of Paper for Printed Library Materials, ANSI Z39.48-1992.

Most Westminster John Knox Press books are available at special quantity discounts
when purchased in bulk by corporations, organizations, and special-interest groups.
For more information, please e-mail SpecialSales@wjkbooks.com.

# Contents

# Practices

# Acknowledgments

Gratitude is an appropriate way to launch this work. Chief among those who set me on the journey to this book are Brother John Mostyn, CFC, and Nancy Wiens; each of your creative visions for the Social Discernment Cycle has influenced this latest iteration, but you are also built into its very foundation. San Francisco Theological Seminary granted me the sabbatical leave to commit this process to writing, and the Collegeville Institute of Ecumenical and Cultural Relations provided the physical and psychological space to actually write down the work of the last twenty years. My colleagues in both of these institutions provided incredible hospitality, encouragement, and challenge through the birth of the original manuscript. To three trusted and generous colleagues, Rebecca Bradburn Langer, Kenton W. Smith, and Sharon Latour, my deep gratitude for reading and commenting on an early draft and saving me from obscurity in any number of places. To Barbara, Barbara Anne, and John, thanks for accompanying me, each in your own way. Thanks also to David Dobson and all the crew at Westminster John Knox Press for shepherding this book so skillfully through its production.

To all those groups and individuals whom I have had the privilege of presenting and accompanying through the Social Discernment Cycle, thank you for sharing your process and the incredible fruit you so frequently received as a result of the process. You kept me going year after year, in the expectation of more fruits. Among this group, I count the Sisters of the Holy Names of Jesus and Mary and Holy Names University, Oakland, California, whose marvelous diversity challenged my presentation of the Social Discernment Cycle in fresh ways and taught me far more than I taught you.

Some of the people who deserve thanks are no longer present with us: Stephanie Egnotovich, editor extraordinaire, who lived until she died too soon, and Mary Garvin, SNJM, who continues to spread her wisdom around. I didn't talk much about this work with either of you, but you would have understood and blessed it

# Introduction

"*H*ow are we to live our lives thoughtfully and faithfully in the midst of all the forces, options, and decisions that characterize modern life? Discernment, the Christian practice of seeking God's call in the midst of the decisions that mark one's life, may very well be the single most important Christian spiritual practice for dealing with this contemporary dilemma." So begins *The Way of Discernment: Spiritual Practices for Decision Making*.[1] There, I proposed that it is possible not only to become acquainted with various forms of discernment from the long history of Christian spirituality, but also, more importantly, to discover practices that work particularly well for you as you discern decisions that arise in your own life. This book is designed as a sequel. Here, the practice of discernment is extended from one's personal life to the various institutions and systems in which we all live.

Throughout the pages of this book, you will engage in the Social Discernment Cycle. It merits the term *discernment* because it is a process for seeking God's call in a particular situation. It is called *social* because it deals primarily with human communities in their social-structural, rather than interpersonal, aspects. It is a *cycle* because one completed round of discernment prepares for the next. The Social Discernment Cycle is particularly apt for any discernment that involves a structure, system, or institution. For example, the Social Discernment Cycle could guide decision makers about whether one institution should merge with another. It could also assist individual persons within the merging institutions to determine how they are called to respond in the midst of these transitions.

I envision multiple types of readers for this book, all of whom dwelt in my imagination as I was writing. Some of you are seeking fresh, faith-grounded ways to approach a decision you are about to make, one that is set in the context of some structure, organization, or institution. Some of you may feel stuck in some structure and need to find breathing room. Some may have found *Way of Discernment* useful and want to extend its perspective from personal discernment to discerning with and in large or small structures. Pastors and spiritual directors, you may find a fresh way to help your parishioners and directees when these seekers bring institutions into your pastoral conversations. I envision leaders of institutions, pastors, chairs of nonprofit boards, and leaders of faith-based organizations turning to Social Discernment for ways to assist your organization to move together into God's future. Finally, I also imagine that those of you who are preparing for pastoral, clinical, or spiritual direction ministries see Social Discernment as a way to minister to the systems and structures that will inhabit your ministries whether you invite them to or not. I hope you take the Social Discernment Cycle into your future pastoral planning.

How is God leading me to act in this particular situation? serves as the guiding question in the first volume. Here, the focus shifts from individual persons to persons in systems, so the question shifts accordingly: How is God leading *us, individually or together,* to act in this particular moment in *our organization*? Rather than offer a variety of processes from which to choose those that fit your personal circumstances and personality, as in the earlier volume, this book focuses on a single more extensive process, called the Social Discernment Cycle or, more simply, Social Discernment. Its multiple steps will make up individual chapters in part 2.

Why this turn? Groups of faithful Christians have always used the best insights of their day and combined them with the wisdom they inherited from the past to develop ways of discerning that meet the needs of their situation. Today institutions and structures are far more complex than those envisioned in the communal discernment practices gleaned from the long history of Christian discernment. In fact, say the authors of *Presence: Human Purpose and the Field of the Future,* the appearance of structures on a global scale is tantamount to the emergence of a new species on earth.[2] Prior to the last one hundred years, there were few examples of globe-spanning institutions. But today, global institutions are proliferating, overwhelming existing cultures, languages, currencies, and means of communication. Even in the close-to-home structures of family, school, workplace, church, and local community, the complexities are often puzzling and our attempts to move these structures forward in mutually beneficial ways stymied. Our political systems today seem forever bogged down in partisan politics. Our economic arrangements are replete with contradictions. We experience a growing distance between the economically advantaged few and a disadvantaged large majority. We face immense structural problems exacerbated by globalization and an ecological crisis that is not easily repaired. Yet our individual actions are mediated and magnified by such structures. What are we to do in the face of such complexities?

The way things are now is not the way they have to be in the future. The good can grow and the destructive can shrink. To move in the direction of the good, it is crucial that our institutions mediate grace, that is, grow the good. By employing an effective institution, we can magnify our power to assist in this transformation far beyond what one individual can do.[3] For example, we can ease the growing disparity between those at the top of the economic ladder and those at the bottom if we adjust the tax code to favor those at the bottom, raise the minimum wage, increase educational opportunities, or provide effective and safe child care. The possibilities and the structures for addressing this one situation are many.

The Social Discernment Cycle is designed to address large and small systems, to help us take concrete steps in the face of systemic complexity, be it in one's family, workplace, neighborhood, school, or church, in local or national politics, or in response to the global ecological crisis. The only way we can affect the future is to do the right thing in the present. Social Discernment helps us discern what the "right thing" might be, and, together, take the first step. It helps us make "little moves against destructiveness"[4] as well as "little moves for constructiveness."

Taking our cue from our forebears' penchant for using the insights available to them in their day, this volume weds the theory and practice of discernment to newer tools now available. The Pastoral Circle provides the inner skeleton of the Social Discernment Cycle. This widely used pastoral planning method originated in Europe after the Second World War as the "see-judge-act method." It was further adapted in Latin American liberation theology and finally made widely available in North America by Joe Holland and Peter Henriot in their 1980 volume, *Social Analysis: Linking Faith and Justice*.[5] The Pastoral Circle cues us to look at groups not as simple collections of individuals but as systems, with the behaviors characteristic of systems. It also reminds us that one of discernment's most effective contexts is pastoral planning. I will introduce the Pastoral Circle more extensively below. The increasingly complex structures in which we live our everyday lives also invite us to use disciplines that did not exist when the discernment tradition was taking shape. The social sciences offer one such tool, social analysis, while mathematics offers a second, systems theory. We will employ nontechnical concepts and practices gained from these disciplines to enhance our discernment in and of systems.

There is a certain amount of overlap between this book and its predecessor because I intend each book to stand on its own. Consequently, I introduce discernment again, but I do so here with particular emphasis on group discernment. I reaffirm the necessity of spiritual freedom because seeking God more profoundly than any penultimate outcome is one of the essential qualities of discernment. Spiritual freedom is as elusive in social discernment as in personal discernment—it remains always a gift from God. So we will learn to ask for it over and over throughout the Social Discernment Cycle. We continue to approach our potential decision in an attitude of prayer, even as we are doing hard critical work on analyzing the structure. The notion of confirmation, that pause where we bring everything we have done to God prior to finalizing our decision, appears here again, but now we consider signs that suggest that an *institution* is moving toward the good, as are the individual discerners.

This is also a book to "work." It is one thing to read about Social Discernment and its history, theology, and biblical basis. It is quite another thing to actually discern. Discerners often arrive at an action that is completely surprising to them. But sometimes discerners arrive at the same action that they were contemplating prior to engaging in Social Discernment. In those cases, common sense would suggest that it is a huge waste of time and energy to engage in Social Discernment. Yet, almost to a person, discerners claim that *they* have been changed in the process. As a result of their work in the Social Discernment Cycle, they engage their structure differently, if only in attitude. The good news of Social Discernment: the listening for God that is the heart of discernment can be amply rewarded even if the system appears to change little in the end. Social Discernment can become, then, a privileged way to find God even in places where we might not have thought to look—right in the middle of the often stubborn structures in which we live and work every day.

To facilitate actually doing discernment, each chapter includes a portion of the discernment process in the form of an exercise to do personally or collectively, depending on your situation. I encourage you to engage this portion thoroughly, keeping personal notes or minutes to record the details—whether facts, insights, graces, or struggles—of this step. The process builds upon itself, and a small insight in an earlier step may prove crucial as the process unfolds. So, work the process.

## The Origin of the Social Discernment Cycle

It is important to make clear from the outset that I am not the originator of the Social Discernment Cycle, simply one who has adopted it as central to my work in discernment. It is the focus of a discernment course in the Diploma in the Art of Spiritual Direction at San Francisco Theological Seminary. Other students preparing for ministry may become acquainted with it through one of the spiritual formation courses titled Spiritual Life and Leadership.

The process came to San Francisco Theological Seminary in a 1992 workshop on spirituality and justice cosponsored by the Program in Christian Spirituality. John Mostyn, CFC, and Elinor Shea, OSU, the facilitators of this workshop, were among those at the Center for Spirituality and Justice in the Bronx who struggled through a process of trying to link social justice and spiritual direction. By trial and error, they discovered that they had to develop a whole new way of thinking about humans and the God-human relationship, as well as a new understanding of spiritual direction, in order to establish that linkage. The result of this struggle is what we have come to call the Social Discernment Cycle.[6] The version I use here has had many hands upon it in addition to those of Mostyn and Shea, most notably Maureen Cleary, Nancy Wiens, and the scores of students who have experienced the process in the course of their studies.

The questions that make up the exercises have a theological grounding. Yet no particular question or wording is intrinsic to the process. These questions have been developed to help elicit the underlying movement of the Social Discernment Cycle with sufficient concreteness. Over the years, individual questions have been modified, dropped, and added, as seemed useful. As I prepared this book, I again tweaked both the exercises and the individual questions. The exercises, then, can be tailored to the individual case, perhaps making them much simpler, if simpler will suffice, but also lengthening them or creating new questions to cover complex or idiosyncratic structures. As you become acquainted with the Social Discernment Cycle, you should feel free to make appropriate adaptations. Nonetheless, I owe a tremendous debt to the participants of the Center for Spirituality and Justice, who persevered through trial and error to develop the underlying conditions, theological perspectives, and original questions.

## The Pastoral Circle

The skeleton of the Social Discernment Cycle is the Pastoral Circle as described Joe Holland and Peter Henriot.[7] This process and its graphic representation in figure 1 share similarities with the praxis circle of Paulo Freire and the hermeneutical circle of Juan Luis Segundo. It illustrates the dynamic linkage between "insertion" (location in the system), social analysis, theological reflection, and pastoral planning.

## Figure 1: The Pastoral Circle

Social
Analysis

Theological
Reflection

Experience

Insertion

Pastoral
Planning

From Joe Holland and Peter Henriot, *Social Analysis: Linking Faith and
Justice* (Maryknoll, NY: Orbis Books, 1980), 8. Used with permission.

In adapting the dynamic of the Pastoral Circle to discernment, we have
tweaked the circle somewhat, as illustrated in figure 2. For our purposes,
"Insertion" becomes "Noticing and Describing." What is going on at present, to whom, by whom? Where and with whom are we locating ourselves
as we begin the discernment? At the beginning of the process, we draw near
to the real-life experience with the system, our own and others'. We want
to know what the discerners and others are feeling, thinking, experiencing,
and responding. To use Holland and Henriot's language, we *insert* ourselves
close to the experiences of those involved.

In order to understand these experiences in all their dynamic linkages, we
move to social analysis. Here we examine the causes, consequences, and history of the entity. We identify actors and those acted upon. We look for how
power flows and what kind of power it is. We try to uncover our assumptions
about what counts as useful information for our discernment. Our goal is
to peer through the murkiness of the structure, exposing the various linkages that together constitute the system. Juan José Luna insists that these
first two steps in the Social Discernment Cycle should not be imposed by

people outside the system. Rather, those who are living it should describe and analyze their experiences in order to develop their power within the system, which is especially important for those who may feel they have little or none.[8]

Holland and Henriot's third movement is theological reflection. The Social Discernment Cycle preserves the important task of theological reflection but enfolds it in an element crucial to discernment, namely, prayer. Discerners are invited to bring all that they have uncovered in the social analysis and theological reflection to personal and/or corporate prayer, laying it all out before God. "And this," as one Jesuit student exclaimed when he saw this addition, "makes all the difference" between problem solving and discernment.

Our version of Holland and Henriot's fourth movement shifts from pastoral planning to deciding (discerning) the single first action that our discernment calls us to. It is not enough simply to pray about the structure; in social discernment we are called to take some action within or on the system. What should this action be? How will we know it is the action we are called to make? Who will be the players in this action? How will we assess the action, once taken? Our final three chapters will add considerable detail to this final movement of the Pastoral Circle as Holland and Henriot originally conceived it.

## Figure 2: The Social Discernment Cycle

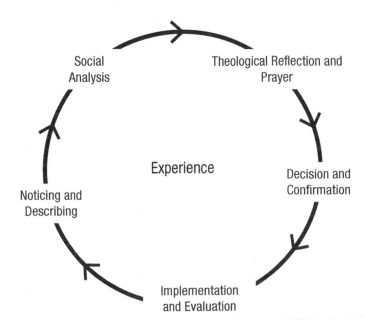

As we move around the circular process, the way we work shifts. As we examine experience, feelings matter immensely, so we seek to notice and reflect on them. Social analysis relies on good hard thinking—which is why folks often complain that this step "isn't spiritual." Theological reflection and prayer shifts us to the heart as we try to respond contemplatively to all that we have learned. Finally, the last movement requires action, with all the accompanying planning, thinking, feeling, and prayer that implementation will require. Figure 3 illustrates these shifts.

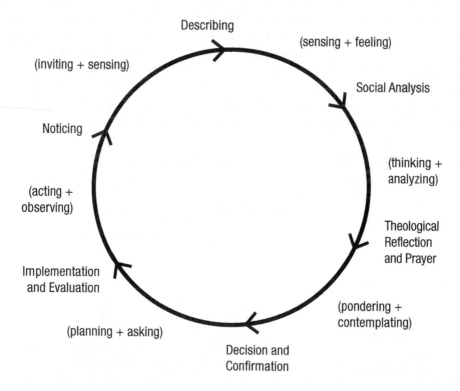

Figure 3: The Social Discernment Cycle
(with Modes of Processing)

This image, however, makes it appear that the circle is closed, that a completed discernment process leads right back where you started. In fact, discernment followed by action always brings about a newly configured structure with a new condition of possibility. In terms of Social Discernment, we could say that an action on a system always elicits a *system* response—the system is somehow different. The modified structure leads to a new situation for discernment. Figure 4 illustrates these dynamic shifts over time.

## Figure 4: Social Discernment over Time

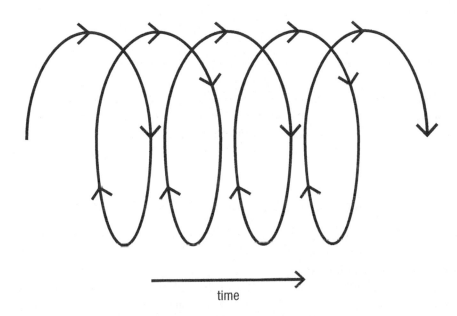

time

Basing the Social Discernment Cycle on the Pastoral Circle offers several advantages beyond providing a skeleton upon which to build the discernment process. Its roots in Roman Catholic social justice teaching and liberation theology invite us, from the very construction of the method of discernment itself, to connect discernment to social justice. Oppression is maintained not simply by a series of individual unjust actions. Indeed, the insidiousness of oppression of all kinds is that it transcends individual actors. Personal actions to repair a damaged relationship, while laudatory, do not get at the root of systemic oppression. Rooting out systemic oppression, as well as making lasting system change that enhances positive elements, requires action upon the whole system. Once we move from personal to systemic analysis, we realize why so many of our well-intended actions either make no difference in the system or invite perverse reactions from the system, making a bad situation worse.

## Typical Cases

In order to keep our discussion from flying off into abstractions, we'll follow two cases throughout the process. Hopefully, these extended examples will spur your imagination as you work with your own discernment.

Most of us struggle with systems in which we are minor players—that is, we are not in a position as a solitary individual to easily alter the momentum of the system. The first extended case example is such a situation. It can help clarify the Social Discernment dynamics in a system in which you are the only actor attempting to discern and act in a given system. Although your discernment will unfold very differently, this example is intended to spark your imagination for your own system.

The second case considers the situation of a group discerning within a structure. Here we add the complexity involved in forming the decision makers into a discernment group—an identity that is not in the job descriptions of most decision-making groups! This example will help a discernment group imagine how they will proceed through their system's discernment.

### Case 1: Group Norms in Eastside High School Sisters' Residence

Sister Joan Peters lived in the Sisters' Residence at Eastside, the local diocesan high school, along with seven other sisters.[9] Five taught or otherwise served in the high school, and three, including Sister Joan, resided there but had ministries outside the school. While several of the sisters had lived at the residence for many years—one as long as eighteen years—others were more recent arrivals. Sister Joan herself had lived at Eastside for three years when the "presenting incident" occurred. It involved her longtime friend Sister Katherine.

Sister Katherine had notified her ministry of her intent to retire at the end of the year. She and Sister Joan talked several times about where she would move after her retirement. Eventually, Sister Joan proposed that she consider Eastside, where she would be able to continue with various volunteer and part-time ministries, particularly the spiritual direction and retreat work to which she had devoted herself for many years. After meeting and discussion with the members of the community, all agreed that Sister Katherine would move to Eastside in August.

August came and Sister Katherine settled into Eastside. She began to publicize her spiritual direction ministry in the local parishes, and new clients for spiritual direction began to call. Many of the persons that Sister Katherine had accompanied in spiritual direction in the past also continued to meet with her, despite the additional travel. Soon she began giving retreats to local parishes and groups. Her ministry was taking off in the new site. But on the home front, tensions were building.

Sister Joan began to notice a general sense of irritation with Sister Katherine and puzzled at its origin. All the sisters had participated together in setting the group rules and expectations for the year, and Sister Katherine's behavior did not seem to Sister Joan to violate these group norms in the least. What, then, was going on? Observing longer, she noticed that Sister Katherine's use of the residence visiting room for receiving those coming for spiritual direction seemed to spark irritation. But Sister Katherine only used the visiting room during the day, when all the others were busy with their ministries; she had not inconvenienced anyone, at least that Sister Joan was aware of.

After pondering for some weeks the responses that Sister Katherine was eliciting from some community members, she began to realize that Sister Katherine was bumping headlong into unspoken group norms. She had no way to know the specifics of "this is how we do it here"; these expectations had never been articulated. She would discover a norm when she had broken it. Once Sister Joan came to this realization, she decided to use the Social Discernment Cycle to help her understand how things came to this impasse and what she should do when her friend unwittingly violated another unstated expectation—as would surely happen if the last few weeks were an indicator. We shall follow Sister Joan's progress through the Social Discernment Cycle over several weeks' time.

### Case 2: Hope Presbyterian Church Pastor Nominating Committee

Hope Presbyterian Church was in transition.[10] Its pastor of fifteen years had announced a year before that it would be his final year. Following Presbyterian polity, Hope installed an interim pastor at the conclusion of that year to see the church through the transition until its new called pastor was in place. Now, under the guidance of the presbytery's Committee on Ministry, Hope's session (the local congregation's governing body) pondered who should serve on the Pastor Nominating Committee (PNC) alongside the member recommended by the Committee on Ministry.

The nominating committee's responsibility, they knew from the Presbyterian Church (U.S.A.)'s *Book of Order*, is to assess the current state of the church and to prepare a Ministry Information Form that accurately describes the church, detailing the kind of pastor most appropriate for the next season of the church's life. This Ministry Information Form is then publicized, and candidates who seem appropriate for the position are culled from all those sending in their Personal Information Forms. From the list of those being considered, the nominating committee narrows the selection to several and checks in with the Committee on Ministry, who must eventually recommend to the presbytery that it receive the new pastor into its membership. The nominating committee next selects the single candidate that they believe is most suited to their congregation. They then interview this candidate, observe his or her preaching in a neutral pulpit, consider letters of recommendation, and follow up on all the appropriate due diligence, including meeting the candidate's spouse and family. Finally, if everything points to this person as the next pastor, they present this candidate to the congregation, who must vote whether to accept this nomination and thereby extend a call.

We shall follow the Hope Presbyterian Church Pastor Nominating Committee's use of the Social Discernment Cycle as they carry out their particular task on behalf of the membership of Hope.

## Itinerary, Theological Grounding, and Note on Language

Part 1 sets out the theology and theory for understanding discernment not just personally or even communally, but *structurally*. The first chapter reviews various understandings of discernment and emphasizes the connection between discernment about institutions, systems, and structures of all kinds and the work of justice. We begin our practices with the Awareness Examen. The second chapter clarifies the role of discerners and how they function in Social Discernment. It demonstrates the difference between an individual discerning about a system in isolation from others and a group discerning together about a system. The practice introduced here asks for the spiritual freedom that underlines discernment. The third chapter defines structure and describes how systems act. At the end of this chapter, I trust it will be clear why the person-to-person interactions we are used to in our personal lives are often ineffective in working with systems. The practice helps select an appropriately framed structure with a scope that will lend itself to discernment.

Part 2 unfolds the various steps of the Social Discernment Cycle. The fourth chapter assists with clarifying the structure and the issue within the structure to be discerned and also raises the issue of the buy-in of the discerners. Its practice invites us to narrate our experience in the system in all its concreteness. The fifth chapter leads us through an uncomplicated social analysis, which can be adjusted as appropriate to the complexity of the system. We also ponder how the process feels to the discerners at this point, with an eye to persevering to the conclusion of the process. It's at this point that people always complain, "This doesn't feel spiritual at all!" The sixth chapter presents the prayer and theological reflection step of the process, the heart of the discrimination that constitutes discernment. This chapter suggests a straightforward process for theological reflection and invites both personal and communal prayer into the heart of the discernment. The seventh chapter challenges our sensibility that a single sweeping action is the preferred goal of the Social Discernment Cycle, proposing that seeking a first contemplative action (as we have sometimes called the outcome of Social Discernment) is a worthy outcome for the process. Here, too, we begin internally confirming the tentative decision about this first contemplative action. In the eighth and final chapter, the notion of confirmation expands through a discussion of signs that institutions and other structures might, in fact, be moving toward God. These signs, and others like them, I propose, are the structural equivalent of the more person-oriented touchstones treated in chapter 7. This chapter also steps back and pulls together this journey called Social Discernment.

Anticipating a variety of readers, from those who just want a way to breathe easier inside a rigid system to those who will lead discernment processes and still others who prepare future leaders, I include several brief essays in the form of appendixes. These essays relate the Social Discernment Cycle to aspects of the social sciences and discernment literatures. They represent some of the topics and figures that have engaged pastoral theologians over the last two decades that I have tried to integrate into my teaching and writing. This small set is by no means exhaustive (for example, family systems theory is not represented), but it may suggest avenues for developing aspects of the Social Discernment Cycle in the future.

Appendix 1 provides a condensed form of the Social Discernment Cycle. It can serve at least two purposes: (1) If you get lost somewhere on the way through the process, wondering how this or that step relates to the whole, the condensed form may help quickly restore your bearings. (2) It can serve as a skeleton for those who desire an outline to use in less complex discernment processes. The second appendix shows how the Social Discernment Cycle exemplifies the dynamic pattern of Christian discernment, using an overview supplied by theologian Mark McIntosh. The third describes discerners and discernment groups in light of Donald Schön's concept of the reflective practitioner. The fourth describes Social Discernment in light of Watzlawick, Weakland, and Fisch's theory of change. Those who have explored developmental theories may find the fifth appendix, "Social Discernment and Transformational Learning," helpful in sketching the relationship of Social Discernment to developmental theories. Appendix 6 discusses the resonances and differences between the Social Discernment Cycle and "social technologies" based on the future, such as Theory U.

In *The Way of Discernment*, I made explicit some of my theological assumptions, encouraging readers to clarify their own.[11] Briefly, these theological assumptions, here tweaked toward systems, include these points:

- God is real, and we can trust that this God is actually alive and at work in the systems in which we find ourselves. Indeed, the Holy Spirit *is* the power of God at work in the world.

- God is the creator of all that is, beginning with the cosmos itself and encompassing the simplest and most complex of systems.
- God did not just create "in the beginning" and then leave the creation to make its own way, but God is continually creating, upholding, and enriching both individuals and systems.
- God created human beings with deep intelligence and with an ability to ourselves reflect on the systems and structures that exist around us in such richness and variety.
- Humans are able to choose, to direct our own future within limits, and to participate in creating systems that enhance life. Yet in that freedom, humans can also choose destruction, sin, rebellion, isolation.
- God's provident care took form in Jesus, who becomes our premier source for understanding not only who God is, but also how we are to live in harmony with God's purposes. Jesus, in his turn, sent us the Holy Spirit to be with us and teach us what we need to know and empower us to carry out our vocations in the world. Jesus concluded his work on earth through his self-emptying and salvific death. But death was not the end: Jesus was raised up, and he continues to live as the Christ to whom all creation is drawn. The work of salvation is thereby accessible to all, sealed through the covenant of baptism. Jesus therefore is the ultimate norm for all discernment.
- Reflecting on God and reflecting on humans are two sides of the same reality; we can know ourselves in God and we can find God in probing not only our own self but also created reality itself.
- Humans can participate with God in cocreating the future in all its complexity and richness, and for this task we have been provided means of grace.[12]
- It is impossible to fall outside God's provident love.

In addition to this list, to which I still subscribe, this volume, stimulated particularly by research into the nature of systems, gives me the opportunity to reflect briefly but more explicitly on the nature of God as Trinity and of the Holy Spirit as the "face of God" at work in our human experience. The Christian doctrine of the Trinity suggests systems and structures as we experience them are faint images of God, who, in the Christian understanding, is simultaneously both three and one (triune). The persons of the Trinity act both in their own right and yet always together as manifestations of the one God. The tensions inherent in describing the triune nature of God cannot be resolved logically, as Christians have affirmed over two millennia, but the very assumptions about God as Trinity in Unity ground within the very nature of God the processes for discerning and acting in all other created systems.

The Spirit has been spoken of as the lost person in the Trinity—at least in Eurocentric theologizing—a loss brought about through failure of imagination. By splitting sacred and secular, and ruling secular out of bounds for theologizing, the theater of the Spirit's activity is vastly shrunk to the Spirit's role in the church and in the individual's own private spirituality. One could also arrive at the same puny role for the Spirit by beginning from the opposite direction: the secular is where the action is, and Spirit has no place in the secular.[13] Again the Spirit is relegated to its role in private spirituality or to its role in the church—which has no standing in the secular world. In fact, it is the Spirit of God who moves us to recognize Jesus as God's Word for us in the first place. This Spirit already dwells in every part of creation, including—especially—in what we have come to split off in our imaginations as "secular." God, as Spirit, is necessarily and intimately involved in every event in the universe. In fact, the Spirit *is* God's power at work in the world. Once our imaginations are set free to imagine the Spirit at work in the world, we have the theological premise to discern about any and every system, including secular ones.[14]

Finally, a word about language for the divine. Any name we choose limits the deity, and English-language pronouns further confound our speech about the divine. In addition, our prayer language and our theological or discursive language for the divine may differ. What facilitates prayer and conversation for one person is off-putting to another. My perspective, and therefore my language, follows from my Trinitarian and Christian perspective, but even among Christians there are varieties of languages for God used in prayer, theologizing, and worship. John Mostyn, CFC, speaks of the "Mystery we call God." While I find this a lovely and satisfying way to speak of the divine, it seems unwieldy to use it throughout the book, though you will see it in the central exercise in chapter 6. I have resolved this issue somewhat ploddingly by simply speaking of the divine as "God" throughout the book—though "Spirit" peeked through here and there. But use whatever name for the divine that assists you to pray.

Shifting the language for the divine may not be enough for some individuals and groups who could profit from the Social Discernment Cycle. The very notion of prayer or the images and metaphors suggested for prayer and theological reflection in these pages may be off-putting. Let the final thought of this introduction, then, be "freedom and flexibility." I invite you always to look for the dynamic under the words and images employed, especially in the exercises, and hold onto it. Then adapt this underlying dynamic to your situation. If "prayer" is off-putting, perhaps "reflection" will open up the central dynamic of the prayer and theological reflection exercises in chapter 6. If a theological explanation doesn't work, perhaps there is another angle that will bring home the point effectively. Our God is big enough to work beyond the system of discernment presented here. Rejoice in that reality, and move forward however you are able.

With these few words of orientation, let us launch our discernment journey. We begin with the ancient Christian prayer beckoning the Holy Spirit:

> Come, Holy Spirit, fill the hearts of your faithful.
> Enkindle in us the fire of your love.
> Send forth your spirit and we shall be created
> And you shall renew the face of the earth.

PART 1    An Invitation to Social Discernment

Chapter 1

# Discernment in an Age of Complexity

*D*iscernment, the Christian spiritual practice of seeking and responding to God's call in the midst of all the forces, options, and decisions that mark our lives, may very well be the single most important Christian spiritual practice for dealing with the complexity of our contemporary lives. Discernment concerns human agency in relation to the Divine. These are huge claims. Let me unpack them piece by piece.

What *is* discernment? What content does this strange word attempt to convey? In a fine book on discernment practices for leadership groups, Ruth Haley Barton speaks of discernment as "the capacity to recognize and respond to the presence and the activity of God—both in the ordinary moments and the larger decisions of our lives."[1] In the case of discernment, "capacity" implies both gift and skill, so we might describe discernment as the gift and the skill in individuals and groups to recognize how God is operative in and around them. In the Christian understanding of God, humans, and the God-human relationship, discernment is a gift. Its author is the Holy Spirit, whose particular role in God's out-facing toward creation is to animate, teach, enliven, provoke, empower, and nourish believers.[2] In this understanding, even the desire to seek God comes first from God, is supported and nourished by God, and has as its goal our greater and greater immersion in God.[3] God desires to provide the tools and support for all people to live in such a way that they live out their destinies as God's beloved children, so we can assume that the gift of discernment is given in some measure to all who ask for it. Our stance as members of God's beloved community is twofold: asking for the gift of discernment and, as it is given, learning to live discerningly until we develop habitually listening hearts and lives responsive to God's call to us as individuals and communities.

Discernment is likewise a skill because it can be developed and honed by prayer and practice.[4] In this sense, discernment is a spiritual practice, that is, something we do repeatedly that helps us move closer and closer to God. Over time we can learn to see more deeply, discriminate more finely between a good and an apparent good, learn the subtleties of how to live without falling into extremes, and learn to unmask the deceptions of the evil one, whom both Ignatius of Loyola and C. S. Lewis have portrayed in their differing discussions on discerning.[5]

Discernment is about distinguishing between goods and choosing the better. We don't, then, use discernment to choose between something that is clearly morally evil and something that is morally good, for the simple reason that God, the author of all good, cannot be calling us to do that which contradicts God's very nature. Choosing between good and evil relies, not on discernment, but on the moral decision-making traditions of our various spiritual and religious traditions. In our contemporary world, however, what constitutes a moral evil is often not immediately clear. In this situation, discernment may indeed help us to clarify how to respond.

I have said that discernment is a Christian practice. Does that mean that only Christians can discern? Christians from such widely differing theological positions as Pentecostals and Quakers and Orthodox have developed systems of discernment, albeit based on different theological assumptions about God and on different spiritual practices. But others besides Christians can also seek a higher wisdom than might be immediately available, and thereby "discern." The outcomes of their discernment must then be judged against some vision of wisdom or the good. In this work, however, I speak as a Christian trying to elucidate a practice that has been present in the Christian tradition since the time of the New Testament. I freely use Christian theological terms, because discernment grew up within communities that used them. Nonetheless, I welcome persons from a variety of Christian traditions, or no tradition, to employ these practices, and I hope that they can find them helpful.

Second, what might it mean to seek God's call?[6] Most Christians have been taught that "God's will" is something that we should seek and follow. But the term "God's will" too easily evokes something static, immutable, and transcending creation that, once discovered, must be followed to the smallest detail.[7] God's will used in this sense is something inscrutable, unable to be influenced by any action of ours. The response can only be to study Scripture for clues about God's will and then do the best we can without knowing whether we have fully carried out God's will. Such an orientation encourages literal readings of Scripture, especially in contested areas of Christian life. Deuteronomy 30:14, however, suggests a different understanding of God's will: "The word is very near to you; it is in your mouth and in your *heart* for you to observe" (emphasis added). I believe, then, that there is a way to understand God-human communication that leaves room for a different understanding of God's will.

This broader understanding begins with the universe as a whole: it is open, flexible, and evolving. On the human level, we experience the boundedness that we call "the laws of nature." But when we look either more macroscopically or microscopically, we begin to see that the universe itself is dynamic and ever changing. Think of the theories of the origin and continual expansion of the universe or quantum mechanics, the mathematical description of the motion and interaction of subatomic particles, including mind-bending notions of wave-particle duality and the uncertainty principle. Since the universe reflects its maker, we can expect that God, too, is dynamic, ever changing, continuously creating—not simply repeating what has already been created. And since we are created in the image of God, we are able to participate, with God, in the creation of our future. So my second claim: discernment concerns human agency in relationship to the divine.

Of course, humans are not free to the degree that God is. We are limited by, for example, a particular genetic structure; the culture, political system, and family into which we have been born; our gender, socioeconomic status, and ethnicity. We are also limited by our own choices: when we choose one thing, we cannot simultaneously have every other option. Yet in the midst of these limitations, there exists in human persons a genuine ability to cocreate with God our particular futures, as well as to contribute to the collective future of our communities and, indeed, of everything living on earth.[8] We exercise this cocreative potential through our choices, limited though they may be. It also means, significantly, that there is no such thing as a minutely detailed template called "God's will" that exists outside space and time, immutable and largely unknowable. Indeed God's will in one's life is cocreated in a dynamic relationship between God and individual persons and between God and the systems that make up life in various cultures, the natural world, and beyond, to the universe as we know it.[9]

Put another way, all humans face an uncertain future, and we must live into it by the decisions that we make. We are creatures whose deepest self-realization comes from moving into God's dynamic future with all the life and skill with which we have been endowed, within the concrete situations of our particular and finite lives. Our fulfillment, then, lies in becoming the deepest, most alive persons that we can be and that our concrete situations will allow, and simultaneously contributing to the flourishing of those we touch. It is this understanding that I am trying to evoke by using the phrase "God's call" in place of "God's will."[10]

The definition at the head of this chapter might imply that there is a single practice that carries the name "discernment." In fact, there are many systems of discernment. A quick overview focused on discernment by and in groups will help locate the varieties of practices that come under the heading of discernment.

## Historical Highlights: Discernment for Groups

Although the notion of discernment is treated briefly in the New Testament—the most obvious group discernment is the Christian community discerning about its common life as recorded in Acts 15[11]—it took several centuries of Christian history before discernment began to be treated systematically. The emphasis in the earliest centuries, and to a large extent thereafter, is on discernment as a means of personal spiritual growth. The classic image for this earliest period is the seeker approaching the Abba or Amma (male or female wisdom figure) asking for a word pertaining to his or her spiritual condition. Yet there are moments in the tradition where discernment with and in groups emerges. In Benedict's Rule (ca. 525), the basic monastic guideline for almost a thousand years, discernment appears under the term "discretion."[12] In this setting, discretion was a kind of moderation, a control on the other virtues, a sensitivity concerning a person's strengths and weaknesses. Discretion was essential for the abbot in order to govern the monastery wisely. So Benedict counsels the abbot to consult all members of the community because wisdom is given to all, even the newest. During this period, the notions of discernment, discernment of spirits, and discretion are firmly lodged in the writings of the early church theologians and their practice located primarily within the monastic setting.

The sixteenth century's religious ferment spilled over into spiritual theology. Echoing the developments in the natural sciences, the first science of spiritual guidance appeared. In this context, Ignatius of Loyola (1491–1556) wrote his immensely influential *Spiritual Exercises,* or directions for a guide to lead a retreatant through an intense period of prayer. Discernment lies at the root of the relationship between the guide and the retreatant. Though Ignatius is often stereotyped as being rigid and controlling, his directions to the spiritual guide set exactly the opposite tone: the guide is to treat each retreatant uniquely, to discern the spirits experienced by each, and to teach this discernment to each retreatant. He tried to be very precise in his Rules for Discernment of Spirits, a series of aphorisms about how to read the various interior movements stirred up in an individual during the course of the retreat. He also developed processes to help retreatants choose ("elect") a vocation; this section of the *Spiritual Exercises* offers wisdom for discerning decision making still effective today and upon which I frequently rely. Ignatius's earliest companions adapted the Rules for Discernment of Spirits and Means of Making an Election to make a series of decisions that would affect their life together.[13] The record of this process, with its roots in the *Spiritual Exercises*, forms one of the clearest examples of a group discerning together about issues of significance to all of them.

The Reformation caused a shift from monastic discernment to the context of the ordinary Protestant pastor and congregation. That move effectively shifted much of the formal practice of discernment from the clerical spiritual director or confessor onto the individual Christian, but largely without the structures and processes for the laity to learn discernment. While discernment did not disappear within Protestantism, this much more diffuse situation did not tend to produce a focused and constructive contribution to the writing on discernment, making it harder to trace its trajectory. A major Protestant contribution to the notion of discernment flows from renewed emphasis on the priesthood of all believers. Among other fruits, baptism was understood to issue in the responsibility to assist other Christians in living out the Christian life. As this doctrine became expressed in practice, those pursuing discernment also shifted from a "spiritual elite" who worked personally with a spiritual director to anyone who desired to know how better to advance in Christian life and holiness.[14]

Slightly later than Ignatius, but apparently independent of the long history and practice of discernment of spirits that culminated in the *Spiritual Exercises*, a branch of the Reformation that rejected both Roman Catholicism and the new Protestant movement did begin to develop a rich and focused practice of group discernment. The followers of George Fox (1624–91), the Religious Society of Friends, or Quakers, as they were soon called, eschewed clerical orders, theology, doctrine, and liturgy, seeking to be guided immediately and directly by the Inner Light. Without benefit of a normative understanding of Scriptures, tradition, theology, or hierarchical structure, they soon found themselves struggling with bizarre behavior in some of their members. How could one assess whether various interpretations of the Inner Light were constructive or destructive if there were no touchstones beyond individual interior experiences of the Inner Light? They settled on one: affirmation by the assembled meeting, thus setting individual discernment within a communal context. The same discernment sensibilities at work in the meeting for worship were carried over to the meeting for business. It could be said, then, that all decisions made during Quaker meetings are a form of group discernment.

A relatively recent practice, the Clearness Committee, developed in response to the need for individual guidance. In this form of discernment, an individual facing a decision brings the decision to a group who assist the discerner in coming to "clearness" through asking a series of unhurried, loving, yet probing questions. As the discerner listens to his or her own answers, dimensions open up that often lead to a sense of a call with respect to the decision.[15]

Methodist spiritual formation groups, called "classes" and "bands," developed mutual guidance to the degree that it became a unique Protestant contribution to both spiritual guidance and discernment. John Wesley recognized how difficult it is for ordinary Christians to live their Christian life in the everyday world. Convinced of the benefits of mutual guidance, he taught "Christian conferencing" as one of the means of grace (prayer, Scripture, sacraments, and fasting are other generally recognized means of grace). Over time, Wesley developed a method of group guidance based on spiritual maturity. Every person was expected to attend the local church and receive the sacraments there, and also to participate in a "class" of no more than twelve persons, usually arranged geographically. The benefits of the large group were thus combined with the benefits of an intimate group; each group assisted with different aspects of soul care. The heart of these class meetings was the personal sharing of each member around the points that had been previously agreed upon, all of which had to do with growing in the basics of living a Christian life. Persons new to the Christian life were "learning how not to say no to God"[16] by means of mutual support and accountability. Based on a lively belief that the Holy Spirit was present as the members met, they expected that both promptings and warnings from the Holy Spirit would arise in their hearts, as well as through the guidance spoken by the leader. Identifying these warnings and promptings sharpened the discernment of the faithful group members. More importantly, the conviction that discernment is best performed in the context of community, whether with a trusted spiritual adviser, a friend, or a small group, finds strong confirmation in this stream of Protestant Christianity. Nonetheless, neither classes nor bands, which Wesley developed for those more advanced in their Christian walk, focused on assisting groups in discerning their common life.

Probably the most fruitful contribution to the art of discernment from the Reformed tradition came from the American theologian Jonathan Edwards (1703–58). In a number of works, primarily *Distinguishing Marks of a Work of the Spirit of God* (1741) and *Religious Affections* (1746),[17] Edwards addressed topics directly related to discernment. He was concerned that false criteria were being used to evaluate spiritual phenomena, in particular, the religious experience of individuals and groups in the Great Awakening. He developed biblically grounded criteria, intuitive to the direct experience of the Divine as given by the Holy Spirit, by which a believer might make a fair judgment about these phenomena. In *Distinguishing Marks,* Edwards focused the fruits of the Great Awakening writ large—was this phenomenon from God? In *Religious Affections,* Edwards clarified the qualities of a saving work of God in the individual. Such criteria become critical at the conclusion of any process of discernment, as the discerner or group evaluates the reliability and trustworthiness of the potential choice before moving ahead.[18]

## Decision Making through Discernment

Elsewhere, I have generalized from these varying systems of discernment the commonalities that I believe characterize discernment brought to bear on decision making. The Social Discernment Cycle will participate in these steps, moving back and forth between them:

- Seek spiritual freedom, the inner disposition often called "indifference," upon which discernment rests and that creates the climate for discernment.
- Discover and focus the options open to decision.
- Gather and evaluate appropriate information relevant to these options.
- Pray in the light of all the information, seeking in the light of faith the better way forward among the options.
- Formulate a tentative decision through an appropriate process. (Since the Christian tradition of discernment contains a variety of methods, discernment can proceed through whatever method helps us reach a judgment, in the light of faith, about how God might be calling in the concrete circumstances.)
- Seek confirmation that this option is God's call in this moment.
- Finalize the decision, putting it into action and assessing the result.[19]

Those knowledgeable in the theory and practice of discernment may be able to detect my strong dependence on Ignatius of Loyola in developing this set of steps, particularly his third "time" for making an election.[20] While in many ways Ignatius simply reworked the received discernment tradition, his creative contribution had to do with election—making choices in light of one's relationship with God. The underpinnings and implications of Ignatian spirituality, and specifically the treatment of election, are immense. First, Ignatius operated on the principle that union with God comes about in the world through the continual discernment of God's call to act in this very world. It follows, then, that from such discernment and choosing flows one's very vocation. Theologically, the place of this union shifts: God "comes down to us" in the person of

Jesus. As Jesus empties himself out for others in this world, he is increasingly united to God, whom he addressed familiarly as "Abba." Likewise, as we pour ourselves out in the world, we are united to God through Christ. We don't "go up" to meet God; we "go out" to meet God, who is right here among us, acting for the redeeming of the world. Our union comes about through "the act and art of 'allowing' oneself to be chosen," says Javier Melloni, allowing God to act through us in all the events of history.[21] If our vocation entails following God's call in the world, discerning how God might be calling us in and through the systems that permeate our lives is indeed part of that vocation.

The authors of *Grounded in God* pose a list similar to mine, using somewhat different language in their orientation toward small discernment groups:

- Formulate the question for discernment.
- Gather information and ideas.
- Explore practical considerations.
- Become still and centered in God's presence.
- Let prayerful silence pervade.
- Pose evocative questions, tapping into the imagination and drawing upon Scripture.
- Provide opportunity for reflective responses.
- Look for signs of God.
- Await consensus.
- Develop a plan of action.[22]

Both sets suggest that a clear question, relevant data, and a plan of action once the decision is made are crucial aspects of discernment in decision making, and both likewise stress the importance of the inner disposition of the discerners, the quality of their prayer and interactions, and the desire to follow the call of God. The first list, however, borrowing from Ignatius's material on election, is more explicit on two aspects. First, it begins with and continually returns to a prayer for spiritual freedom, that is, for the freedom to put God first in the choice. It also inserts a definite pause point before finalizing any decision, where the discerners take their tentative choice back to prayer to await some further discernment by way of confirmation or disconfirmation. Discernment following the first set of points is the "slow food" of discernment, and, I trust, equally nourishing.

## Living in Systems Today

This all-too-brief survey makes clear that discernment is deeply rooted in Christian life and teaching. We have, then, very serviceable and widely used systems from the tradition. In addition, we have a number of contemporary processes to aid a group to discern its life.[23] Why would we then want to create another communal discernment process? This question raises the issue of systems and their complexity. Follow me in a thought experiment.

In an age of instant communication, our lives seem to spin faster and faster. If we try to focus or to extricate ourselves from the seemingly perpetual motion, we find that we are deeply embedded in multiple systems that both free and constrain us. If we have reason to pay attention to genealogy, we tend to be aware of the generational linkages in our families of origin and marriage, but they are there even if we never advert to them explicitly. We participate in the capitalist economic system with its stocks and bonds, retirement accounts, checking accounts, student loans, and mortgages. When we are ill or break a bone, we rely on the health-care system, HMOs, and health insurance. If we have small children, we may struggle with child-care arrangements, and sooner or later we become acquainted with the local school system and specifically our own child's school principal, teacher, and classmates and their parents. Every four years we are drowned in reminders of national politics, but when we call 911 or drive without fear down the streets at night, we participate in the effects of local government. That I can use a single transit pass to travel on Bay Area Rapid Transit and various local transit systems and use one bridge transponder to pay my bridge tolls in several bridge districts illustrates regional government. If I get a traffic ticket, serve on a jury, or participate in the Sunday worship at the neighboring federal prison, I become more aware of the justice system. If my neighbor's gardener is suddenly absent, having lost his petition to stay in the United States, the immigration system impinges, as it does when a potential graduate student has to abandon international study plans for lack a visa.

"No man is an island," wrote the sixteenth-century English poet John Donne.[24] True then, true now. What is new is the complexity of the systems that impact our daily lives. Communications are instantaneous and global. Economic systems are likewise global, and some corporations are now bigger than many countries. Migrations and refugees affect every part of the world. Wars, even if the fighting happens across the world, are likewise global, as witnessed by returning veterans and the skewing of the budget toward defense from bigger or craftier enemies. Ecology is systemic at root: no one has told the salmon, for example, to migrate within the boundary waters, please, so that the United States can regulate the population effectively. We are just beginning to insist that each landowner on every watershed avoid contaminated runoff and keep sufficient vegetation in place along riverbanks so that the juvenile fish can live long enough to make their voyage to the ocean.

✳ —    To bring this home in your own life: list all the systems you can think of in which you participate. Did you remember to include your own body, and all the subsystems within it?[25] Did you include the system of the atom with its subatomic particles? On the other end of the scale, did you include the earth? The solar system? The universe itself?

We might not think this expansively or this intimately about systems, either because they work well or because they change so slowly that we don't notice. But a hurricane, a devastating flood, a war, a catastrophic illness, the death of a child, the loss of a job, the closure of a manufacturing plant, or a deep recession brings home the transitory nature of systems in a particularly painful way. You might try drawing the nesting and overlapping of the systems you listed. Complicated, isn't it?

I claim that discernment might be a critical tool for dealing with multiple levels of complexity. Why? Our survey of discernment traditions makes it clear that there are many nuances and practices, each suited to their original cultural, social, and theological contexts. Our contemporary social, economic, and spiritual cultures differ widely from those of the past and from each other. Even in my lifetime as an academic, for example, I have seen immense changes in the complexity of the system that is called a university. It used to be possible to run an undergraduate institution with little money and lots of donated services—Roman Catholic sisters did it all over the United States in the nineteenth and twentieth centuries. But the amount of regulation now demanded by accrediting agencies dictates that even small institutions must have departments dedicated solely to research and assessment. Endowments are necessary to ensure insulation from the vagaries of the economy. An extensive system of scholarships and tuition waivers ensures that students whose families have few economic resources have access to higher education. Housing sufficient books to support scholarship is enormously expensive, now complicated by the move to technologize teaching and learning. IT departments must turn over hardware every three or four years and constantly update the systems, adding ever-stronger firewalls and servicing "smart" classrooms all over campus. Science departments need new and ever-more complex (and expensive) equipment to ensure that students graduate with the necessary skills and experience. And this is just one example from one arena of life.

In the time of Ignatius of Loyola, a hypothetical university faculty might have gathered themselves together and gone through a manageable process of decision making similar to that which Ignatius and his first companions used to come to a common discernment about whether they should bind themselves by vow and become a religious community. What did they do? First, all the companions had to gather in one place (to work face-to-face, as will we),[26] they had to figure out the method (as will we), and they had to dedicate sufficient time to come to their resolutions (and so will we). They were a diverse bunch (we may be too), and it was not particularly easy to come to decisions:

> We decided to come together for some days before separating to discuss with one another our vocation and manner of life. After doing this for several days, we were divided by different ideas and opinions concerning our state of life, some of us being French, others Spanish, others Savoyards or Portuguese. There was unity of mind and purpose: to seek the gracious and perfect will of God according to the scope of our vocation; but there were various opinions concerning the more effective and more successful means both for ourselves and for our fellowmen.[27]

Mentioned almost in passing is a crucial observation: "There was unity of mind and purpose: to seek the gracious and perfect will of God according to the scope of our vocation." This unity of will and purpose, this coming together around mission, did not arise spontaneously; it was the fruit of each spending considerable time with the *Spiritual Exercises* and with each other, sharing what was on his heart and intently listening to the others, taking all that was said back to his own prayer. Such unity of mind and heart around a common purpose is not easy to achieve in most of the systems in which we live. If we examine Quaker decision making, we find a similar dynamic: it works because Quakers share a common experience, the meeting for worship, and they are committed to a process that is built on the common experience of listening for God, however they might speak about its dynamics.[28]

Spiritual director and longtime staff member at Shalem Institute Rose Mary Dougherty names one aspect of this unity of mind and purpose clearly:

> Whatever we say of individual discernment we must also say of communal discernment. Ongoing prayer and attention to their shared life in God must be the grounding of those who come together to discern. What they identify as their shared life in God must be articulated so that their decisions can flow from the sense of who they are together in God. A group, like an individual, may feel it is time bound to make a decision, while recognizing that it doesn't have the grounding it needs to do so. This recognition can be the wake-up call that the group needs to seriously nurture its spiritual identity. . . . In my own experience, one of the most challenging but necessary practices within groups engaging in discernment is that of honest dialogue, what I call "contemplative dialogue."[29]

We face a two-pronged challenge: Can we develop a discernment process, based in the Christian discernment tradition, that actually brings discernment to bear in the midst of the complex reality of the multiple and overlapping systems in which we live our ordinary lives? And can we develop our understanding of discerning groups so that they themselves function as discerning *systems* for dealing with systems?

In the third chapter, we will take up the notion of systems, getting a sense of how they work. For now, however, let us note a couple of realities: In a system, change is seldom linear. Even if our discernment group includes a person with authority to make decisions on behalf of the group, that person's actions may or may not change the system in ways we expect. Second, most of the systems that "pinch" us are composed of actors who do not share our desire to follow the call of God in the system, and if we proposed that as a goal, they would either laugh us out of the room or dismiss us as crazy (yes, in many religious structures, too!). In this climate, how will we create the prerequisites for discernment that Rose Mary Dougherty mentions? Third, most systems have a huge number of actors, each influencing one part of the structure. How do we get this crowd together to discern? Who leads it? How do we keep the players invested?[30]

Since we face such immense obstacles to discernment in and with systems, why not simply reserve discernment for those intimate groups where folks share the same religious sensibilities, and can, with good leadership and some prayerful time, develop into viable discernment groups for assisting one another's spiritual growth? The short answer, to which I have alluded in the introduction: because it is *systems* that preserve both justice and injustice. Oppression is maintained not simply by a series of individual unjust actions. Rather, the insidiousness of oppression is that it transcends individual actors. Personal actions to repair a damaged relationship, while laudatory, do not get at the root of systemic oppression. To do so requires action upon the whole system. Systems, by their very nature, also have all sorts of unintended consequences. We think that pushing here will fix the problem. It may (or may not!) alleviate the original problem, but it may also produce grievous unforeseen and unintended consequences. So, for example, with good intentions, the United States set out to stem the international flow of drugs over its borders. But the chosen solution not only has not stemmed the flow of drugs across the borders, it has made drug running ever more lucrative and saddled the United States with an unwinnable but extremely costly war on drugs. The drug trade routes and profits have fanned out into even more lucrative trafficking in human persons, who, after all, can be sold not just once, but over and over again.

Do we do nothing, then, in the face of complex systems? In issues of justice, Christians and all people of goodwill are called to exercise their best thinking—and discernment, I contend—to address systems, either to weaken unjust systems or to create or strengthen competing just systems.

Furthermore, only through systems will humankind create the breakthroughs that will ultimately allow us to live together peacefully and sustainably. The Social Discernment Cycle proposes one way to discern systems.

## The First Spiritual Practice

We close this chapter with a key spiritual practice, often called Awareness Examen. The first example is for individual use. Eastside's Sister Joan had long practiced Awareness Examen every evening, and hopefully the members of Hope's Pastor Nominating Committee also adopted this exercise among their own personal spiritual practices. Following this version for individual use is another designed for discerning groups. Hope's Pastor Nominating Committee adapted this second version for their use at the conclusion of each time they met together.

### Awareness Examen

There are many versions of Awareness Examen.[31] This spiritual exercise is usually done in the evening, looking over the day, but you may use it to review with God any period of time or activity.

1. Slow down. Stop. Prepare yourself to pray by becoming aware of the love with which God looks on you. . . .
2. Note the gifts God has given you today. Give thanks to God for them. . . .
3. Ask God that the next few minutes be a time of special grace and revelation. . . .
4. With God, review the day. Look at the stirrings of your heart, your thoughts, and your choices as the day progressed. Which have been of God? Which have not? What does God want to say to you about both? . . .
5. Ask God for forgiveness for any failure or omission, and for healing from their effects. . . .
6. Look forward to the following day, and plan concretely with God how to live it according to God's desire for your life. . . .

A few comments about this process may help us understand its significance in discernment and help us develop an analogous process to fit Hope Presbyterian Church's group-oriented discernment. In the practice called

Examination of Conscience that some of us learned as children while preparing for our first confession, the focus is on individual sinfulness. We learned to ask ourselves, what have I done to offend God? But here the focus is on what God is doing in one's everyday life. We and our sinfulness are not the center; God and God's graciousness is—a huge shift! As you begin easing into the prayer, the sensibility you are cultivating and trying to sink into is the love with which God looks at you. Next you look for God's gifts for you during this day, allowing thankfulness to begin to bubble up. Asking for what you desire—another contribution from Ignatius of Loyola—is not because God doesn't already know your heart, but because it is an exercise for *you* in knowing and tutoring your desires. Then comes the heart of the prayer. With God—very important—you review your day. There is a place for contrition, but now it arises in light of God's presence and grace alive in you.

How is the Awareness Examen connected to discerned decision making? It helps us know ourselves in the light of God and therefore to know God more intimately. It hones our ability to notice what God is doing in even the minutiae of our daily lives.[32] To the degree that this practice becomes habitual, it functions in discernment analogously to the stretching and weight training that an athlete does, day in and day out, in order to be as strong and limber as possible at the time of the athletic event. In a very real sense, Awareness Examen becomes one's daily practice of discernment.

Sister Joan, already in the habit of praying the Awareness Examen, allowed her reactions to what was happening at Eastside Sisters' Residence to surface in her examen every time her friend received a sharp remark or a cold shoulder. She first noticed her puzzlement but soon also became aware that she carried a tinge of anger. She also noticed her desire that the living group tend more carefully and hospitably to a new member whom it had, in fact, welcomed into its midst. As she wrestled with the tension inherent in what she was noticing and feeling, the Awareness Examen provided the context for her eventual "aha" that the group's unspoken expectations lay beneath the otherwise puzzling lack of hospitality shown to her friend. At this point, she began to use the formal steps of the Social Discernment Cycle. As she proceeded through those steps, the Awareness Examen continued to serve as a prayerful context for understanding how God was addressing her concretely, inviting her to action within the structure. Only a bit into the process, for example, did she begin to surface her own complicity in the dynamics through her own reluctance to speak out. But we are getting ahead of the story.

Hope Church's Pastor Nominating Committee could profitably practice a group version of the Awareness Examen as it went about setting up its tasks and settling into its meetings. Below is a sample Awareness Ex___ for group practice. The meeting chair or any member can lead the process. It can easily be adapted to different kinds of groups.[33]

## Awareness Examen for Discernment Groups

At the conclusion of your time together, commit to a brief period of about ten minutes to review the quality of your work together. You may wish to adapt the exercise to both the group itself and to the actual task it has just worked on together.

1. Signal the end of your work time by putting away your meeting materials. Prepare yourself to pray by taking several slow deep breaths while also flexing your shoulders, straightening your back, putting your feet on the floor—whatever helps you mark this time as one of recollection. . . .
2. Become aware of the presence of God, who, in fact, has dwelt within the meeting. Allow the gifts that God has bestowed on your institution or organization to surface in your imagination. Speak them briefly in turn, and give thanks for them. . . .
3. Ask God that the next few minutes be a time of special grace and revelation. . . .
4. With God, review the meeting you have just completed. Review the stirrings of your heart, your thoughts, your actions during the time of the meeting. . . .
5. Ponder which of these thoughts, feelings, and actions created openings for the work of the Spirit in you individually and in the group. . . . Speak these aloud into the group.
6. Ponder which of these thoughts, feelings, and actions created blocks for the work of the Spirit in you individually and in the group. . . . Speak these aloud into the group.
7. Ask God for forgiveness for any failure or omission and for healing from their effects. . . .
8. Look forward to the next occasion this group will be together, and ask God to nourish your group's life even during the time apart. . . .

Peter Senge and colleagues describe a practice of "seeing with the organization," which bears strong similarity to Awareness Examen, though couched in nonreligious language (which may assist some groups in creating a version that works for them).[34] Regular practice of Awareness Examen for Discernment Groups will, over time, sensitize your group to the ways God works with you and will help you become more adept in cooperating with the richness of life that God intends for your group. You will notice some similarity between this spiritual practice and the one in the next chapter, designed to aid the group in coming to shared spiritual freedom. Groups that habitually practice Awareness Examen for Discernment Groups will have already begun to develop their hunger—and their taste—for spiritual freedom.

Chapter 2

# Discerners: Who Are You?

Who may discern? With what attitude do we discern? What skills do we need to bring to discernment? These are the questions that occupy us in this chapter.

The first question may be answered very simply. All may discern. Discernment is not some magic process that only those initiated into its mysteries can access. Nor is it reserved for a spiritual elite. Discernment is for all who are serious about inviting God into their lives right where they live. It's also true that no discernment process is sacred in itself. Seeking God in the midst of our lives, however we do it, is the sacred task. Discernment is a means to this end.

You may, however, have been discerning without giving it that name. Anytime you have seriously tried to find out what God might want as you head into a decision, large or small, you were discerning. You might have participated in a group that has discerned. Hope Church will ask itself, Is this the person God is calling to be our new pastor? Posing this question places these church members in the midst of discernment even if they do not call it by that name. An executive team might be seeking the deepest purpose for their business—though they might not all be Christian and have never heard the term "discernment." Nonetheless, if they are seeking the deepest purpose of their company, they may be very close to the Christian practice of discernment.[1]

If this latter statement seems like a category mistake, slipping between good management practices and spiritual discernment, it's perhaps because we need to establish a theological foundation for working with systems. To begin constructing this foundation, I rely on the work of biblical theologian Walter Wink[2] and, in later chapters, the work of Irish theologian Donal Dorr, who will be particularly helpful for understanding the qualities of an institution that is responding to God's call. Why Wink? Wink brings together three critical components: (1) serious biblical exegesis, offering and model-ing responsible engagement with the Bible as we enter into our discernment; (2) fearless determination to take experience of and in systems seriously, particularly his own experience working in dehumanizing systems; and (3) the ability to avoid the contemporary malaise of reductionistic materialism that both undermines the ancient biblical view and empties the contemporary understanding of systems of their deeply spiritual aspects.[3]

## Wink's Contribution to a Theology of Systems

Wink names all systems and structures and institutions "Powers." He takes this name from Ephesians 3:10; 6:12; and Colossians 1:15–20. "Powers" is a biblically derived term with the potential to serve our understanding of struc-tures by healing the pervasive contemporary split between the inner and outer aspects of structures. Wink summarizes his notion of Powers as follows:

> I will argue that the "principalities and powers" are the inner and outer aspects of any given manifestation of power. As the inner aspect they are the spirituality of institutions, the "within" of corporate structures and sys-tems, the inner essence of outer organizations of power. As the outer aspect they are political systems, appointed officials, the "chair" of an organi-zation, laws—in short all the tangible manifestations which power takes. Every Power tends to have a visible pole, an outer form—be it a church, a nation, or an economy—and an invisible pole, an inner spirit or driving force that animates, legitimates, and regulates its physical manifestation in the world. Neither pole is the cause of the other. Both come into existence together and cease to exist together.[4]

Wink speaks of "the Powers that Be," reminding us that we all deal with them. They staff hospitals, run the city government, head our families, collect our taxes, run our schools. They are more than the people who run these insti-tutions; they are the *systems themselves, the institutions and structures* that weave society into an intricate fabric of power and relationships. They are necessary. They can be helpful. They can also be the source of many evils.

Wink makes the following crucial assertion: Every structure has a call to serve the good of God's creation. Institutions are created through human agency, but ultimately they are held in being by God's agency. Thus, insti-tutions, and indeed all structures, must be good at root because their ends are ultimately to serve God's creation. Yet it's clear that structures also per-petrate suffering—there is ample evidence that structures, like the humans who so often created them, are fallen, that is, no longer manifesting God's

life. But deep within them lies a call, just as deep within each of
call. Structures, like individual persons, are called to promote the reign of
God by promoting the welfare of the rest of God's creation, including other
humans. And again, like humans, structures get deflected from their call.
The "demonic," for Wink, is the spirituality produced when an institution
turns its back on its divine call and starts to serve another end. Positive social
change does not necessarily consist only in casting out the demonic, but also
in recalling the structure to its divine calling. As structures return to their
divine call, they are redeemed. Structures, then, are essentially good, Wink
believes, yet fallen, and so can be redeemed—all three ideas must be held
together to portray accurately the spirituality of systems.

   We could think that, as Christians, we could not in good conscience
remain within structures acting demonically. But we cannot escape all structures, and all structures are fallen. What are we to do? And how are we to act
so that we do not become the very thing against which we are acting? There
must be a way to exercise our Christian vocation with respect to institutions,
because Christians—indeed all humans—would otherwise be in an impossible bind. And there is: we can work nonviolently to call the institution back
to its divine calling. We might at times do that from within the institution,
at other times do it from without. We can also encourage and foster those
aspects of an institution that do, in fact, reflect its divine calling. Again, we
can do that from within or from outside an institution.[5]

   Wink spends considerable energy in his trilogy[6] looking at how Powers
operate. In the biblical view, Powers are at one and the same time visible and
invisible, earthly and heavenly, spiritual and institutional (Col. 1:15–20). In
the ancient biblical world, the referent of the phrase "principalities and powers" was, in fact, the actual spirituality at the center of the political, economic,
and cultural institutions of their day. Powers, as the soul of systems, are also
all around us today. As Christians, we need to learn to identify them, to discern
their vocations,[7] and to discern our response—a way to talk about the Social
Discernment Cycle. But note that Powers can carry both positive and negative
values with respect to God's reign—they are both good and fallen. Our task
in Social Discernment is to strengthen the positive and weaken the negative.

   Powers are strong, invisible, and difficult to dislodge. Likewise contemporary structures, by their very nature, tend to keep in place the interrelationships
out of which they are constituted—that is, both the values and the problems
are embedded in structures. You can recognize how true this statement is
if you consider the global economic system of capitalism. In the absence
of any significant competing economic system, capitalism has become the
very economic air we breathe. Even if we were to totally reject capitalism

as an ideology, we still could not escape such capitalist structures as money, banks, insurance, merchandising, and international economy. If the values perpetuated are "Kingdom values," the institution or structure more readily mirrors the "governance of the Trinity."[8] If, however, its values are antiking-dom, then we have to do far more than reach individual persons—we have to change the structure or have the work we do for the reign of God constantly undone. When our efforts are constantly undermined, it's easy to become hopeless or cynical, especially in dealing with large, complex, tightly inter-related systems of structures. And indeed, experience suggests that a tempta-tion to hopelessness may creep up on you as you delve more deeply into your system in the Social Analysis step of the Social Discernment Cycle.

Evil, therefore, is not just individual but structural and spiritual. It is not simply the result of individual human actions but also the consequence of huge systems over which no individual has full control. Only by confronting the spirituality of an institution and its physical manifestations can the total struc-ture be transformed. Any attempt to transform a social system without address-ing both its spirituality and its outer forms is doomed to failure, Wink believes.

Furthermore, since Powers/institutions/structures transcend individuals, we need to band together in order to increase the likelihood that confronting them will succeed in transforming them. According to Ephesians 3:10, the group that exists specifically for the task of calling the Powers to their divine vocation is the church, which must perform this task despite being as fallen and idolatrous as any other institution in the society. But the church is not by any means the only organization given this task; it is the vocation of all Christians, indeed, it could be said that it is a call present in all of us by virtue of our very humanness.

To summarize Wink's argument: God not only liberates us from the Pow-ers but also liberates the Powers from their destructive behavior. Powers can be redeemed. The task of redemption is not restricted to changing individuals in a structure but also involves changing the fallen institution itself. Redemp-tion understood structurally means actually being liberated from the oppres-sion of the Powers, being forgiven both for one's own sin and for complicity with the Powers, and setting about liberating the Powers themselves from their bondage to idolatry.

Put in somewhat different language, systems and structures are part of how humans organize society. Systems as such are ambiguous—at the same time they can foster the reign of God, they can hinder the reign of God, or they can be neutral, neither fostering nor hindering the reign of God. Typically, they fos-ter and hinder at the same time. Christians must approach structures with their eyes open, using their analytic abilities to see what is there in order to know how they ought to respond. We come prayerfully before God, seeking God's preferred future for us in this institution and for the institution itself. We enter into discernment not simply about our own personal lives, then, but also about the structures and institutions that permeate all aspects of our lives.

You will notice an absence of the language of sin in this discussion so far. Constructive theologian Eleazar Fernandez, among others, believes that we must redefine the notion of sin beyond individual actions to include the notion of systemic sin, for which he employs the terms "evil" and "social sin." Not to do so obliterates or at least minimizes the enormous power of systems to maintain and perpetrate evil. It also allows dominant individuals and groups to avoid coming to terms with their complicity in these systems—they may not personally sin, but the system does it for them. In light of these convictions, Fernandez defines sin as "the violation or the breaking of the web of life that sustains us and makes us whole; it is violation of right relations."[9] By locating the nature of sin in broken relationships, Fernandez provides a way to think of the notion of sin in systems, which, by definition, are organized arrangements of relationships.

Likewise—and this brings us directly to the Social Discernment Cycle—individual repentance is not sufficient; what must happen is social conversion or transformation. Social conversion embraces and transcends the personal, as well as the various avenues that have made us the person that we are. Fernandez does not want to argue for the priority of individual conversion nor for its opposite, the priority of social transformation, but for their simultaneity: "the social is personal, as the personal is social through and through."[10] Thus, as we proceed through the Social Discernment Cycle, we must allow ourselves to be converted individually even as we seek the conversion of a sinful social system. Likewise, our experience of personal conversion nourishes us in the difficult and time-consuming task of calling systems into their rightful vocations in the reign of God.

Wink focuses a good bit of attention on the negative potential in systems, for which he tends to use "Powers" as shorthand language. But it is possible to approach structures in a manner that focuses on their developmental possibilities. Such a theological perspective can be found in Irenaeus of Lyons (ca. 130–202), who held that humans move from lesser to greater perfection, nourished by Jesus Christ. Graced existence means that humans are in a continuous state of becoming. They have the freedom to choose to follow the path that involves spiritual relationships—or the spiritual aspect of institutions—and they can choose those they wish to pursue. As humans choose spiritual aspects of systems, we receive from those systems the gift of becoming more like God, whose incarnation is Jesus Christ. Theologian

Mark Graves sees "God's likeness" as "an emergent collection of human tendencies that is perfected by following Christ."[11]

In a tightly reasoned argument based on Irenaeus's theology, Graves describes how such emergence works for a community:

> In Irenaean spirituality, the individual begins imperfect and develops in successive stages. Likewise, for a community, its spirit develops through the free choices of its individuals, the memories they create and share, and their interpretations of the communal process. Some interpretations may necessarily build on other interpretations and conflicts between various interpretations may lead to group selection of the one (or ones) that resonate most closely with the group's ideal for itself and its future. The selection of interpretation . . . provides growth and strengthening of the relationships comprising the community both interpersonally and via extended communication using writing and artifacts. As the interactions, self-organization and selection of self-regulatory subsystems abound, the community can focus its activities on functional behaviors that increase the emergent qualities of the system and recover from prior processes that close the system off from continued emergent relationships that move the system toward its spiritual ideal.[12]

This perspective of emergent systems suggests that certain kinds of processes can, over time, create a discerning *system* out of a collection of individuals. At this point, though, let me remind you that it is not that we execute the Social Discernment Cycle perfectly, or that we reach the best decision (whatever that may be), but that we seek and find God—this is the most important responsibility that each Christian has. In so doing, we will inevitably move closer to our own deeply held values and to each other. We have seen that, because God is involved in all of our life and thus God's call precedes us even in the most "secular" activities, we can expect that God is already at work in all our systems, structures, and institutions long before we become part of them. We believe that God has a plan for us, for society, and for the world. It is our call first as humans and then as Christians to join God's work in the world, to enhance the spiritual aspects of the structures in which we live out our lives.

## Creating Discerning Systems

The established Christian traditions of communal discernment have a good deal to teach us as we seek to develop discerning systems out of decision-making groups. Communal discernment has traditionally been designed for groups that share religious language and values and can meet face-to-face over time. These conditions, constituting what Mark Graves calls a "community," may mask some of the nonpersonal aspects of a group's behavior, so we may not think of them as structures.[13] Yet communities—groups with high social cohesion and shared values and norms—do act and respond in many ways more like a whole person (that is, a system) than as a collection of individuals. This observation suggests why discernment processes created for individuals can sometimes be extended to communities. One of the clearest examples of group discernment grew out of just such a community; I noted in chapter 1 how the deliberation of the first Jesuits extended the application of the Rules for Discernment of Spirits and Rules for Making an Election (aspects of *The Spiritual Exercises* of Ignatius of Loyola) to group decision making. Nonetheless, if we can keep in mind the differences between "communities" and other decision-making groups, Christian group discernment practices can also ground the use of the Social Discernment Cycle by groups composed more broadly—potentially including our hypothetical executive management team, if it grasps the inherent power of a structure to hold both evil and good.

While the qualities that foster discernment in small groups are similar to those for individuals, the challenge comes from moving from individuals in proximity to each other to a group that discerns as a single unit. In other words, it is necessary to create a discerning *system* that acts as a whole through the members' prayerful intuitions and insights converging in unity. The creation of this discerning system is always intentional on the part of the group members; it never happens by accident. That it happens at all is a grace conferred on the group by the God who desires to cocreate with systems as well as with individuals.

What are some of the qualities in individuals that foster discernment? And what analogues can we imagine for both communities of shared religious values and groups that may have lesser, but still significant, ties? The ability to embrace silence, self-knowledge, knowledge of the group, self-revelation, and vulnerability, the communication skills to engage in deep conversation and contemplative listening, the ability to solve conflicts within the group, and the willingness to honor a group covenant seem to me to be key to the formation of both discerning individuals and groups. A discussion of these qualities will engage us for the remainder of this chapter.

*The first quality includes space for silence.* While sufficient freedom from the press of daily responsibilities can make possible outward silence, and group processes can have silent times structured into them, the quality I am pointing to here is an inner settledness, a calmness characterized by an absence of internal chatter, a readiness to listen for the subtle traces of God's communication, however they might come, and even a sense of expectancy at what God will do in the silence. Both individual discerners and discernment groups need enough comfort with silence to be patient with prolonged silence, recognizing that there are some things that can only be learned through it. Our reliance on electronics may be making silence harder and harder to befriend, with instant communications fracturing the possibility of silence even during sleep.[14] Individuals and groups alike may have to *practice* silence in order to develop a thirst for the inner richness that flourishes in it.

*The second quality is self-knowledge.* This kind of knowledge comes over time through the habit of self-reflection and from welcoming the honest and loving feedback of friends and colleagues. Age can season this self-knowledge, but age is by no means a guarantee that it exists. Furthermore, there is always more to discover and own about oneself, no matter one's age. Such individual self-knowledge is also crucial to the discerning group; even a single member who lacks self-awareness will hamper a discerning group's ability to listen deeply for the presence of the Spirit, because the Spirit often shows up in the inner motions of the individuals in the group. Awareness Examen, practiced regularly both by individuals and by discerning groups, fosters such self-knowledge.

*Third, the discerning group must know the individual members who make up the group, which requires self-revelation and vulnerability.* This may be the single most important step as a group begins to form itself into a community of shared vision and values. How might a group do this? A variety of ways exists, and groups will find their own path. Two practices that lend themselves to forming a discerning group are slow conversation and, in the explicitly religious group, faith sharing. In both of these practices, we are engaged in the unhurried engagement of one person with another, in which each is interested in the others' stories, in learning what makes them tick, what gives them deep joy and causes them deep pain, their values and deeply held beliefs. We desire to go deeper than our surface knowledge, untested assumptions, and judgments about others. "This kind of sharing comes from the heart and soul, not the mind," says Trey Hammond. Such conversations "are the act of entering into the mystery of someone else's being and seeing where theirs connects with yours."[15]

Jesuit John English, who worked for many years on the *Ignatian Spiritual Exercises for the Corporate Person*[16] and consulted widely with Christian Life Communities and other decision-making groups, offers some wisdom about faith sharing and its ability to form a communion of like-minded people. English believes that the primary instrument for creating community and a privileged instrument for ongoing communal discernment is sharing the story of each member's personal life and the story of the group's common journey with God. Sharing stories, he states clearly, is not easy; it requires vulnerability, a belief that one's story is intrinsically worthwhile, and the skill to articulate what is happening inside. But even when told haltingly, the result is the ability to begin to see the unique ways that God relates with us as individuals. One's life as an individual and our lives together then become a source of revelation. They become God's word to us as we see them in the expansive perspective of God's creative presence. All history is graced history, claims English. God is present in it all, the graced and the sinful alike: "Our experience is where God has been with us and so it becomes matter for our prayer whether it brings sorrow or joy."[17]

Even if the group is formed in nonreligious contexts, much of the quality of faith sharing can be reached by deep conversations. Even science, thought to be the bastion of experiment and the antithesis of conversation, is based on deep conversation.[18] In fact, science may give us a way to understand the deep meaning of a very old concept, dialogue. Dialogue, says quantum theorist David Bohm, is one of two types of discourse, the other being discussion. Discussion takes place when ideas are batted back and forth and a subject of common interest is analyzed and dissected. Each participant attempts to forge a strong position that ultimately prevails over the positions of the others. Clearly discussion is useful, and there will be a place for it in discernment. Discernment groups, however, thrive on dialogue. Dialogue takes place when a group, in Bohm's words, "becomes open to the flow of a larger intelligence." In dialogue, participants do not seek to win, only to participate together in a larger pool of meaning that is always developing. This larger pool of common meaning cannot be accessed individually.[19] In dialogue, the whole organizes the parts—a case in which a system perspective is more encompassing than an individual perspective. Dialogue, in this rich sense, forms individuals into a learning system that can serve as an effective analogue to a traditional faith community.[20]

*Fourth, the discernment group must have appropriate communication skills.* Margaret Wheatley has spent considerable time teaching the art of conversation to diverse groups of people out of her conviction that conversation can take us to a deeper realm where we remember we are part of a larger whole and discover collective wisdom that we may have forgotten or never known. The more diverse these conversation groups become, the better. They need not share the qualities of "communities" in the sense in which Mark Graves uses the term—so Wheatley's simple model can be used in groups in which there is little or no unity at the beginning.

For conversation to take us to this deeper level where community begins to form, Wheatley offers several principles that also can assist in the formation of discernment groups:

- We acknowledge one another as equals. No one is the expert in dialogue. Natural power dynamics are acknowledged; the person with the most institutional power suspends its use, and the person with less institutional power claims voice and agency.
- We try to stay curious about each other. Others are always more than they seem.
- We recognize that we need each other's help to become better listeners. If we listen only to our own voice, we hear only our own voice.
- We slow down so we have time to think and reflect. Contemplative dialogue is often punctuated with silence as we treasure what was just said before we prepare any response.
- We remember that conversation is the natural way humans think together.
- We expect it to be messy at times. We will certainly not always agree and may sometimes passionately disagree on the way to a shared vision.
- We develop the willingness to be disturbed. We may not like what we hear, yet we believe that it is important to hear it.
- We are willing to not know. Conversation partners are ultimately mysteries in their own right, and not knowing can open us up to change or possibility, even hope.
- We value being surprised.[21]

I add, from my experience:

- We are willing to become vulnerable. Vulnerability invites like vulnerability from others. Vulnerable conversations immediately shift to a deeper, more intimate level.
- We are committed to seeking and speaking the truth and remaining in conversation through the inevitable struggles to communicate.
- We trust in ourselves and in other discerners, knowing that a better approximation of truth will arise from many voices rather than just one.

These points are stated from the perspective of the initiators in the conversation. Imagine being on the receiving end of a conversation punctuated by the above points. You would experience yourself validated as an equal partner in the conversation, essential to its outcome, given room to speak, and taken seriously for your unique contribution when you do. You would be met with vulnerability from your conversation partners, who clearly trust you to hold sensitive information carefully and who signal regularly that they are not only interested in what you say but actively encourage you in the saying of it. Feminist theologian Nelle Morton spoke of such quality of listening as "hearing one another into speech."[22] If you have been in this situation, you will recognize the powerful affirmation that it conveys, the gift that it indeed is.

Such conversation skills, what I have called contemplative listening, can be learned. As they are practiced, they continually deepen the quality of the discernment group. I frequently suggest the following guidelines for contemplative listening in groups, but they hold equally well for conversations between two people:

- Take time to become aware of God's presence. Ideally, settle your body in a comfortable but alert position, and set aside your inner chatter. Several slow and deep breaths can assist in this settling in. Intentionally turn your focus to God, asking God to be present with you and in the conversation. If the conversation happens spontaneously, even a momentary intention to listen deeply helps set the context.
- Listen to others with your entire self (senses, feelings, intuition, imagination, and thought processes). When you notice that your attention has shifted away from the other, gently bracket your own inner dialogue and return your attention to the speaker. You can return to your own story later.
- Do not interrupt. Allow a pause between speakers to absorb what has been said. Do not formulate what you want to say while someone else is speaking. Deep listening is a much slower process than everyday conversation because it inserts sufficient silence and sufficient inner and outer space for the effect and intention of the other to resonate and deepen prior to any response.
- Respond first to another's offering with a simple statement acknowledging both the content and the emotional valence with which it was said. This kind of first response indicates to the speaker that you either have, indeed, understood the comment or are seeking to understand it.
- Speak for yourself only, expressing your own thoughts and feelings, referring to your own experiences. Speak as concretely as possible.
- Generally, leave space for anyone who may want to speak a first time before speaking a second time yourself. Deep listening in a group is about gleaning shared wisdom.
- Listen to the group as a whole—to those who have not spoken aloud as well as to those who have. Allow the whole group's experience to inform your later responses.
- Hold your desires and opinions lightly. Be willing to allow the emerging shared wisdom to change your perspective.[23]

Such conversation and listening skills serve us well in straightforward conversations, but they are also crucial in extremely complex situations, such

___ the South African population immediately following the lifting of apartheid. Indeed, process consultant Adam Kahane believes that the only way to solve such dynamically, psychologically, socially, and politically complex problems is through "opening up our talking and our listening." That, he says, is the only way to move through such intractably messy situations peacefully.[24]

Appreciative Inquiry (AI) also can assist in the formation of discerning communities. Appreciative Inquiry proposes that organizations are not, at their core, problems to be solved but entities created to fill a need in society. It begins with the positive assumption that organizations, as centers of human relationships, are alive with immense constructive capacity.[25] Thus the philosophy of Appreciative Inquiry is highly compatible with the perspective that systems have unique God-given vocations and that divine creative energy is at work in systems, however covered it may be in a given moment. As AI consultant Sue Hammond notes, individuals and groups alike have been highly trained to seek out the negative and focus almost exclusively on fixing those elements. Appreciative Inquiry helps counter this deeply ingrained tendency and release the energy contained in working positively.[26]

I have earlier noted that discernment can either focus on removing a block to following God's call (a problem-solving approach) or, as AI encourages, focus on how to foster the positive movement involved in enhancing the mission. Of these two options, the ability to spot how God's call in the system is already being manifested is far less developed than the ability to see what is blocking it. Put theologically, Appreciative Inquiry's orientation reminds us to keep searching for signs of how God is already at work in the structure, gracing it and helping it live into its vocation. We then commit ourselves to the first contemplative action that joins in the work God is already doing, then the next, and the next.

Appreciative Inquiry also raises the issue of the ideal size of the discerning group. In AI, all the affected people are brought into the room and work the process. It is usually messy to gather and winnow everyone's perspective and can require skilled leadership to keep the process moving. The benefit is high buy-in of all the participants who, after all, will themselves have formulated the points of decision and action. All are freed to be heard, to be known, to offer their unique perspectives, to dream in community, to contribute, to act with support. This strong buy-in and shared positive perspective unleashes power in service of positive change.[27]

But it is often not feasible to gather everyone together for purposes of discernment. Mancur Olson's classic work on systems reports on research about the effect of group size on the buy-in of the participants. In general, the larger the group, the less the individual participant will feel that his or her participation will matter in the final outcome—a reality that AI attempts to overcome by having all participants be involved in the writing of the propositions and the decisions. Groups should be large when influencing opinion is the goal, but small if action is the goal. It turns out that the optimum size of an "action-taking" group is quite small—five to eight people.[28]

These varying perspectives on group size are instructive for discernment groups, I believe, not because we need to adopt one or the other perspective, but because reflecting on the way size affects group behavior gives us insights into the optimum size of the discerning group and suggests the kind of group processes that would most effectively lead to the formation of a discernment group—a size that may differ depending on the focus of the discernment. In my religious congregation, a group of about fifty delegates (a "large group" in Olson's terms) forms a discernment group at the time of the General Chapter (the legislative body that meets every five years to set direction and elect the next leadership). In Hope Church's process for selecting a new pastor, a "small" group, the Pastor Nominating Committee, does the heavy lifting of the formal discernment process, at least in part because this group will deal with much confidential information. The wider church membership is involved in the selection of these committee members (who then function as a type of representative for the purpose of discernment), and the congregation has the final word through the congregational vote. If the congregation has sufficient data and if there is a real possibility that they could turn down the Pastor Nominating Committee's candidate, the congregational vote could be considered a key component of confirmation. We will speak extensively about confirmation in chapter 7.

*Fifth, as individuals commit themselves to this kind of deep conversation, disagreements will inevitably arise; these conflicts must be resolved.* Having a constructive way to deal with this expected part of any group's process is crucial to its long-term growth. Again, there are many strategies for conflict resolution, and the means a particular group uses will need to be fitted to the group. Ruth Haley Barton, reflecting on her experience of leading Christian groups in spiritual discernment, opens her observations with the theological reality that Jesus has promised to be with groups praying together (Matt. 18:20), and that includes when these groups face conflict. Groups might intentionally seek ways to be open to the divine presence among them through, for example, committing themselves to helpful opening and closing rituals, taking time for silence at key points in the discussion, framing the conversation in terms of seeking to understand the other person and to understand the demands of Christian love in this situation of conflict, and committing to staying open to God and to the other when everything in us wants to shut down and shut the other person down as well. Participants can commit themselves to direct, face-to-face communication rather than resorting to conversations in the hallways and parking lots that serve only to play persons off against each other. They might commit to involving an objective third party, if necessary, one who is trusted by each party in conflict. Groups can also commit to being proactive about developing skills and practices related to conflict transformation, knowing that God can be working a deeper unity precisely through their conflicts.[29]

Groups with members belonging to other traditions than Christianity, or to no specific religious tradition, will need to speak about the religious, spiritual, or value foundations that can unite them. Time spent on this conversation will pay off amply when the going gets rough. Indeed, identifying the basis of unity beyond the task at hand and beyond any individual religion, spirituality, or life philosophy may be the most important task in the formation of a discernment group. Mancur Olson notes that selfless behavior that has no perceptible effect is sometimes not even considered praiseworthy.[30] But as the discernment group develops a common vision, it can create a culture that rewards the kind of selfless behavior so essential to discernment. It can also set the expectation that spiritual freedom, the ultimate form of selfless behavior, will ground its work together.

*Finally, to formalize and strengthen the effects of such deep conversations, groups would be well served to commit to a covenant of their own making.* In the Jewish and Christian traditions, covenant making is itself a spiritual practice. Speaking of covenants forming discernment groups, Ruth Haley Barton notes, "Our covenant is, first of all, a covenant with God. Before God *and* with the people of God we make certain commitments regarding how we will honor God, each other and our relationships as brothers and sisters in the family of God."[31] Such a covenant might include agreements on attendance, participation, confidentiality, topics to be covered, leadership, whatever aspects foster that group's purpose. A covenant makes the group commitment clearer on a deeper level than does conversation. Since it contains process guidelines that the group itself has agreed upon, the group can claim shared ownership for their behavior. Indeed, a well-crafted covenant protects the members and discerning community as a whole.

All this, just to form a discernment group? Yes! Discernment is about desiring God, first and foremost. Everything we do to form a group unified in this purpose and skilled in communicating among the members contributes to this end. The individuals and the group both become closer to God in the process of preparing to begin a formal discernment process. The time is never wasted when seen from this faith perspective; indeed the process, more than just preparation, *is* the product itself.

The discernment group as a human creation will likely be far from perfect. Yet if discernment is a grace as well as a skill, as I suggested earlier, then the group can proceed in faith, recognizing that they have done the best they humanly could to proceed in unity in responding to God's call as they understood it. Furthermore, actually discerning, as well as carefully reflecting upon a completed discernment process, can deepen the discernment group's ability to function as a discerning system in the future. We practice so as to become more skilled artisans. As we gather ourselves to answer the question, What is God leading us to here and now? we will find that our faith in God, our willingness to work together, and our willingness to let go all deepen—leading us toward the first step in any discernment process, spiritual freedom.[32]

## Seeking Spiritual Freedom

Spiritual freedom is the structural analogue to the Ignatian concept of indifference.[33] Indifference, in the Ignatian sense, does not mean not caring but rather being willing to hold everything other than God as penultimate. Biblically, indifference is evoked by the parable of the Treasure in the Field (Matt. 13:44). When the householder finds such a treasure, he goes out and sells everything he has and buys that field. He becomes "indifferent" to all his other possessions because he has his eye on the treasure. In discernment, spiritual freedom or indifference is the inner attitude of looking for God and being willing to "sell any other possession" to move toward God's heart for you, whether individually or collectively. Reaching the point of indifference in discernment simply (and profoundly!) means no longer being bound to any single option, outcome, point of view, ideology, person, or strong impulse toward any single outcome.[34] Note, though, that the tradition considers indifference something that is given us by God, not something we can achieve by pulling ourselves up by our own bootstraps.

Theologian Eleazar Fernandez offers a refreshing metaphor for spiritual freedom. He speaks of "a heart as large as the world." A heart as large as the world is a heart that sees the connections of our lives wherever we are located on this planet. It is a heart that knows that we live in the intersection of the global and the local and knows that we share common vulnerabilities. A heart as large as the world is a heart that experiences the pain of the world, especially the pain of those who have suffered the most. It knows that, at the most elemental level, we connect with people in their joys and sufferings. Making our hearts as large as the world requires a major reorientation that involves shattering our narrow world and becoming centered in the interconnections of communities around the world. It is for this we pray when we pray for spiritual freedom.[35]

The following spiritual practice is designed to help individuals reach the inner climate in which spiritual freedom can take root. [36]

## Seeking Spiritual Freedom

The importance of desiring to follow God's call through your decision making cannot be overstated. The attitude of indifference, that is, being willing to choose what God desires over all the other, lesser things we might also desire, is the essential starting point for discernment. As indifference takes root, it flowers into the spiritual freedom to respond freely to God's call. This prayer helps you form and deepen your indifference.

1. Ask for God's Holy Spirit to be with you as you seek to understand what God calls you to do and be.
2. Consider the following statements. Turn them over in your mind, and then allow them to take root in your heart. Speak personally to God about what they mean for your life. Spend enough time on each that it becomes a statement that you believe and accept as your own.

   - You, God, have created all that is and are even now creating me, just as I am.
   - You desire that I become my truest and most authentic self.
   - You put in me my deepest and most authentic desires, Creator God. I can know what you desire, God, as I ponder and understand these calls of my heart.
   - Yet some of my desires lead me away from my truest self, where you, O God, dwell. I do not always desire what you desire.

3. Using your own words, ask God to deepen in you the *desire* for what God desires.
4. Commit yourself, here and in all the subsequent prayer exercises that mark the successive steps of your discernment, to ask for the gift to desire what God desires and, as God's desire becomes clear, to choose it.
5. Give thanks to God for any new clarity and freedom that comes through this prayer.

Sister Joan approached this exercise with a sense of recognition, acquainted as she was with the concept of indifference from Ignatian-oriented retreats and workshops. Once she made the shift of language from "indifference" to "spiritual freedom," she found it helped clarify where she wanted to be interiorly as she continued through the steps of the Social Discernment Cycle. Getting there, however, proved a bit more difficult than just wishing for it to happen. She found that it was necessary to focus not on the other sisters, or even on the community as a structure, but on God and God's outpouring love for her and for the other sisters. As she did that, she was able to sense a bit of God's love for the other sisters rising in her—God's desire. When she let her attention shift to the problem or the sisters through whom the problem was manifested, she began to grasp for solutions, and her spiritual freedom vanished. "I guess," she recounted to her spiritual director, midstream in the process, "I am getting a lesson on who really is in charge here!" She fell into the habit of beginning each step of the process with a little prayer: "Remind me, Gracious One, who is really in charge here. Let me see with your eyes, and love with your heart."

Sister Joan's experience, even that she had a noticeable experience that she could relate to her spiritual director, is hers alone. You may have a very different experience or no experience at all that you can put your finger on. No matter. Simply express your desire to follow God's call when it becomes clear, or, if you prefer to make this step more religiously neutral, to be ready to move toward the "right" thing when you become aware of what that is. As you find yourself grasping for a solution, arguing with other real or internal voices, aggressively defending a point of view, feeling anxious or bitter or defeated, or, ironically, checking out and giving up, return to a form of the prayer for spiritual freedom. Imitate Joan only insofar as you make this prayer your own.

Spiritual freedom is so crucial to discernment that commentators on group discernment regularly note the significance of each member's spiritual freedom; indifference in all the discerners is presented as a prerequisite for discerning groups. Thus, though the exercise above might be done privately, as Sister Joan did it, it can also profitably serve as a corporate prayer, with individuals sharing how the experience went for them, as well as their sense of their readiness to be a part of a larger discerning group. Yet, in keeping with our structural perspective, I suggest that the discernment group will need to ask for spiritual freedom *as a group*.[37] The following exercise is designed to assist discerning groups in their prayer for spiritual freedom. It works best with small groups that have established comfort with faith sharing. You should feel free, however, to craft a prayer for spiritual freedom that fits the identity of the group. You will also notice the similarities between Awareness Examen for Discernment Groups and this spiritual practice seeking spiritual freedom. Awareness Examen looks back over the just-completed time together, while this practice looks over the entire history of the discerning group's life, asking for increasing spiritual freedom, seeking signs that this gift may be growing in the group, and living gratefully within that grace.

## Seeking Group Spiritual Freedom

The following exercise is designed to assist discerning groups in their prayer for spiritual freedom. It works best with a small, intimate group that has spent some time together. You may need to rework it for large, diverse groups of multiple stakeholders or for the first meeting of a discerning group that does not yet have a history together.

1. Ask for God's Holy Spirit to dwell within the group as you seek together to understand what God is calling you to become as a discernment group—a group heart large enough and free to together follow God's call as it becomes clear.
2. Looking back over the group's life, what signs of God's presence among you can you notice? Name these signs aloud. Reflect together on what these signs may be saying about how God is at work among you. Give thanks.
3. Looking back over the group's life a second time, what impediments to God's life can you notice?

     Each member individually: Reflect silently on such impediments in you (such as fear to speak, irritation at another's manner, holding on to a past hurt, overpowering less powerful members of the group). Silently confess these failures, and ask God's forgiveness and empowerment for the future.

     Then the group members collectively: Examine your group behavior for impediments in the group's life. Bring them to light and collectively ask for God's forgiveness and empowerment.
4. With new realism regarding your group as beloved community that has at times fallen short of its vocation, ask God to enliven you collectively to desire what God desires.
5. Commit yourselves to asking for this gift frequently throughout the discernment process.
6. Give thanks to God for any new clarity and energy that comes through this prayer.

Hope's Pastor Nominating Committee decided to open each session together with a brief time of prayer that created space for the members to formulate silently their personal prayers for spiritual freedom. Leaders also spoke aloud the desire that spiritual freedom undergird the group and unite their work together. Each member took a turn preparing this opening prayer. As they began to recognize their group patterns through the Awareness Exa- ⫽ men, some leaders spontaneously began to name the patterns, inviting God's grace to dwell in the midst of their work together, however imperfect it might have been in a given meeting. After particularly difficult meetings, the convener used the exercise above in place of the usual Awareness Examen, because it invites an explicit review of the whole arc of the group's dynamics.

These practices are presented as discrete and somewhat formal steps, as if they are to be done once at the beginning of the discernment process. However, spiritual freedom is elusive and never within our own control. We may experience it partially or momentarily, only to have it slip from our grasp. So we practice continually, opening ourselves regularly to receiving this grace. Each phase of the Social Discernment Cycle opens with a reminder to return to the prayer for spiritual freedom. Every time we renew this desire, we place before our minds and hearts the ultimate goal of our discernment, namely, following God's call, allowing this goal to pull us forward. Indeed, spiritual freedom is one of the distinctives that distinguishes discernment from other patterns of decision making. I encourage all members of discerning groups to ask for moments to renew spiritual freedom in the midst of the process, whenever such a prayer might be needed. It can be done as simply as requesting a moment for silent prayer.

With this desire for spiritual freedom, then, we move to considering the nature and behavior of structures at a deeper level.

Chapter 3

# Systems and Structures: What Are They?

*T*he Social Discernment Cycle is designed to address the dynamics of systems as distinct from the dynamics of one-to-one interactions. Organizations and institutions of all kinds are subsets of this more inclusive category of system. In order to grasp the unique value of Social Discernment, we need to understand what systems are and how they work. In what follows, I make no attempt to discuss system behavior with mathematical rigor. Instead, this discussion creates examples through analogy.[1]

Systems thinking is a discipline for seeing wholes, for seeing interrelationships rather than things, for seeing patterns of change rather than static snapshots of events. One of the cornerstones of systems thinking is to see ourselves as part of the feedback process, not standing apart from it. We are always part of the system. A corollary of this statement: any individual agent (including you or me) is not responsible for the way the system operates; responsibility is a function of the whole system itself. Searching for someone to blame for the way things are, then, is fruitless. But what we can do is look at the big picture and the long view. We can look for leverage points, where a small action can produce seemingly outsized results. We can learn to distinguish high from low leverage points in highly complex structures, seeing through the complexity to the underlying simplicity of the structure.[2] We can learn to look at both the whole forest and individual trees at the same time, resisting the easier course of looking at only one or the other. This chapter is designed to assist in gaining these new eyes.

I first became aware of the system quality of some kinds of change (or lack of it!) while studying human development. In the group of theories labeled "structural," namely those theories following the pattern set by Jean Piaget,[3] I soon learned that there is a kind of human developmental change that follows structural rules. When we try unsuccessfully to solve some problem, our tendency is to try the same strategy harder and harder. When increasing our effort brings no result, we may, figuratively speaking, step back and take a wider look. Over time and with repeated attempts, we may eventually change our way of making sense of things, that is, the worldview that holds the problem. Once we see the world differently, we are able to construct a new solution for the now reframed old problem.[4] This change in worldview is a structural change, that is, a change in the way we structure the world so that it makes sense to us. An experience of making multiple carefully discerned but unsuccessful attempts to change structures provided the urgency to create what we have come to call the Social Discernment Cycle.

Systems are interlocking collections of forces and relationships that function in relationship to each other. Merriam-Webster.com defines "system" as "a regularly interacting or interdependent group of items forming a unified whole."[5] The notion of "unified whole" is key, as this whole governs the behavior of the parts. Systems can involve people, so we can speak of a social system, a political system, or an economic system, but the role of humans in systems may also be nonexistent or minimal, as in a number system or quantum mechanics. Groups of organs that work together to perform a vital function are systems; the stomach can't perform its work independently of the rest of the system, and likewise the smooth functioning of the rest of the digestive system depends on the stomach working correctly. We also use the term for a group of related natural objects or forces, such as a weather system or a river system or a tidal system, and we frequently learn to our chagrin that disturbing something that looks insignificant disrupts the entire system, sometimes catastrophically. Finally, we call an organized set of doctrines, ideas, or principles usually intended to explain the arrangement or working of a whole a system. If we "swim" inside a system, such as capitalist economics, we may be totally unaware that what appear to us as viable options remain within this economic system, rendering us unable to perceive any options outside that system. We are the proverbial fish, unaware of the medium, the properties and limits of the water we swim in. To us, swimming away, it is just the way things are.

The word "structure" focuses on the interrelationship of the parts, "the arrangement of and relations between the parts or elements of something complex."[6] Two of Merriam-Webster.com's definitions are relevant here: the "organization of parts as dominated by the general character of the whole" and "the aggregate of elements of an entity in their relationships to each other."[7] It's clear from these definitions that systems have structure. In fact, a system's structure is the source of its system behavior, which we can spot by watching a series of events over time.[8] Once we understand how structure impacts systems, we will focus on structures as the operative feature of systems.

In the preceding chapters, I have been using the word "institution" in the same breath as the words "system" and "structure." Sociologically, an institution is a configuration of social interactions that provides stability, coherence, order, legitimacy, and shape to human social interactions. Institutions emerge out of social interactions and are perpetuated over time, indeed over human generations. Constructive theologian Eleazar Fernandez, citing Wolfhart Pannenberg, notes other functions of institutions: they "stabilize society; solidify the interactions so that they do not become haphazard; raise reciprocity to the level of obligation; order meaning; mediate the relations of individuals to each other into a meaningful and coherent whole and regulate relations among individuals in connection to basic and secondary needs."[9] As an academic institution, my seminary provides such structures as curricula that guide and constrain both students and faculty; student services to ensure sufficient welfare to those who seek to study and live in our community; and faculty handbooks, contracts, and diplomas to "raise reciprocity to the level of obligation." Clearly institutions are a subset of systems.

In our attempt to understand what makes systems work, the first thing that we need to know is that systems, by definition, produce their own behavior over time—this characteristic is one of the ways that a system is distinct from a machine, which does exactly the same thing each time. The behavior of a system will be characteristic of that particular system. The corollary is equally thought provoking: the same force applied to another system will produce a different reaction. Nor do systems necessarily respond in a linear cause-and-effect manner, something that regularly catches us off guard when there is an unintended consequence to our action.

A second crucial observation: Structures, by their very nature, preserve their form. They are resilient, which is not the same as saying that they are static.[10] But they do resist structural change. Imagine a fishnet. Now imagine that this net is held by persons stationed every few feet around its entire circumference, pulling it taut. If one person on the circumference yanks the net hard to the left, what happens to the nice flat net and the people holding it? The nodes near the force absorb some of the force, but when the force exceeds the combined power of the net to resist, the net moves—more close to the force, and less farther away from the force. What the net doesn't do is move neatly in a straight line in the direction that the force pulls it. In fact, the force travels through all the nodes, those in front, to the back, and to both sides. It ripples throughout the net. But relatively quickly, the net returns to its original shape. This property of structures helps explain why the effect of a single intervention to a well-established system can appear to vanish, leaving the system looking as if nothing changed.

But, despite this penchant for order in systems, the universe is governed by *disorder*. How can this be? Over the last thirty years, this question led natural and social scientists to a third crucial observation: dynamic systems share some common elements across their immense diversity. (1) They are *complex,* composed of many different agents interacting with each other in many different ways simultaneously. (2) The richness of these interactions allows systems to *undergo spontaneous self-organization*—so our modern university is a different order of complexity than its nineteenth-century counterpart. (3) These self-organizing systems are *adaptive,* turning whatever happens to their advantage. (4) They are also unpredictable in their attempts to adapt, operating on *"the edge of chaos,"* as complexity scientist Chris Langton puts it.

The process works like this: For all dynamic systems, order quickly settles down into stasis, while chaos leads to too much randomness, preventing patterns from forming. Between too much and too little order is a state of enough but not too much, called "complexity," that allows patterns to form, re-form, and improve in relation to all other forces operating simultaneously. The pattern is immediately recognizable in the chemistry of water. Ice occurs in the "order" state, with all the molecules lined up in lattices; steam is chaotic, with molecules banging into each other in no pattern whatsoever; and liquid water illustrates complex state at the edge of chaos where the molecular bonds form and re-form according to the rules of fluid dynamics. In life forms, the pattern looks like this: Statis (no life) $\longrightarrow$ Life/Intelligence $\longrightarrow$ Too "noisy" for life forms to cohere. In dynamic systems of all kinds, order and complexity emerge from the bottom up, not the top down, and thrive on the edge of chaos.[11]

The fourth crucial observation: in order to understand system behavior, it is necessary to grasp all the aspects of a system whole. The classic fable of the blind men and the elephant—each blind man, grabbing a different part of the elephant, was sure he could describe "elephant" accurately—reminds us that each one's certainty was anything but accurate. Often our attempts to influence a system are foiled by the fact that we perceive only part of it, act on what we see, and are surprised when our action doesn't produce the expected response.

Systems theorist Donella Meadows insists that, though jargon about systems abounds, we do intuitively understand systems at some level and have worked with them all our lives. In fact, as children, we master systems as a matter of course. She brings that point home by translating some system jargon into common folk wisdom:

> Because of feedback delays within complex systems, by the time a problem becomes apparent it may be unnecessarily difficult to solve.
>
> —*A stitch in time saves nine.*

> According to the competitive exclusion principle, if a reinforcing feedback loop rewards the winner of a competition with the means to win further competitions, the result will be the elimination of all but a few competitors.
>
> —*For he that hath, to him shall be given; and he that hath not, from him shall be taken even that which he hath (Mark 4:25).*
>
> or
>
> *–The rich get richer and the poor get poorer.*

> A diverse system with multiple pathways and redundancies is more stable and less vulnerable to external shock than a uniform system with little diversity.
>
> *–Don't put all your eggs in one basket.*[12]

What makes a system rather than a simple collection of things? You know you are dealing with a system if you can answer positively the first three of these questions. The fourth is a clincher:

> Can you identify parts? . . . and
>
> Do the parts affect each other? . . . and
>
> Do the parts together produce an effect that is different from the effect of each part on its own? . . . and perhaps
>
> Does the effect, the behavior over time, persist in a variety of circumstances?[13]

A system, then, is more than the sum of its parts. But it's the interaction of the parts that makes systems so puzzling. Sometimes it's a flow of information and other forces of which we are not aware; at other times, functions or purposes elude us. Sometimes systems are nested inside systems. These subsystems may have different purposes from each other and from the larger system, and the net effect of all these various forces and purposes may add up to surprising—and from a planning point of view, unpredictable—system behaviors. In fact, says Meadows, the least obvious part of a system is its purpose, but a system's purpose is often the most crucial determinant of the system's behavior. Changing the purpose of a system often brings radical change in behavior. For example, if a seminary changes its mission from educating leadership for the church to educating the laity in the church, the entire curriculum must shift, the faculty be employed differently, and support services reorganized to the needs of a different student population. A well-crafted mission statement that clarifies the mission of the institution, then, is crucial, as it clarifies how the parts of the institution are ordered in service to the mission. Changing the mission statement brings about the possibility that the ordering of institutional resources actually changes as well. Notice that I said that there is a *possibility* that the parts of the institution will change in relation to a new mission statement. More about that possibility later.

The relationship between the various elements of the system is also crucial. Changing the behavior of one element can sometimes bring radical changes to the system over time.[14] If humans kill off all natural predators in an area, the deer population will escalate (unless held in check artificially) until it eats everything in sight, and then it will crash.

In order to understand two other elements of complex structures, stocks and flows, imagine a bathtub full of water with its drain plugged and its faucets turned off. Over time, the water level remains the same (to keep the model simple, let's ignore evaporation). When I take out the plug, the water drains steadily until the tub is empty. But if, when the tub is only partly empty, I turn the faucet on a little, the water level drops more slowly because I am replacing some water as more flows out. If I turn the faucet more and replace water faster than the drain allows it to escape, the water will gradually rise until it exceeds the original waterline and hits the emergency overflow, thereby increasing the outflow again. If I add water at exactly the same rate at which it is exiting the tub, I have caused the system to be in dynamic equilibrium, with the water level staying the same while water is flowing through the tub. A classic example of dynamic equilibrium played out in the U.S. political system at the time of the 2013 government shutdown. The Republicans refused to pass a "clean" resolution to balance the budget unless the Democrats defunded the Affordable Care Act, which they refused to do. Neither side could work its will on the other—individual actors moving furiously but the government as a whole going nowhere.

In the bathtub model, water is the stock. A stock is the material or information that has built up in a system over time. Stocks change over time through flows, that is, the filling and draining (or deposits and withdrawals, births and deaths, purchases and sales, growth and decay, etc.) in the system. We can spot stocks easier than flows, but it is the flows that determine what actually happens to the stocks. Both the inflows and outflows—not just the inflows—change the level of the stock. So we can build roads (inflow to the stock of highways), or we can repair roads in a timely manner and delay the moment we have to build a new road (decrease the outflow)—"a stitch in time saves nine."

A stock doesn't have to be physical. A company's name recognition and its reputation are stocks, as is the reserve of goodwill that causes people to cut some slack for a colleague's Monday morning cranky behavior. Stocks do have finite limits: for example, the debt ceiling sets the limit on the stock of money that the U.S. government can spend without special permission from Congress.

In Social Discernment, the hoped-for outcome can be a decrease in negative system effect—in system language, slowing the rate of decrease of a positive stock by slowing its flow out of the system. Likewise, we want to encourage a positive effect on the system, the equivalent of raising the size of a positive stock (increasing a flow in the opposite direction)—or both simultaneously.

Now that we know what stocks and flows are, it is possible to add the element of time into our picture. Back to our example of the bathtub full of water, with the plug in and the faucet off. When I pull the plug, the water doesn't vanish instantaneously. It takes time to flow out, and the amount of time has to do with the properties of water and the size of the drain, and so on. The point is that stocks take time to change, because flows take time to flow. That means that stocks act as buffers, delays, lags, ballast, and sources of momentum in a system—for better or for worse. I forget about time lag when my computer program is opening slowly and I impatiently click the mouse several extra times. Now not only does the original program need to open, so do three more copies, further delaying my work. Changes in stock set the pace of the dynamics of the system. We can overdraw water from the aquifer for some time before the aquifer is damaged, and we can heat up the atmosphere worldwide for some years before the melting ice caps reach the point where rising ocean water swallows up island nations. The lags imposed by stocks allow room to maneuver, to experiment, and to revise policies that aren't working—that is, if people actually believe that stocks are being drawn down at an unsustainable rate.[15]

Getting a sense of the rate of change in the stocks in a given system has several benefits when discerning systems. Knowing that things can't change any faster may mean that we don't give up too soon. Or it may help us refrain from pushing harder and harder and causing resistance to increase apace. But we may also be able to use the time lag to effect a positive outcome by riding on the momentum. We know, for example, that Social Security will run short of money sometime in the future, so we can choose to make small adjustments to the system now and avoid a major catastrophe later.

Complex systems involve multiple sets of stocks and flows, not just one. The interaction of these "system systems" is called a "feedback loop." Meadows defines feedback loop as "a closed chain of causal connections from a stock, through a set of decisions or rules or physical laws or actions that are dependent on the level of the stock and back again through a flow to change the stock."[16] For example, when the inventory in a business falls below a set point (equivalent to Meadows's "rule"), the stock clerk orders more, so that there will be sufficient inventory on hand to cover future sales. When the number of mice, rats, voles, and moles expands, so does the population of foxes and raptors, thereby keeping the population of rodents from getting out of hand. Every stable system has balancing feedback loops—it's the interaction of the feedback loops that keeps the system in or moving toward dynamic equilibrium. If the positive feedback loop gets enhanced (through adding another element or through decreasing the negative loop), it will either expand exponentially or experience runaway collapses over time—as in the example of the deer population lacking any natural or artificial mechanism to check its numbers.

An important feature of feedback loops is that the information delivered by a feedback loop can only affect future behavior of the stock, not past behavior. The stock clerk in our imaginary store can only affect the future amount of the merchandise on hand. He or she can never deliver a signal fast enough to correct behavior that drove the current feedback. So the flow must be set appropriately to compensate for the draining or inflow of the stock over time. This set can never be perfect, causing oscillation in the size of the stocks—they get a little low, triggering the stock clerk's order, and, when the new merchandise arrives, the stock is a little overfull. This, in turn, triggers a sale to lower the stock to a manageable size, it eventually drops below the danger point, the stock clerk orders, and so on.

Any delay in balancing the feedback loop makes a system likely to oscillate. Surprising system behavior can be caused by these kinds of oscillations. In our imaginary store, suppose the supply company inadvertently sends an incorrect order, constituting a major delay in the feedback loop. In the time it takes for this mistake to be remedied, the store runs out of the item completely and must issue rain checks. By this point, an ordinary-size order will not cover the usual rate of sales plus fulfill all the rain checks, so the clerk must order a larger amount to cover the backlog. The stock oscillates due to the delay in the feedback loop. Decreasing the amount of time it takes information to flow through the system makes each approximation closer to the trigger and lowers the oscillation of the stock in and out of the stock room.[17]

Peter Senge puts these somewhat esoteric stock, flow, and feedback concepts into colloquial if somewhat counterintuitive statements about systems and their behavior, which hopefully now make some sense:

- Today's problems come from yesterday's "solutions."
- The harder you push, the harder the system pushes back.
- Behavior grows better before it grows worse.
- The easy way out usually leads back in.
- The cure can be worse than the disease.
- Faster is slower.
- Cause and effect are not closely related in time and space.
- Small changes can produce big results—but the areas of highest leverage are often the least obvious.
- You can have your cake and eat it too—but not all at once.
- Dividing an elephant in half does not produce two small elephants.
- There is no blame.[18]

There are no separate systems, says Meadows; the whole world is a continuum.[19] So how do we draw a boundary around a system in order to examine it and its behavior, as we will want to do in Social Discernment? The purpose about which we discern determines where we draw the boundary. For example, if the Pastor Nominating Committee is to discern the next pastor for Hope Church, clearly Hope Church needs to be the basic structure. But Hope Church isolated from the structures in which it and its members are nested may lead to a strange choice for the next pastor. So the committee would do well also to analyze the structures in which Hope Church is a subset, such as the Presbyterian Church (U.S.A.) and the neighborhood, as well as the systems that together constitute Hope Church, including the session, the paid and volunteer staff, the various ministries and committees, and the individual family units. To achieve this picture, the committee needs not only to see the major systems that constitute Hope Church but also to "stand outside" Hope Church and see it as nestled within other systems. Only by looking at a larger order and a smaller order of system can we get an effective picture of Hope Church for the purposes of the committee's work. Determining at what level of the structure to focus in order to achieve the desired end is part of our task as we begin the Social Discernment Cycle.

Donella Meadows gives us one more gift as we seek to understand how systems work. She analyzes various ways that systems can get frozen, "system traps," as she calls them, and offers sometimes counterintuitive ways to break these logjams. Four examples follow:

Policy Resistance. *Trap:* When various actors try to pull a system state toward various goals, the result can be policy resistance. Any new policy, especially if it's effective, just pulls the system state farther from the goals of other actors and produces additional resistance, with the result that no one likes, but that everyone expends considerable effort in maintaining [here's why a new mission statement may not actually result in a realignment of the structure]. *The Way Out:* Let go. Bring in all the actors and use the energy formerly expended on resistance to seek out mutually satisfactory ways for all goals to be realized—or redefinitions of larger and more important goals that everyone can pull together toward.

Escalation. *Trap:* When the state of one stock is determined by trying to surpass the state of another stock—and vice versa—then there is a reinforcing feedback loop carrying the system into an arms race, a wealth race, a smear campaign, escalating loudness, escalating violence. The escalation is exponential and can lead to extremes surprisingly quickly. If nothing is done, the spiral will be stopped by someone's collapse—because exponential growth cannot go on forever. *The Way Out:* The best way out of this trap is to avoid getting in it. If caught in an escalating system, one can refuse to compete (unilaterally disarm), thereby interrupting the reinforcing loop. Or one can negotiate a new system with balancing loops to control the escalation.

Rule Beating. *Trap:* Rules to govern a system can lead to rule-beating—perverse behavior that gives the appearance of obeying the rules or achieving the goals, but that actually distorts the system. *The Way Out:* Design or redesign rules to release creativity not in the direction of beating the rules, but in the direction of achieving the purpose of the rules.

Seeking the Wrong Goal. *Trap:* System behavior is particularly sensitive to the goals of feedback loops. If the goals—the indicators of satisfaction of the rules—are defined inaccurately or incompletely, the system may obediently work to produce a result that is not really intended or wanted [a case of "garbage in garbage out"]. *The Way Out:* Specify indicators and goals that reflect the real welfare of the system. Be especially careful not to confuse effort with result or you will end up with a system that is producing effort, not result.[20]

It is important for us to understand not only the nature of systems but also how systemic change happens. Usually, we see a problem, apply a corrective to the problem, and expect the problem to vanish. This strategy is what Paul Watzlawick and colleagues call a "first-order change." But in a system, a problem is only a symptom of something else. In order to affect the underlying system, not just the symptom, we need a "second-order change," that is, a change of system itself.[21] A second-order change is applied to what, in first-order-change perspective, appears to be the solution—which is precisely the real system problem. First-order change appears to be based on common sense while second-order change often appears counterintuitive, weird, or puzzling. In a first-order change, the system is tweaked but remains essentially the same; in second-order change, the entire structure may be reorganized, resulting in new properties, new rules of order, and new change agents.[22]

In second-order change, moreover, we deal with effects, rather than assumed causes. That is, "we can take the situation as it exists here and now, without necessarily understanding why it got to be that way, and in spite of our ignorance of its origin and evolution, we can do something with (or about) it."[23] Instead of asking, why is it this way? we first ask, what is going on? and only much farther into the analysis, if at all, ask why this might be the case. Transformation of the system occurs in *what* happens, not in *why* it happens. In science, the question "why" is almost enshrined in dogma, yet simple explanation, by itself, does not bring about innovation. Likewise, in human behavior, insight only contributes to an explanation of the problem, not to its solution. We recognize this difference in the all-too-common statement: "I am this way because of how my parents raised me." Meanwhile the same problematic behavior continues unabated, now justified by the explanation.

In complex (including living) systems, we can add several important nuances to our understanding of change. These systems, it turns out, emerge from the bottom up. They respond to local forces, which makes it possible for small local interventions to have disproportional effect on the whole system. And, since these systems never reach equilibrium, the challenge is to focus more on the change itself than on the goal of the change and on the establishment of networks rather than single outcomes. "The power lies in the connections," says scientist Paul Farmer. It's more important to look at how systems behave, not how they are constructed, and then attempt to tune the internal agents so that they operate at the edge of chaos. It's here where optimal adaptation occurs under the ideal proportion of stability and chaos.[24]

Social entrepreneurs point to similar systems dynamics but use quite different language. They might put their system learning into the following "rules": (1) *Accountability and commitment:* people will work hard for and be accountable to that which they help create. (2) *Learn from one another:* begin with a diverse sample of persons who represent the world you want to create and invite them to own their own process. The future begins to show up in the process itself. (3) *Bias toward the future:* pay less attention to the past and how things got to the present situation; once you have described the present, focus on the possibilities for the future. (4) *Pay attention to how people engage:* spend time and energy here rather than in studies and experts. Relatedness is the foundation of all social achievement. (5) *Small scale and slow growth*: this scale allows for internal adjustment and learning to emerge at every step and ultimately results in a more long-lasting and pervasive change.[25]

The goal of Social Discernment can be stated in terms of changes in systems: We will be seeking the first contemplative action that addresses the system so that it then moves toward God's call for that system. Thus we need to understand not only systems and how they work, but also how they may be changed. The steps of the Social Discernment Cycle are designed precisely to assist in this process.

We have just learned one of the most important prerequisites for effecting change in systems: to see the system "whole" in order to see how the various parts interact to form that whole. Senge, Scharmer, Jaworski, and Flowers go further, claiming, "What is most systemic is most local." That means, then, that the emerging whole can be served by paying attention to what is right within one's own awareness.[26] A word of caution: the system is composed of more than the sum of the various actors. What assumptions are guiding the actors? What mental models[27] do they use to simplify complex reality, but which also thereby distort it to some degree? What goals do they hold? Do they match the stated mission of the institution and the goals of the other actors? What are the various loops that feed back into each other? As we move into the Social Discernment Cycle, such questions will assist individuals and groups in analyzing their respective structures in such a way that important linkages and blockages will become more evident.

Once we have a sufficiently accurate picture of the system, the ways of intervening can be tailored to the system blockages. We might quit fixing the symptom and look at the larger system maintaining this behavior in the first place, that is, we might reframe what we see as the issue. We might redefine the purpose of the system, supply improved information, reduce time delays, or, alternatively, slow down the process of change to allow for greater reflection, ownership, and integration of people and systems. We might apply leverage to the system. We might quit shifting the burden or lowering the vision to compensate for a system that is figuratively dragging its feet. The next paragraphs briefly treat each of these possible ways to intervene systemically.

One of the first things we might do is *change the frame of what appears to be a problem.* We can change the size of the system in which to address the problem or the conceptual or emotional setting in which the change is experienced. A perfect example of conceptual reframing is attributed to King Christian X of Denmark during the Nazi occupation. In reply to the Nazi emissary for "Jewish questions" who wanted to know how King Christian intended to solve the "Jewish problem" in Denmark, King Christian is reputed to have said, "We do not have a Jewish problem; *we* don't feel inferior." Later, as the story goes, when the order came down that all Jews were to wear the Star of

David armband, the king announced that there were no differences between one Dane and another, and therefore that the German decree applied to all Danish citizens. He was reputedly the first to wear the Star of David, and the population overwhelmingly followed his example. The Nazis were forced to cancel the order.[28] The story, though unfounded, does illustrate how one might reframe a problem—here changing the membership of the class "Jew" to membership in the class "Dane," thereby making the order unenforceable. As Peter Senge succinctly puts it, "Leverage often comes from new ways of thinking."[29]

Sometimes system changes are not difficult once we see what the real system issues are. A new goal, if it effectively captures the purpose of the group and is owned by all, will change the output of the group in both significant and subtle ways. Sometimes *supplying improved information or reducing time delays in receiving information* makes an immense difference in the system. Student services in our seminary improved noticeably with the addition of a simple structure, a biweekly student services staff meeting. The only agenda for the meeting was that each person in turn told the others what was going on in his or her area of responsibility in the next two-week period. Everybody then knew the same information at the same time, and the sense of being blindsided or left out of the loop diminished immediately. The staff began spontaneously to offer to help each other in crunch times, and the sense of a team united around excellent student services grew noticeably. The time invested, ninety minutes approximately every other week, paid off amply in improved morale and service. Sometimes, paradoxically, it is important to slow down the rate of system change. Time to ponder, respond, shift mental models, and otherwise regroup, and even to play, can be exactly what injects new life in a sluggish system.

Another way to foster system change is to *look for points of high leverage, in contrast to points of low leverage*. A point of high leverage is one in which a relatively small change produces a proportionately large system effect.[30] In Social Discernment, we sometimes speak of this point as the "soft spot in the system." This phrase indicates the point at which a strategically placed action may change the dynamic preventing an institution from following God's call more closely. Finding these points of high leverage, however, is often difficult because the overt system (the system on paper or that is immediately visible) may not be the system as it actually functions. The actual system may have all sorts of subtle and unacknowledged feedback loops and resistances preventing the system from operating as it appears that it should on paper. Here is where the analysis of the system is crucial. But just as crucial is the role of intuition—our best logic often gets blown out of the water by system behavior. The Social Discernment process makes room for both careful rational analysis and intuition as the discerners ponder and pray their way through the process.

So what are some places of high leverage? One point of high leverage is around rules, both the power to make rules and the power to enforce them. That's why lobbyists congregate around legislative bodies when they are crafting legislation. It's also why petitioners gather around decision makers, as, for example, when a student seeks relief by going to the dean rather than to the director of student services, or a faculty member skips the department head and the dean to head directly to the president. Note that, if successful, the petitioner may have the solution he or she wanted (or not), but more importantly from a systems point of view, the subsidiarity within the system has been effectively weakened. Why go through the system, why obey the rules, if you can directly influence the rule maker?

We might *quit shifting the burden or lowering the vision to compensate* for a system that is figuratively dragging its feet. This pattern is, in essence, treating the symptom rather than the cause. The underlying problem grows worse, masked because the symptoms appear to improve, even clear up—Senge's "behavior grows better [symptom] before it grows worse [underlying problem]." But the system eventually loses the ability (or the will) to maintain the improvement, without having developed the ability to solve the underlying problem. A classic example is the welfare state, where the problems leading to chronic unemployment and homelessness are never addressed, while the homeless and underemployed are subsidized, thereby improving their condition and getting them off the street. After some time, say, several generations, we find that the state is now responsible for subsidizing a whole class of people. A local government that has taken great pains to deal with the problem of its homeless will serve as a magnet for more homeless, increasing the burden on the government, which now has more than its share of homeless. The only way to stop shifting the burden is to address the underlying issues that cause homelessness in the first place, and doing so in sufficiently wide scale that the problem doesn't simply migrate to another part of the system. In the case of homelessness, sufficient affordable housing stock, living wages, sufficient jobs, job training, an educational system that actually prepares students for the workplace—these are tougher issues whose solution is not so easily managed.

Or, we might try something as simple as shifting our perspective from looking at the problems to looking at the possibilities.[31]

Systems are not magical or irrational, though they may at first appear so. It is possible to begin to see at the system level, and our ability to do so can increase with practice. The Social Discernment Cycle is designed to bring these system insights to the process of discernment, joining our prayerful search for God's call to the very systems that we inhabit.

So let's begin. The first task for both individuals and groups is to select the system that you will discern. The following exercises will help you do that.

## Selecting the Structure

This exercise helps you arrive at a structure in which you now participate and define its boundaries sufficiently that you can focus on the structure in the subsequent steps of the Social Discernment Cycle.

1. Let the silence deepen around you. Enter into it. Renew your desire to follow God's call as it unfolds through your reflection/action. Do not rush. Simply turn your attention to God, as you experience God, and address your desire to God. Invite God to direct you to the structure in which you will concentrate your effort.
2. Notice the many structures in which your life takes place. Perhaps an event stands out that is more than it seems and suggests a particular structure. Or notice which structures in your life carry the most energy and concern or evoke in you the desire to improve them.
3. Allow one of these structures to present itself for your consideration. Describe this structure and the place you hold in it.
4. Is this a structure in which you are a regular player? What about this structure could bear improvement?
5. Bring this event and structure to God and attend to any sense that arises in you.

Note: A social structure is a formal set of rules, regulations, and relationships that exists— consciously or unconsciously—between and among people and is not dependent upon the personalities of specific individuals. These structures live on even after individuals depart from them. Examples include committees, corporations, towns, congregations, schools, and so on but also normative patterns enforced by laws and mores, such as distinctive ethnic or regional cultures, racism, sexism, corporate culture, and globalization.

We saw in the last chapter that Sister Joan's awareness that something was amiss at the Eastside Sisters' Residence surfaced through her practice of Awareness Examen. Gradually, the examen helped her crystallize the awareness that what was happening was more than personal, leading her to this exercise. As she reflected on these more structurally oriented points, she realized that something in the way the group's norms were stated was simply not covering the situation, because Sister Katherine was honoring all the group's norms. Once Sister Joan identified the structural nature of the issue, she was only a step away from naming this structure as "the unspoken expectations of this living group." In Sister Joan's situation, a presenting incident pointed toward the structure, which would not have surfaced in her attention had there been no conflict among the sisters.

If you are attempting to grasp the Social Discernment Cycle for the first time, I encourage you to learn the cycle by focusing first on how God might be calling you within one of the systems that permeate your own life, be it a work situation, a neighborhood problem, your child's classroom, a committee in your church, or the local political action group to which you belong. Later, you can add the complexity of group decision making. The above exercise is designed to help you select that structure.

In the Hope Church example, the Pastor Nominating Committee's structure and work was detailed ahead of time, so its members did not have to spend energy on selecting the structure. Nor did they need a presenting incident to focus their discernment, as did Sister Joan. But other groups may need to clarify if there is something that they should attend to through a discernment process or if they wish to use discernment to move forward with something that is within their group's decision-making purview. Sometimes a crisis arises that the group must address. In these kinds of situations, it will be important to clarify what is at issue and surface the underlying structure that upholds it. The preceding exercise has been modified below to assist such groups. It assumes a leader who will introduce both the silence and the points of sharing and bring the exercise to a close. The leader should also feel free to further adapt the questions to fit the situation of the group more closely.

## Selecting the Structure for Groups

This exercise helps you arrive at a structure in which you now participate and define its boundaries sufficiently that you can focus on the structure in the subsequent steps of the Social Discernment Cycle.

1. Let the silence deepen around you. Enter into it. Renew your desire to follow God's call as it unfolds through your reflection/action. Do not rush. Simply turn your attention to God, as you experience God, and

address your desire to God. Invite God to direct you to the structure in which you will concentrate your effort.

2. Perhaps an event stands out that is more than it seems and suggests a particular structure. Or notice which structures carry the most energy and concern or evoke in individuals or the group the desire to improve them. Surface all these structures.

3. Allow one of these structures to present itself for consideration. Perhaps it is a structure where something is not going well, or it may be a structure that is performing beautifully but that your group would like to enhance. Describe this structure and the place your group and its members hold in it.

4. What about this structure could bear improvement?

5. Bring any precipitating event and the structure to God. Attend carefully to any thoughts or feelings that arise in the group members.

Armed with an understanding of discernment, systems, and the Social Discernment Cycle itself, we are now ready to discover how God is calling in and through the system.

PART 2    The Social Discernment Cycle

Chapter 4

# The Situation and the System

*P*art 1 laid groundwork for a basic understanding of discernment, particularly as it occurs in a group setting. You now know the steps composing discerned decision making, no matter the specific method used. You have begun to pray for spiritual freedom, for a "heart as large as the world" that grounds discernment. You now have an initial grasp of the power of systems to resist or foster change and some sense that systems have their own change dynamics. You have begun to search out the issue and system that you will discern. It is time to begin the Social Discernment Cycle.

The chapters in part 2 walk you systematically through the process, for process it indeed is. These chapters are laid out differently than in part 1. Here, each chapter begins with a spiritual practice that captures the dynamics of that phase of the Social Discernment Cycle. These exercises form the heart of the discernment process. Reading them over will give you a measure of insight into the dynamics of the Social Discernment Cycle, but not until you work the process will you actually engage in discernment. Spend as much time as you need on each exercise, keeping notes about the thoughts and feelings elicited by each question. Some questions will seem relevant and fruitful; others may not. I recommend that you attempt all questions, as sometimes the relevance of a question comes to light later in the process.

Only after you have prayerfully digested the questions, turn to the discussion that follows. When you turn to the commentary, you will be filtering it through the lens of your or your group's own prayer, intuition, imagination, storytelling, and analysis. Working in this order minimizes the possibility that the text dictates what you imagine or think about your structure. Put theologically, this order—praying and sharing, followed by reading and discussing the commentary—allows maximum openness to the Holy Spirit working through the process to bring out the aspects most salient to your discernment situation. The text comments on the theology behind various questions so that you can further understand their relevance to the process and illumines the dynamics of each step as you do it. You will read the text differently in the light of the Spirit's action on you or your group, particularly when your experience of prayer and reflection is fresh and vivid.

Each chapter also continues the two case examples begun in the introduction so that you can see how discernment processes for an individual and a group might unfold. Your discernment, however, will be unique to you, your structure, and your situation.

I strongly recommend that both individual and group discerners record your reflections in a journal for easy reference as you proceed. Sometimes a key insight emerges early, but its importance does not appear until later in your prayer and reflection. Your journal record ensures that seemingly unimportant observations and connections are not lost. If possible, I encourage individual discerners to share your answers and anything that strikes you from your reflections with a spiritual companion, pastor, spouse, or friend. This sharing will help you notice things that otherwise might escape your attention, especially if your spiritual companion is able through the contemplative listening skills described in chapter 2 to help you move more deeply into your own responses. In both cases, however, take care to maintain appropriate confidentiality, sharing such information only in confidential settings.

If you are working in a discerning group, I suggest a two-step process: In the first step, all members work through the questions individually, keeping their own notes, sharing highlights with the other members of the discernment group. The group keeps a record of these comments, then takes a collective step back from their comments, and the participants share what strikes them about either individual comments or the comments seen as a whole. The goal of this two-level procedure is to begin distilling the core insights from the multiple individual contributions.

We begin with further reflection and prayer about the system, focusing on the particular matter for discernment that is showing up in the system and how it is appearing in the system. Both individuals and groups may employ the following exercise. This reflection will assist in examining the structure through an experience within it. The goal is to surface what is going on and how you feel about it. The first step here, and in all subsequent practices, is to renew your desire for spiritual freedom, for "a heart as large as the world," so that as the call of God becomes clear, you will be ready to respond. But remember, spiritual freedom is a grace!

## Looking at the Current Situation

Prayerfully answer the following questions, recording the answers in an appropriate format for later use.

1. Prepare yourself to address God and for God to address you. Renew your desire to follow God's call once it becomes clear. Ask God for guidance to see deeply into the structure and to respond with honesty and freedom.
2. Who are the players in this structure? What roles do they play? How are these roles and players related?
3. What is the physical environment like?
4. What concrete behaviors are happening to you and to others in the structure that you have chosen? Is there a story or a situation that captures these behaviors?
5. What are your feelings about these realities and behaviors?
6. What subjects (people, structures, tasks, ideals, etc.) in this structure or in this situation do you connect with? Who or what do you avoid?
7. When you think or talk about this structure or situation, who or what do you tend to leave out (certain people or subjects)? How do you feel when this happens?
8. Given the current situation in the structure, how are you responding physically, emotionally, intellectually, and spiritually?
9. Who are marginalized, suffering, powerless, neglected, ignored, invisible, trivialized, or ridiculed in this situation or in this structure?
10. Stand in the shoes of these marginalized subjects and look at the structural situation you have just described. From this perspective, what do you see differently about this structure?
11. As you become reflective and prayerful about the situation, note the tugs and pushes of your heart. Write them down *after* you reflect and pray.

"Looking at the Current Situation" is our name for the first formal step of the Social Discernment Cycle. It also could be called "Describing the Current Structure," because this title also accurately describes the discernment task of this first step. We want to get a snapshot of the structure at this point in time. We want to know the players in the structure, human and otherwise, to notice how they interact, to see who is in and who is out, and what is really going on that is unspoken or is going on precisely because unspoken. We want to overhear the conversations in the hall and the break room, at the watercooler or in the parking lot, as well as listen to the official rhetoric. We want to become acquainted with the players we haven't really known, rarely interact with, or actively ignore, which may require extra effort to step out of our respective comfort zones. And, especially in this step, we want to pay attention to the feelings stirred up by the situation or the system.

In the literature on the Pastoral Circle upon which the Social Discernment Cycle is based, this first step is called "Insertion"[1] and "Contact."[2] Authors Joe Holland and Peter Henriot were approaching systems from the outside, as pastoral agents looking for the critical point for intervention. By this choice of language, they were attempting to describe the process of coming close to the real people and dynamics of a given system. From this perspective, one "inserts" oneself into the system as it really functions in all its concreteness. For example, Henriot describes how the small Christian communities that have been set up in a very poor Zambian parish are inserted into the life of their community through stories. The group members who gather for their weekly meeting are invited to listen to the story of Mrs. Amai Banda. Mrs. Banda sells tomatoes by the side of the road in order to earn a little money to feed her family. Her daily activities are described, her real-life struggles illustrated. Then the group members are asked if they know anyone like Mrs. Banda. Perhaps some in the room have had similar experiences to Mrs. Banda. The participants are given the chance to share how they feel about such struggles in their own lives and in the lives of their neighbors. The participants in the small Christian community do not know Mrs. Banda personally, but they know others like her—indeed, some others like her are in the room. Henriot concludes his description of this step: "This is the moment of *contact*, the anecdotal, the asking of *what* is happening."[3]

In a later essay, James Hug uses the term "experience" to describe this first exposure to the structure.[4] This term suggests that one is already in the system but is examining it with fresh eyes, newly attuned to the structural dynamics. Although we call this step "Noticing and Describing," our purpose is the same. At this point, we want to have contact with the players in the system, to let them evoke feelings, indeed, our empathy. In order to achieve this close contact even when not physically present, we invite real stories of concrete behavior.

This first step, by whatever term we use, invites us to "walk around" inside the system, to listen to its stories, yes, but also to tell our own stories of what it is like in this system from our various perspectives. Where and with whom are we locating ourselves as we begin our process? Whose experience is being considered? What feelings are evoked?

You may notice that the questions slip back and forth between asking you to describe a structure and to describe a situation that has occurred within the structure. Using both of these terms, while a bit awkward, is intentional; each offers a somewhat different path to describing the system. You may be clear what the system is that you wish to focus on in your discernment. In that case, as you describe the system, you can also describe a situation that exemplifies the system behaviors. This story, then, provides a solidity, a concreteness to what can so easily be a collection of vague abstractions—an occupational hazard when working with systems.[5]

There is another reason to associate a system with a concrete incident that occurred in the system. Relating to something as abstract as a system is often very difficult. How do you have empathy for something so impersonal? Encountering a real person, as revealed in one or more concrete instances within the system, humanizes the system. Being able to empathize with the experience of a real person within the system can also provide the impetus to stay with the Social Discernment and resulting actions over the long haul that it often takes for systems to change.

But rarely do we set out to examine a structure for its own sake—usually something has happened that suggests that we should do so. Likewise, you may not yet be clear about what the system is. When an incident has occurred that bears reflection, then identify the system that holds the incident. In this case, the incident leads to the system. Sister Joan's situation at Eastside Sisters' Residence exemplifies this latter option: Because the assumptions underlying the sisters' behavior were unarticulated, perhaps even unconscious, they were both powerful and puzzling. She would not have noticed them—and that they formed a system—had it not been for the criticism her friend's behavior elicited. As Sister Joan concluded the last exercise, she named her system "the unnamed assumptions about how we live together." Once she had named the structure, she could profitably undertake this new exercise.

The incident or situation the exercise asks for, then, may either illustrate typical system behavior or point to the as-yet-unnoticed system underlying the behavior. Note, however, that we are much more prone to isolate a negative incident than a positive one, as Sister Joan did. Social Discernment may indeed offer ways to address a negative situation, but we also want to focus discernment energy on looking for what is working in the structure, what is already bearing fruit, and nourish that positive movement. At this point, you might intentionally make space for a positive incident to drift into your mind. In fact, if you give yourself permission to tell a number of stories about life in your structure, both negative and positive stories may show up, giving a fuller picture of the underlying structure and evoking a variety of emotional responses.

Incidents also encourage us to focus on the event level, and we may try to manage the system by managing the individual events. Peter Senge calls this penchant "the fixation on events."[6] In Social Discernment, however, we want to do something quite different with the incident: namely, to unearth the system that is framing it and countless other incidents and to connect to the system with immediacy and empathy. Hearkening back to the systems discussion in chapter 3, we will not be trying to fix the causes of any situation or incident, but instead we will address ourselves to the underlying structure. It is at this second level that systemic change occurs. The remainder of the Social Discernment Cycle will assist us in examining the system that maintains this particular framing incident and then searching for the point where our action may be able to best leverage the system toward greater fulfillment of its vocation.

The exercise encourages us to identify the marginalized subjects in the system. Often we focus on persons as we answer this question, but the wording leaves open the possibility that the marginalized might be some other facet of creation, or even creation itself. What do I mean by "marginalized"? Two emphases are possible; which one makes the most sense may be a factor of the size and complexity of your system. At one level, the marginalized are those pushed to the edges of society for whatever reason. The materially poor are economically disadvantaged, and the economic system is set up in a way that ensures that they individually, or others like them, will remain at the bottom of the economic ladder. In a smaller-scoped system, it may be more useful to define the marginalized as those most powerless to affect the systems that control their lives. Children who are the victims of bullying are unable to affect the system that brutalizes them. They are pushed to the edges of the classroom or peer social system.

Why would we want to identify the marginalized subjects in our system? Marginalized individuals function as the proverbial canary in the coal mine. They signal where the system is holding injustice, where it is causing pain, where it is preventing the fullness of life — sometimes even extinguishing life itself. They signal that unjust powers and principalities (using Wink's language), or anti-Kingdom forces (using Dorr's language), are at work. Their condition is not God's will. Since they are, by definition, the ones not at the table, we will need to invite them to the table of our discernment. We begin by inviting them, at least in our imagination, to fill out our description of the system; their perspective will shed a very different light from the perspective of the system's movers and shakers.

But there is another significant reason to identify the subjects in the structure who are marginalized. These subjects bear the weight of the sin held by the structure. If the institution is to fulfill its vocation, it is there that the effect of its collusion with sin is the most pointed. It's there, as well, that our own personal vocations will come clear: to come alongside the marginalized subjects as God does. We are called to solidarity with these marginalized ones who point the way forward. There, with these subjects, is where God's heart already is.[7]

Another question invites us to describe the physical environment. We are embodied; our location and the qualities of our location matter, often more profoundly than we realize. For instance, in a famous experiment, a doctor tracked the rate of hospital patient recovery via three observable factors—number of days in the hospital, dosage of medications and number of negative nurse notes—and determined that patients randomly assigned to a hospital room that looked out on trees fared noticeably better on all three scales than patients assigned to a room that looked out on a brick wall. If you need another example, ask my friend who suffers from seasonal affective disorder what it feels like and how she functions in the middle of the gray winter days in Medford, Oregon.[8] She never knew she had this condition until she accepted a call to serve a church there and became nonfunctional the first winter. Finally, our campus center is at the top of a hill. The chapel, classrooms, and library, as well as student lounge and faculty and administration offices, are all clustered a few steps from each other at the top of the hill. After the 1989 Loma Prieta earthquake, we had to vacate all the classrooms and offices at the top of that hill. We were forced to relocate these offices and people around the bottom of the hill. For the years we were dislocated from the center of the campus, we seldom saw clusters of students, or clusters of anyone, for that matter. We lost the physical center of the campus, but we lost the communication heart as well. We functioned like discrete individuals, always reaching out for some physical sense of the community that we knew before the earthquake. Physical environment does matter.[9]

Is the space that the system occupies beautiful or ugly? Homey or institutional? Does its configuration promote communication or isolate individuals? Invite interaction with nature or inure actors against nature? Contribute to community or fracture community? Foster hierarchies or egalitarian relationships? Promote creativity or resignation? These are the kinds of observations that may be surprisingly significant in our future analysis.

Looking for the source of irritation, Sister Joan first sought a simple answer in the physical location of the room Sister Katherine was using. Was she disturbing the persons whose bedrooms were above? No, she used the visiting room only in the middle of the day. Was she preventing others from using it? Unlikely, because the others were almost always at their own work sites at that time of the day, and Sister Katherine always notified everyone in advance when she wanted to use the room. Sister Joan herself had used the room in a similar manner and suffered no repercussions. Examining the physical layout of the house suggested that it was not, in this case, the key element.

As you begin to explore the system description, it will be important to attend to one more level of preparation. It does not come out directly in this spiritual practice, but I have laid the foundation more generally in chapter 2 as I described the formation of discerning groups. In Social Discernment, both individual discerners and members of discerning groups need to make explicit their values, perspectives, biases, and stances because they influence the questions that we ask, the judgments we make, and, indeed, what we actually see. "No social analysis is 'value free,'" say Holland and Henriot;[10] likewise no discernment process is free of the influence of the discerners and their perspectives. But a time of clarification brings such perspectives into the conscious awareness of the group. As the group articulates the values it will subscribe to as a group (including biblical texts, denominational statements, the vision and mission of the structure, and other statements of value), they also continue to form themselves into a discerning *system*, with interrelated persons and perspectives, yet functioning as a single discerning unit.

It might sound as if the ideal is a discernment as little contaminated by the perspectives of the discerners as is possible to achieve. I am not making this assertion. Such a group would be impossible to form on scientific grounds; we know from quantum mechanics that all objects influence neighboring objects, making an unbiased group impossible. But such an ideal is problematic on theological grounds as well. As discerners, we remain finite, fallible humans. In our humanness, with all the limitations of our unique perspectives and biases, these particular people are our companions in discernment. In our very humanness, we seek to understand, as best we can, what God desires of us in this particular situation. Discernment never brings certainty; it never ceases to be an act of faith—faith that we can make an adequate determination at all and that the actions we take as a result are actually used by God. "Whatever details we need to focus on in the pastoral circle," says theologian Jon Sobrino, meditating on the life of Oscar Romero, "the most important thing is to let ourselves be affected by what is most real in reality. This affectedness is prior to methodology as such; it can be seen in our openness to conversion, our honesty toward reality, our faithfulness unto death toward reality, and our openness to what reality gives us, that is, grace."[11]

Many Quakers, in fact, actively seek out diversity when they are forming a Clearness Committee.[12] They honor the reality that different people will see different aspects of the situation and will bring out different aspects of the structure. Far from being an impediment, diversity is an asset in discernment if—and this is an important if—the discerners are willing to seek constant conversion toward greater spiritual freedom. Hence, we place this reminder at the beginning of each step of the Social Discernment Cycle.

As individuals begin sharing, the moment of truth quickly arrives. What do we actually *do* with the diversity in the group? Quaker wisdom can help us again. Quakers hold, as a basic tenet of discernment, that "there is that of God in every person."[13] Thus, the wisdom the group needs is dispersed throughout the entire group. The least likely person may hold a crucial piece of wisdom for discernment. In that belief, all offerings are received respectfully, though all may not receive the same weight going forward. The contemplative listening guidelines remind us neither to interrupt nor to contradict the comment of another. Instead, we simply offer our own piece of wisdom and take our hands off of what happens, figuratively speaking. We trust the Spirit to guide the group to move forward on the best wisdom of the group. This way of proceeding is indeed countercultural.

We left Sister Joan's process at the point at which she began to examine the characteristics of her structure. She quickly named the persons, but naming the roles was more subtle. There was no "superior"; the group governed itself collectively. Some roles had to do with the teaching assignment in the high school, but they didn't seem to affect the living dynamics in the house. The dynamics seemed more related to the number of years that the sisters had lived together, with the tightest group having spent more than a dozen years in the same living situation. She could quickly identify those with whom she connected and those she avoided, because this situation had threaded in and out of her daily Awareness Examen for a number of weeks. "Of course," she said to herself, "I feel loyal to Sister Katherine. We've been friends for a long time and I was the one who suggested that she come here in the first place." When she got to the question asking for her personal response to the situation, she wrote in bold letters across her journal, "FRUSTRATED!"

The question about the marginalized seemed easy, too: Sister Katherine was clearly marginalized. But Sister Katherine was perfectly capable of speaking up for herself, so the cause of her marginalization was more that she did not have access to the unspoken dynamics. "But," Sister Joan mused, "if the dynamics were unconscious, neither did any of the rest of us." Nonetheless, she began to imagine what it was like in Sister Katherine's shoes: not feeling "in," unable to quite relax in her own home for fear that she would provoke another comment, unsure about what reaction she would receive if she spoke out, and likely missing the comfort and companions of her last ministry and living situation.

Sister Joan's discernment process so far is straightforward compared to the dynamics of Hope Church and its Pastor Nominating Committee, to which we now turn.

## The Pastor Nominating Committee Begins Its Work

The members of the Pastor Nominating Committee (PNC) recognized that they had several discrete but mutually related tasks as they began meeting. They needed to form themselves into a discerning body, which meant knowing each other at more than a surface level. In particular, they needed a sense of the inner life and faith commitments of their colleagues. They also needed to develop a common understanding of discernment and some clarity on the steps they would need to go through between their early meetings and the point at which they would be able to present a candidate to the congregation. At the suggestion of their liaison from the Committee on Ministry, they began with some faith sharing, using the common prompt, "Describe a time when your faith was encouraged: What happened, who assisted, what was the fruit? Describe a time when your faith was sorely tested: What happened, who was involved, what was the outcome?" They agreed to some simple conversation rules based on contemplative listening with which to receive and respond to each other's faith stories.

Recognizing that this foundation would serve them well throughout the process, they decided to devote two full meetings to this time of establishing the faith orientation among them. At the close of the second meeting, they offered some general comments on what they noticed. A third meeting was devoted to understanding the basic dynamics of discernment, sharing their emerging understandings and reservations and anxieties. At the conclusion of the third meeting, the assembled committee members elected a chair whom they specifically titled "convener" to signal the equal states of all the members.

They also developed a covenant to reflect their consensus on their ways of being together. They decided to begin each of their meetings with a prayer time designed to assist them both individually and as a group to deepen their desire for spiritual freedom and to close with a brief Awareness Examen looking back over their time together that evening. They also committed themselves to the confidentiality required of their proceedings.

Meanwhile the interim pastor, recognizing that the committee would be well served by fresh congregational data and congregational self-reflection, worked with the session to initiate small-group conversations. These groups, each staffed by a session member charged with setting a prayerful, open atmosphere and keeping a record of the comments, would provide an informal setting for all members to comment about what the church has meant to them and what they would like it to be in the future ("What's working and what might be added or strengthened?"). At the conclusion of the PNC's third meeting, about half of these conversations had been held, including several with the children and youth.

Using a standard instrument,[14] the session explored the demographics of their setting, discovering that a surprising number of young adults had moved into the neighborhood. The racial-ethnic diversity had also increased significantly, with the largest number of nonwhite residents now coming from Korea and Mexico, but with noticeable upticks in those from other Latin American countries and from East Africa. They also noticed an increase in the number of children in the neighborhood, as determined by school enrollments. Since there had not been a corresponding change in the congregation's demographics other than its gradual aging, the session concluded that the congregation needed to explore new ways of being in the neighborhood and reaching its increasingly diverse neighbors, including children and youth.

The session also assembled for the nominating committee copies of the last ten years of congregational reports, as well as demographics and financials and session minutes from the last several years. The support staff compiled this documentation into several substantial notebooks and scanned the material so that it could be easily accessed by each committee member as needed. This material, as well as the summed reports of the informal small-group conversations and other material that the committee itself solicited, would form the foundation of the Social Analysis step of the Social Discernment process.

Looking at Hope Church's process from the outside, we would only see the session's data gathering. The PNC's internal formation was going on out of sight. The meat of the discernment process, however, lay in the committee's answers to the questions in the Looking at the Current Situation exercise.

When they shared their personal responses to the exercise with each other, several things stood out. Only one person had noted the maintenance staff in their naming of roles. They then did a quick review of the segments of the church that one or more of them had overlooked. These omissions, they decided, appeared to be mostly a case of how detailed a picture each had

decided to construct. One committee member had taken the time to analyze the lists of those participating in the various ministries and noted that 5
percent of the congregation was involved in two or more of the ministries.
They realized that this 5 percent accomplished a good bit of the ministry
emerging from this congregation and determined to ponder this reality during their social analysis. They found their observations about the physical
plant unsurprising and somewhat mundane, but when they moved wider than
Hope Church, they realized that it would be important to pay attention to the
changing neighborhood demographics as they proceeded—the changes had
happened so gradually that most of them had simply not noticed.

The collated results of the congregational conversations helped the PNC
members get a feel for the living stories in the congregation about the congregation. But they determined to tell their own stories about specific behaviors
happening to them personally as members of the congregation. At this point,
the tensions residing within the congregation began to surface in the committee itself. The anxiety level within the group rose noticeably at this point,
a reality they were able to name during the evening's Awareness Examen.

Some members of the PNC were reluctant to share negative emotions,
sometimes out of embarrassment and, in one case, out of a sense that doing
so would be a "downer" in the group's process. Others realized that they
had glossed over some of the parts of the question asking for their personal
response to the situation, with the greatest puzzlement around "spiritually"—
what would it look like if their spirits or their spirituality were affected?
When one member noted an area of congregational life that made her feel
hopeless and defeated, another said, "Oh, I get it. Let me go back to that
question this coming week."

A lively discussion ensued around the task of identifying the marginalized,
neglected, ignored, invisible, and not taken seriously within the structure
of Hope Church. They wryly observed that, depending on the perspective,
almost everyone at Hope Church was marginalized in some way! Yet one
member called them to notice whose voice was never heard and who was
never at the decision-making table. When put that way, they agreed that
among the staff it was the maintenance personnel, among the congregation it
was the frail elderly widows unable to come to church, and in the neighborhood, it might be the Somali family that recently rented a small apartment in
the vicinity.

The Awareness Examen concluding their evening offered them a surprising gift: they were able to thank God that their group process so far had
prepared them to hold the tensions surfaced so abruptly within the committee itself. They acknowledged that these same tensions were alive in the

congregation, something for them to take into account as they moved through the discernment process. What does God mean for us to do about these tensions? they wondered.

They left the evening with the next set of reflections on social analysis. Given that the congregational conversations were still continuing, and in light of the various reports and demographic studies that they would need to digest, they set their next meeting for two weeks later.

Chapter 5

# Social Analysis

*T*his next step addresses one of the distinctives of the Social Discernment Cycle. We will employ social analysis to illumine the structure, seeking to cast a light on how the system is formed of interlocking parts and is in turn nestled within more comprehensive systems. We want to see how the players we surfaced in the last exercise contribute to and are controlled by the system dynamics. And we shall do all of this analysis in a posture of prayer. A tall order!

The following exercise may be used by both individuals and groups. You are cued again to keep a record of your responses to the various questions. Later parts of the Social Discernment Cycle will refer back to these responses, inviting you to bring them into the process at that point. The exercise also asks you to remember the feeling tone with which you concluded your last reflection and to renew again your desire for spiritual freedom both in your system and in this process of discernment. These initial steps are integral to the discernment, not simply warm-ups to the real process. My experience suggests that you may have to resist the temptation to rush through these points, to get to the "real questions." These *are* real questions for discernment.

### Social Analysis

This reflection helps you to understand what is happening by getting at the facts and connections. Prayerfully answer the following questions, recording your answers and observations as they occur.

1. Recall the feeling tone at the end of the Looking at the Structure exercise. Record it in your journal as you begin these reflections.
2. Again, prepare yourself to address God and for God to address you.

Renew your desire to follow God's call once it becomes clear to you. Seek God's deep freedom for your life. Since this desire is so essential to all aspects of discernment, do not hurry through this point. Notice how you are feeling as you begin. Record it in your journal as an integral part of your discernment.

3. Ask for God's help to analyze the situation with creativity and hope.

4. Write a brief history of your structure.

5. Identify the traditions and cultures that have been operative in this history. These might include spiritual, religious, philosophic, economic, ethnic, scientific, humanistic, gender, familial, and other traditions and cultures.

6. What is the stated vision or mission of your system (if it has one)? How does this vision or mission statement match your experience of the institution or structure? How does it not?

7. As a created reality, each system or institution is called by God to participate in God's ongoing creation. What would you say is God's deepest call for this institution or structure; that is, what is its *vocation*?

8. What assumptions are made by people in this structure? (For example, "big brother is watching," "leave your sexuality at home, "only clergy are holy," "might makes right," "money talks," "everybody is entitled to their own opinion," "get ahead while you can," "don't make waves," "family comes first," "we've always done it this way," "everybody does it," "we're the best!")
What are your feelings surrounding these assumptions?

9. How are these assumptions connected with the tradition as identified in the fifth question?

10. What social relationships are involved in this structure, such as class, race, gender, ethnicity, age, sexual orientation, societal role? How do these social relationships interact with each other?

11. How is power being exercised (e.g., power *over*, power *with*, power *for*)? Who has it? What are the means or signs of power (e.g., dress, office, budget control, naming and defining reality)? Who makes the decisions? Who benefits? Who pays? How? With what?

12. Are there any trends emerging in you and/or the structure?

13. What will happen if the situation continues as it is?

14. Note how you are feeling now as you work with this phase. Take your feelings into prayer. Look for any signs of creativity and hope that may have caught your attention. Write them down.

I've been speaking of social analysis from the beginning of this book. It's time to give this phrase a proper definition. Social analysis can be defined as *the effort to obtain a more complete picture of a social situation by exploring its structural relationships, including how it came to have its present configuration.* In social analysis, we examine causes, probe consequences, identify actors, illumine linkages, put our experiences in a broader perspective, and draw the connections between the linkages. "Social analysis," say Holland and Henriot, "is simply an extension of the principle of discernment, moving from the personal realm to the social realm."[1]

The Social Discernment Cycle, which takes this statement by Holland and Henriot as its organizing rationale, likewise shifts attention from the interpersonal (that is, relationships among face-to-face individuals) to the social (the structure of the social relationships). Thus, while we start with people serving in various roles, we shift quickly to the roles themselves. Marlene Smith becomes division manager, Jim Nicholsen becomes the seminary president, and Doug Riebe a member of the buildings and grounds crew. Of course, Marlene and Jim and Doug are still Marlene, Jim, and Doug, and of course our personal relationships still matter, but we now bring the roles of division manager, president, and member of the maintenance crew to the fore.

Another important shift occurs as we move into this phase. Recall the figures in the introduction that describe the Social Discernment Cycle. The third figure notes the changes in our *posture* as we proceed through the cycle. In the first phase of the cycle, our way of proceeding is anecdotal, impressionistic, inclusive, curious, full of feelings. As we move to the social analysis phase of the cycle, we shift from anecdote to analysis, from storytelling to critical reflection, from a preponderance of feeling to a preponderance of thinking. Our way of proceeding now becomes analytical, critical, dispassionate, clear-sighted. At this stage, we want to avoid value judgments (good, bad, right, wrong, appropriate, inappropriate, moral, immoral) as much as possible.[2] We are still curious, but now we are curious about how the pieces fit together.

At this point, discerners often complain, "This isn't spiritual!" (Others, of course, will have made the opposite complaint, "This is too spiritual!" long before now!) But thinking and critical analysis, including the "aha!" that comes from careful analysis, are indeed spiritual—just not particularly warm and fuzzy, which won't serve adequately for analyzing a system. At moments such as this, the "discipline" in "spiritual discipline" comes into play: we practice the discipline whether it feels satisfying or not.

But feelings do not disappear completely; they reappear at the conclusion of this exercise, when you are asked to note how you are feeling as you conclude the hard work of analysis. Even in this most heady aspect of the

Social Discernment Cycle, feelings still play a critical role. Emotions[3] actually underlie our thoughts, though we may not be aware of them until we are asked to reflect on them. Emotions, perhaps strong or contradictory ones, are likely to be evoked by the analysis, and they will be a crucial motivator in any actions to flow from what we are uncovering. We will check in with our feelings all along the way, because feelings, especially desire, consolation, and desolation, lie at the very heart of discernment.[4]

The kind of social analysis employed by the Social Discernment Cycle has been called "pastoral" to contrast it with "analytical" social analysis. Analytical social analysis describes rigorous scientific examination, either as an end in itself or for use in other scholarly endeavors. Hope Church's session consulted analytic social analysis provided by a nonprofit offering up-to-date demographic analysis. The Social Discernment Cycle, however, invites us to look at our structures from an involved, historical, and committed perspective (despite what I said above about being dispassionate in the social analysis). We are trying to understand what is going on in order to choose a strategic action that will enhance the vocation of the structure. The Pastor Nominating Committee used the analytic social analysis as part of its pastoral social analysis in service to its ultimate goal of bringing the next pastor to Hope, the one whom they discerned that God was calling to preach and teach and convene its leadership in the immediate future.

As we move through the analysis of the structure, we also pay attention to how time affects the structure, examining the history of the structure and noticing the results of our actions over time. We also notice the space dimension; that is, we ascertain the shape of the structure at a given moment. This exercise has questions to elicit both dimensions of your structure.

The questions on the history of the structure help fill out the time dimension. Where has the structure come from, and where is it going? Over what period of time? Are these changes proceeding so rapidly as to leave us breathless or so glacially that change seems nonexistent? Adding the historical dimension to our social analysis reminds us that any social structure is always in flux, is a truly dynamic system, even when our experience of the structure makes it seem more like a brick wall. A historical perspective, then, can relieve us of a particularly nasty demon, the idea that we are powerless in a structure ruled by "invisible forces" (which are actually the actions of others on the system). History helps us recognize that we can become subjects of our own history, actors in our own structures.[5]

We next ponder what might have been in the minds of those who came before us—the conscious intentions and the larger forces operating at the various points in the structure's history. We do this as best we can from a chronological distance not because the historical players need this analysis, but because *we* need it in order to guard against the temptation to read our present issues back into another moment in the institution's history. We need it to illumine how this particular configuration came down to us in the form that it did. We also need it as fodder for pondering if there are trajectories that might take the structure into the future, a process of deduction and imagination that the twelfth and thirteenth questions begin to make explicit.

The social relationships that form the structure are crucial. The arrangements that govern understandings and responses to class, race, gender, age, and societal role hold whole groups in place in the structure. A particularly vivid example of this ability of the structure to hold fast whole peoples occurs in the 2013 movie *The Butler*. The Cecil Gaines character, loosely based on the real-life Eugene Allen, who served thirty-four years as a White House butler, is juxtaposed with that of his oldest son, Louis. Over these same years, Louis becomes increasingly radicalized by the civil rights movement. At several points, the director alternates shots of Cecil's White House domestic work and Louis's increasingly radical protests, bringing home the huge upheaval in social relations necessary to advance the status of black people in America. Cecil himself asks time after time over the three decades of his White House service that the wages of the black people employed there be raised to match the white employees' pay. He doesn't succeed until he can finally bring himself to take this request directly to the president. He is only able to make that step because of the decades of protest and dozens of imprisonments endured by his son Louis and many others, a movement he has vehemently resisted for years. Familial, generational, class, and racial dynamics all intertwine in this story, where character is slowly forged over a lifetime. Social relationships are a key element in social analysis.

We are interested not only in the externals of the structure—that is, the things that can be observed from the outside—but also in the values, ideologies, and assumptions that can only be uncovered by being inside the system. The stated mission of your particular structure, the topic of the exercise's sixth question, is "external" because it is, presumably, a public document. But the difference between the stated mission and the way the system actually acts (also in the sixth question) gets at insider information that may be completely hidden from external view. Our goal in attempting both outsider and insider social analysis is to uncover the assumptions and biases that inform the system and its actors. These assumptions heavily color both the external and internal actions, often unbeknownst to the actors themselves. The Eastside Sisters' Residence members had not stated—and likely were not conscious of—some of their assumptions, which contradicted their stated assumptions and norms. Hence, the exercise contains a question that asks you to identify the system assumptions as best you can.

The theological perspective developed in chapter 2 reminds us that there is much more at stake and a deeper reality at play than is apparent even to insiders. To stop with insider perceptions and assumptions would be to assume that a structure will readily yield its inner reality to human observation. Walter Wink tackles this issue: "Every Power [Wink's biblically oriented term for structure] tends to have a visible pole, an outer form . . . and an invisible pole, an inner spirit or driving force that animates, legitimates. and regulates its physical manifestation in the world. Neither pole is the cause of the other. Both come into existence together and cease to exist together."[6] Elsewhere, Wink asserts: "Only by confronting the spirituality of an institution *and* its concretions can the total entity be transformed, and that requires a kind of spiritual discernment and praxis that the materialistic ethos in which we live knows nothing about."[7] We are attempting to put our finger on that inner pole. What we are searching for is no less than the spirituality of the structure. Will we be able to name it accurately? Possibly, possibly not. Yet because the reality that we are attempting to name is a spiritual reality, the attempt itself is a deeply spiritual task.

Taking Wink's biblically oriented metaphor, Powers, somewhat literally, we may, in fact, be able to get a sense of the spirituality of the institution by looking at how power flows in structures.[8] Wink's strategy suggests that looking at how power functions in this structure will be instructive for us as well. Hence the eleventh question in the exercise.

As a starting point, we need to observe what kinds of power are at work, recognizing that the authorizing sources of these kinds of power and their effects are very different. Theologian Donal Dorr suggests that we investigate at least four kinds of power: money power (who controls the purse?), political power (who governs?), idea power (who controls ideas?), and religious power (whose speech has the authority of the sacred?).[9] The authorizing power of money is the economic system in which the structure is set. Examining money power invites further questions that will be particularly relevant in some structures: Who has money (or other kinds of purchasing power)? What does the money buy? Who controls what the money buys? Who or what controls who has money? "Follow the money trail" has become common folk wisdom for discovering who controls the system economically.

Political power is authorized by constitutions, rules, or laws. Who gets to run the organization? How does one come to be in this position? What power is conferred by that role—and equally important, what power is not conferred by that role? What checks and balances exist in the system, and are they doing their intended functions? If not, who does the imbalance favor? What happens if political power is concentrated in one or a few roles? Astute observers of political power will immediately notice the frequent intersection of money power and political power. Rarely do these two operate in completely separate worlds.

One would think that idea power is authorized by the logic, relevance, or usefulness of the idea. But many people have really good ideas that never catch on or, even more frequently, that few ever know about. This observation alerts us to a different kind of idea power: power over the communication and marketing of ideas. When a relatively small number of people control the mass media, the editorial policy of major newspapers, the articles accepted into scholarly journals, and the content of daytime talk shows, this small group can effectively shut off the dispersion of ideas they don't like and, conversely, spread those they do. The connections between idea power, political power, and money power are increasingly visible in U.S. politics as corporate and individual contribution limits are abolished and candidate spending limits are removed. Political pundits of all stripes and negative advertising flourish on the human penchant to believe whatever one has heard repeated frequently and strongly—whether or not it has any logical basis in truth. This confluence is likely to show up in much more immediate systems as well.

Religious power is authorized by appeal to the sacred. But whose sacred? What kind of adherence is expected? What are the sanctions for not believing? What happens when one sacred story supplants another or when two sacred stories conflict? Those who hold political power (or desire it) also seek to have themselves authorized by religious power. In the United States, the religious right has recently created a formidable political force by linking religion, patriotism, and money. In your structure, you might look at whose word is "sacred" and must be honored no matter what. It may not be the person who holds the most political power or money power, though, because there also exists a kind of persuasive power that some can exert by virtue of age, experience, wisdom, or charisma.

Donal Dorr comments on the structural linkages among the four kinds of power. Imagine, he says, four pyramids all set on a common base, as if they were four mountain peaks resting on the same plain. At the top of the first pyramid are the small number of people, countries, and companies dominant in the economic sphere; at the top of the second pyramid are those officials who run governments; at the top of the third are the small group who control ideas and their dissemination; and at the top of the fourth are those holding ecclesiastical power. Those at the top of the pyramids negotiate regularly about how things will be, but they rarely if ever communicate directly with those down on the plain, even at the base of their own pyramid. (Pope Francis seems to be an exception, but the fact that the media responds so strongly when he meets with someone at the bottom of the pyramid proves the point.) We might call this relatively small group of privileged people "the 1 percent," a term popularized during the 2012 U.S. presidential election.

Folks in the large middle of the pyramids are those employed by the powerful and their structures: they are the "service personnel" who keep everything in their respective pyramids running smoothly. They act in the name of their particular pyramid's elite, making sure their interests are maintained. Consequently, it is in some way in their self-interest to continue the status quo because, at least in their particular pyramid, they have a relatively greater power compared to the mass of people at the base.[10] Outside of their own pyramid, however, they rank with all the rest of the common people. This huge group of service personnel frequently suffers from structural injustice and the farther from the top of their pyramid they are, the greater toll structural injustice takes.

The interlocking system that maintains the 1 percent fits Wink's definition of a Power perfectly: it's complex, powerful, and difficult to dislodge, capable of much good but also of much evil. This system also has a call, the welfare of humankind, though it is easily deflected from it. But even the 1 percent can be redeemed by being invited to return to—or first express—its call.

The individuals at the peak of the pyramid have most responsibility for any structural injustice in their pyramid because they have the most power to change the system. But they are also the ones least likely to change the system, because they stand to lose the most by any change. Those at the bottom of the pyramid, those with the least power in the system, stand to gain the most from any change. But they may struggle simply to survive. The vast middle, these "service people" who have some access but who, because of their dependence on the dominating system, often continue their service within it—it is they who will be the most able to effect structural change.

Who are these "service people"? They are, for the most part, *we ourselves,* as the Cecil Gaines character in *The Butler* finally realized. We have some structural power, however limited. We have some awareness of how things are, now enhanced by social analysis. We have been graced with some desire that things be improved. What we must do is claim the power and insight we do have and risk putting it at the service of God's call for the structure. To do that, however, we will need to disentangle ourselves from the injustices in the structure, no small challenge.

Donal Dorr offers three practical suggestions for this effort: (1) Concentrate as far as possible on the present structure. Do not be tempted to look elsewhere. In your own sphere of influence will come your personal call.

(2) Recognize that the crucial thing is to maintain your own personal integrity—a deeply personal process. No one can tell you how to do that or what actions it leads you to. Let this be a part of your prayer as you move forward in your discernment. (3) Begin to construct alternate structures—precisely the goal of the Social Discernment Cycle taken as a whole.[11]

Power analysis also sheds light on how we pray. Ideally, we pray in freedom, the freedom that we have already spoken about as a gift of the Holy Spirit. But there is another kind of prayer: prayer of sheer desperation. There is little or no freedom in this prayer. The situation is so sudden or so intolerable that the prayer simply bursts out of us, born of a situation that should never exist. If I find myself in this situation, I am entitled to be scandalized— we know this from the lament psalms, full of railing at God and at injustice. Even if I cry out against *God,* the very act of crying out is an implicit act of faith. Why bother if there is no God at all or if God is so distant and unrelated to us as to be completely impervious to any prayer? Faced with the fact that so many of the world's people are forced to pray the prayer of desperation, Dorr reminds us to be a little suspicious of prayer born of freedom: is it really spiritual freedom, or is it complacency? In the end, however, the Spirit prays through any truly human prayer. I need only come before God with my hands open, expressing what is on my heart. God can work with any sincere prayer to lead us to the next step in liberating action.[12]

Conversion also looks different when analyzed through the lens of power. Conversion for those with the most power lies in renouncing privilege and its gains, distributing power and resources for the common good. For the powerful, renouncing pride and power is the heart of conversion. But conversion among the powerful and the powerless are very different. The kind of humility appropriate to the powerful only further disempowers those at the bottom of the pyramid, who suffer not from pride but from lack of self-respect and powerlessness. Their conversion lies in taking up responsibility and learning that they do have power. Their newfound responsibility includes not falling into the traps of the powerful; they too must exercise their newly acquired power for the common good.[13] The significance of the question inviting an analysis of power, therefore, cannot be underestimated. It provides a crucial complement to the reflection on the marginalized begun in the last exercise.

Of course, there are other ways to think of power. The collaborators who created the Ignatian Exercises for the Corporate Person suggest pondering five types of power, each of which can be exercised formally or informally:

- Coercive power: fear of sanctions
- Reward power: anticipating money or other return, such as higher status in the group, for one's investment

- Expertise power: knowing how, what, when, or why to act
- Friendship power: power of relationship, personal power
- Commitment power: the commitment of individuals to goals and objectives that they have freely chosen, which in voluntary groups requires freeing structures, procedures, and attitudes[14]

A third, and for our purposes final, view of power comes from theologian Lee E. Snook. In trying to imagine other forms of power than dominating power, he identifies truth, freedom, justice, love, and beauty. These kinds of power are the secular forms that the Holy Spirit takes in the world. All forms of power, he claims, including dominating power, have their author in the Spirit of God, but they also have the potential for misuse. Evil is simply misusing any of these forms of power. He concludes with a striking description of the Holy Spirit: the Holy Spirit *is* God's power at work in the world.[15] In our discernment, we are trying to sense how the Spirit of God desires to work more fully in us and in the structure.

As you reflect on the various manifestations of power in the system, you can be alert for leverage points. In what may appear to be an impenetrable wall of interlocking dynamics and forces, we can look for the soft spot, that node where a small correction can evoke a disproportionate shift in the system.[16] High-power roles are obvious candidates for such nodes, but often they are not accessible to us, especially when the system is large, complex, or diversified. Furthermore, we have seen that the persons in the high-power roles may fiercely resist any change perceived to cost them power, prestige, money, or other less tangible status symbols. So the persons in these roles may not be the best points of leverage. Sometimes commitment power can be called on, especially in a moment of crisis. Another strategy is to set in motion a feedback loop, a moderating force that gradually checks the excesses in a system. These feedback structures need not be highly complicated. Even such a small change as regular evaluation or reporting might serve as a useful feedback loop. In effect, we implement Dorr's third suggestion by creating an alternate interacting system or altering the behavior of the existing structure, however minutely.

A word of caution: even though you are on the lookout for such leverage points, now is not the moment to decide on working with a particular leverage point or a feedback loop or any other strategy. The most appropriate locus for your particular action will be the one that you are called to as you continue to reflect and pray—the next step of the Social Discernment Cycle. Continue to work each part of the Social Discernment Cycle in turn, resisting the temptation to shortcut the process by jumping into action at this point.

Need social analysis always be complicated and scientific? Not necessarily. Nor need you be an expert in analytic tools. Once you understand what the social analysis is designed to uncover, you can streamline the analysis accordingly. Peter Henriot offers an approach based on ten jargon-free questions, which will suffice in many cases. I have set these questions in the form of an exercise. You may wish to substitute this exercise for the more complex one at the head of the chapter, depending upon the circumstance and the complexity of the structure you are discerning. It was originally designed to stand alone, so if it is used in tandem with the exercises in chapters 1–4, you may wish to delete parts that are repetitious.

## Social Analysis: A Simpler Version

This reflection helps you to understand what is happening by getting at the facts and connections.

1. Recall the feeling tone at the end of the Looking at the Structure exercise. Record it in your journal as you begin these reflections.
2. Prepare yourself to address God and for God to address you. Renew your desire to follow God's call once it becomes clear to you. Seek God's deep freedom for your life. Since this desire is so essential to all aspects of discernment, do not hurry through this point. Notice how you are feeling as you begin. Record it in your journal as an integral part of your discernment.
3. Ask for God's help to analyze the situation with creativity and hope.
4. What do you notice about the situation here today? What are people experiencing?
5. What changes have occurred in the past twenty years? What have been the most important events?
6. What influence does money have in our situation?
7. Who makes the most important decisions around here?
8. What are the most important relationships people have here?
9. What are the most important traditions of the people in the system?
10. What do people want most in life?
11. What will things be like in ten years if they keep going in the same way?
12. What did you learn from all this?
13. Note how you are feeling as you work with this exercise. Look for any signs of creativity and hope and write them down as they come to you.[17]

However complex or straightforward your social analysis may be, its ultimate purpose is to see the new underlying structure waiting to come into being. Once you sense this vision, the "stuckness" that sometimes dogs this step of the Social Discernment Cycle dissolves. In its place arises a sense of a right action. The context for sensing this new vision comes in the next step, theological reflection and prayer.

## Social Analysis of Eastside Catholic Sisters' Residence and Hope Presbyterian Church

Sister Joan began her analysis of the unspoken assumptions in the living group by recalling the history of the sisters' arrival at Eastside Sisters' Residence in 1949 with the opening of the high school. The structure was built like typical convents of the era: small bedrooms with limited closet space and a sink in each room, common bathroom and shower/tub facilities, kitchen, dining room, and living room, which they called their "community room." There was a small room off the front entrance to receive visitors, since when the residence was built, it would not have been common to have anyone other than sisters in the residence proper. In the early days, all the sisters taught at the high school. But recently, others had come, Sister Joan included, whose ministries were located elsewhere. Over the years, with an increase in the number of nonfaculty residents, the sisters' presence in the residence gradually assumed a traditional landlord-tenant arrangement, with the sisters renting the convent space from the high school. Several members of other religious congregations had also lived at the residence at various points.

When Sister Joan arrived to live at Eastside, she was aware that there were longtime arrangements about the way things happened, who associated with whom, and who controlled various aspects of the space. It had, in other words, its own culture. At the time, being the "newbie" and not teaching in the school, she simply paid attention to these arrangements and tried to fit into most of them without challenging them. In fact, she noted in her journal that she usually did not feel free to challenge them. She also noted that she, along with everyone else, was proprietary about the space she "controlled"; the kitchen, which she cleaned, was her "domain." She recalled her struggle to claim an empty bedroom for an office space in which to do her writing and course preparation. It took a number of months and some arguments to solidify the space and settle in. The rest of the dynamics, she simply learned to live with. But Sister Katherine's arrival, she realized, asked her to examine the way she had chosen to adapt to much of the unspoken living arrangements.

Sister Joan was not aware that the sisters' living group had a vision or mission statement other than general ones in their order's constitutions about common life and caring for all members, so she left that question blank. As for the assumptions of the living group, she mused that the group met at the beginning of the year to set up mutually agreed-upon rules. When there was a question, or if an exception was desired, someone brought it up at the next house meeting, where it was aired, discussed, and appropriate accommodations agreed upon. The system was sound enough, but somehow it wasn't working sufficiently well in this case.

Since Sister Joan's structure was all about assumptions, her list of the group's assumptions was rather specific, including these:

- Sameness is better than change.
- We talk about what is important to us (sometimes we don't).
- We all have the same amount of power (we don't).
- Common life is important to us.
- Common life undergirds our ministry (but sometimes gets in the way).
- We support each other (true for some and less true for others).
- We talk about problems among us (certainly true when the community united behind one sister when she began treatment for alcohol abuse).
- We are direct with each other (often not the case).
- We pray together.
- We participate in the larger congregation's life.
- We like it the way it is (true for some but not for others).
- We go with the house rules (if you know them).
- We are open to newcomers (as long as they don't rock the boat too much).

Besides noticing which group assumptions were honored in the breach, Sister Joan also noticed some of her own assumptions being uncovered by this situation, including contradictory assumptions about conflict:

- I assume that conflict will be destructive to me.
- I assume that I am powerless.
- I assume that we will struggle on behalf of newcomers to our group.
- I assume that solidarity will grow among us and will grow in or despite conflict.

At this point, Sister Joan realized that she needed to attend principally to her own issues and assumptions, focusing on the group's dynamics only as a foil to looking at her own behavior, which, after all, was the only thing in her control.

When pondering social relationships, Sister Joan noted that she was the youngest member of the group, was a relatively recent arrival, belonged to a different province (geographic governance structure) than the other sisters, and did not have a ministry in the school. Sister Katherine, though the most recent arrival, was older than some of the other community members but did not exercise a ministry in the high school. Sister Joan assumed that these relationships left both her and Sister Katherine at a power disadvantage. In this leaderless group, power was exercised by the silent person, whose position could not be ascertained, and by the assertive person who continually asked for what she wanted or needed. The one who comes to this (or any) group as a latecomer, she realized, pays by having to make all the adjustments, until such time as when the newcomer has "paid her dues." But when was that? What were the dues?

One trend that she identified caught her attention: how much personal and group power she was abdicating. Her codependent smoothing over and withdrawal was enabling the dynamics to continue. Over time, she might very well identify with one or two members against the rest—she already noticed her tendency to side with Sister Katherine against the others. Sister Joan wondered how she could be more direct, yet do so respectfully. She was a bit sobered by the realization that she was implicated in the situation and that her responses matter.

Let's next pick up the work of Hope Church's Pastor Nominating Committee as they moved through their social analysis. To fill out the historical trajectory, each member read the history of the church's foundation and early years that was produced at the time of the church's centenary celebration. The session minutes and annual reports filled in the recent past. In order to create a common sense of this history, they put up a long sheet of butcher paper in the education building, and on it marked off decades. Along this timeline, each wrote in black marker what he or she perceived to be the significant events in their history. Next, one of them took a purple marker and noted the tenure of each pastor. When they had completed this much of the timeline, they stepped back to notice what was there, filling in omissions as they occurred to them.

To add texture to the bare facts, they began to tackle together the traditions, which they noted in red, and the cultures, noted in blue, that would have been operating during each of the decades, as best they were aware of them. They noted the 1983 reunion of the two major strands of Presbyterianism in the United States, the Presbyterian Church U.S. and the United Presbyterian Church U.S.A., which many of them had experienced firsthand. Then they realized that they had to bookend that reunion with the fracturing occurring in recent years because of the General Assembly decisions on marriage equality and the ordination of self-affirming gays and lesbians. As a result, several entries about the changing understanding of sexuality appeared on the timeline. In the 1970s, they noted an increase in single-parent families; by the 1980s, there were more families in which both parents were working full time and a corresponding shift in the tradition of women volunteers in the church's various ministries. Women, they mused, first appeared on the session more than fifty years ago but on the pastoral staff only in the 1980s. They also noted that they had never had a female senior pastor, nor any pastor who was not white. The issue of race caused them to note that their membership was also overwhelmingly white, and in the last five years, noticeably more so than their neighborhood. They wrote on their timeline the session's observation about the rising number of children in the neighborhood without a simultane- ous rise in the numbers within Hope Church. "Either we don't have our eyes open, or we must think, at some level, that we are just fine the way we are," one observed—and onto a sheet for assumptions went the statement: "'People should come to the church' not the 'church should go to people.'"

The mission statement, they realized, had not been refreshed in fifteen years, and it had not been used publicly for at least the last ten years. They doubted that it was effectively guiding the congregation or the session any longer—if it ever did—and suspected that many members and elders did not even know that it existed. One member noted: "Against what vision should the decisions guiding congregational life be made—other than the Bible, of course, and that doesn't tell us what to do on the ground. How do we evalu- ate our decisions?" Another said: "That whole flap about who gets to use our facilities that bedeviled us last year probably could have been settled much sooner if we had remembered to consult our mission statement. It actually would have set the parameters much more clearly than the pressure tactics of the various vested interests did." As a result of this conversation, they decided to remand to the session this issue of the "lapsed mission statement," as one put it, and ask that the session begin to ponder with the interim pastor the best way to refresh or rewrite the congregation's mission statement.

They struggled with naming the congregation's vocation, since they didn't trust the mission statement to articulate it for them. Was their vocation to their members, to reinforce their sense of identity, their understanding and love of the Word, their sense of personal discipleship, and their ability to raise their children in the faith? Was it to be a leaven to the neighborhood? If so, they hadn't done a very good job recently. Was it to be a witness to the wider world? If the latter, they realized that their witness wasn't very robust. Could the congregation's vocation somehow encompass one or two or all three? They noted moments in their congregational timeline when one or another of these emphases was particularly evident. Unable to resolve this larger conundrum within the confines of their meeting, they resolved to ask the session to weigh in on how they would articulate the congregation's vocation.

Once they began to get the feel for how to tease an assumption out from under external behavior, they began to develop a tentative list. They also realized that church fights are sometimes precipitated by unarticulated but fervently held assumptions, which, if they could be articulated, might be able to yield to conversation, prayer, and confession. Their list of assumptions included the statements:

- We will always be here.
- Our members like each other.
- There are also cliques in our congregation.
- Because we like each other, we think other people will too, but we don't do much about inviting others.
- Those who drift away from the congregation are the ones not invested in it.
- Our senior pastor should be white, male, and well-educated; preach well; and have a lovely wife and kids.
- Children's Sunday school should be operating during the Sunday worship service.
- Sunday school should be focused on children.
- It's like pulling teeth to get volunteer teachers for Sunday school.
- High school youth group needs a young, jazzy youth minister.
- When the gospel is presented to children at their own level, they respond.
- Mission takes place overseas.
- We are generous to mission projects.
- Our kids go away to college and never come back to church, and we don't know why this is.
- We are a well-educated congregation.
- Children are safe in our church.
- We care for our congregation's ill and suffering.
- We don't like to hear about money from the pulpit.
- Church time should be from eleven to noon on Sunday—and maybe one other night per week. We are too busy for more.
- The church staff should keep everything going; that's what we pay them for.

They realized that they should keep this list growing as they moved through their process, because it was more revealing than they expected about not only the good qualities of the congregation but also the ways they had taken the church for granted. They noticed that, in a number of cases, the assumption didn't match the church's behavior, so assumptions should not be taken as true assessments, but only as indicators of the operative logic behind behavior, conscious or unconscious.

Instead of arguing the validity of the assumptive statements, each member instead named one assumption that he or she identified with positively, meaning it was an accurate and attractive statement about the church, and one that raised discomfort because it was both accurate and discouraging—again without trying to resolve all the differences that this exercise surfaced. What they did agree on was that this level of nonagreement was usually well covered over. Could conflicting assumptions be uncovered, and once that was done, could they work with them in a positive way? Or would the disagreements lead to stronger factions in the congregation? Several admitted during the Awareness Examen that this line of discussion made them anxious about the future of the church. But others also noted that surfacing assumptions actually made some of the church's behavior make sense for the first time and that recognition was actually liberating.

The recent demographics gave them insight into their own church's social relationships, yet they had to check a tendency to read the demographics back into their church. In fact, they were whiter, older, more established than the demographics of the neighborhood suggested. And, they realized, that really wasn't the point of the question. It was to notice not what class the members of the church belonged to but *how* the structures of class (and race, gender, ethnicity, age, and sexual orientation) played out in their congregation. That reframing elicited a bunch of observations and questions, including these:

- The session is at the top of our governance hierarchy. They work hard and are often burned out when their terms are up. Sometimes former session members move their membership to another congregation or drop out of the church altogether. We tend to ask professional people to serve on session.
- The pastoral staff usually agrees among themselves, and the other church staff is quiet if they don't agree with the direction the pastoral staff is suggesting. They will, however, contribute about how to implement decisions so that it works for them.
- Some people feel free to challenge the pastor, but most don't. The ones who do are usually considered the pastor's friends.
- If you are older, you generally have more power in the congregation. The most disenfranchised group in the congregation, however, is middle-aged singles, because our congregation is organized around families.
- We are not an official "Open and Affirming" church, but we know of

several gay couples who worship here. They don't, however, exercise much leadership in the congregation. Why might that be?

- We are really white. How would we have to change in order to have that reality change? We don't think it will be enough just to invite our nonwhite neighbors into our midst.
- We've got really good facilities for children, but we like to keep our children over in them and not in the sanctuary. And the number of children is down—is that just the effect of smaller families, or is something else going on?

By the time the committee got to the power question, they were wrung out. Knowing that they were far from finished with the social analysis, they agreed to meet again in one week. The intervening time was to be given to further pondering and prayer on the questions on power and on how all this material was making them feel. "But," cautioned the convener, "I think we should try to do both of those questions as prayer. I don't know about you, but I really need a good dose of grace about now." Someone also commented that she thought they would need one more step in their process, a step in which they identified, from the social analysis, the qualities that would be ideal in their next pastor. Too tired to figure this out, they put it on the agenda to design the step that will help them get to the qualities they would look for in their next pastor. Their Awareness Examen, however, recognized that their hard work was nonetheless graced: "We are learning important things, not all of them easy to absorb. But important."

After another week of prayer and reflection on the remaining questions, the committee reconvened. As they had agreed, they began with prayer to be open to the revealing word of the Holy Spirit through their conversation. The convener then reported that the clerk of session would put their question about the vocation of the church on the agenda for the next session meeting and would get back to them with the results of their conversation. He also said he had been reflecting on whether they needed to add a step to get to the qualities they would be looking for in their next pastor. It seemed to him that they could continue in the Social Discernment Cycle asking the most immediate question, namely, the qualities. Once they had discerned the qualities, they could set in motion the next steps, including writing the official job description. Meanwhile, the session would weigh in on the vocation of the church. Once they had candidates' names, they could then review everything they had done to get them to this point. Then they would bring the candidates' dossiers to the prayer and theological reflection step with the new question: Which candidate is the one that we should bring to the congregation? This plan seemed to clarify the way forward sufficiently. They could continue modifying it as they went along, given what the process uncovered. Then they turned to the issue of power.

At first they named the obvious kinds of power: the power of the pastor to focus the worship and to set the tone of the congregation through preaching, the governance power of the session, the kinds of power that the staff have over the routine functioning of the church's administration. The purse strings were managed by the treasurer and overseen by the session, as provided for in the *Book of Order*. None of this was at all surprising or particularly illuminating, used as they were to the division of powers embedded in the Presbyterian system of governance. They observed that the denominational power was not very strong; they tended to set their own direction, debate their own positions without much attention to the issues being debated at the denominational level. The major departure from this trend had been the conversation engendered by the need to position themselves with respect to the ordination of gays and lesbians. They relatively quickly determined that they would vote not to remove their congregation from the Presbyterian Church (U.S.A.). That issue did cause them to lose two families who each joined one of the churches that were leaving the denomination for The Covenant Order of Evangelical Presbyterians. They did, however, take pride that their teaching and ruling elders were active on presbytery committees and that there were a disproportionately large number of committee chairs held by their presbytery representatives.

Moving toward the more subtle ways power was diffused throughout their congregation, they noticed the power of one family linked to the endowment. At the point of disbursing the endowment funds, the committee evaluating the requests tended to defer to whatever family member was sitting on the committee at the time. That caused one member to note the forceful voices that spoke out when there was a congregational meeting—"that's a power of persuasion." That caused several more names to surface: "Mary Tomicek has a lot of common sense and can sway the session by a well-timed intervention, I think because she usually has the pulse of the conversation before she speaks." And another: "The 'loyal opposition' is headed by Tom Peterson. No matter what the issue is, he's against it. I think that role gives him status in the congregation. And sometimes, he is actually right, in my opinion." And another: "Now that you mention different kinds of power, Alexander [the homeless man who had taken to panhandling outside the church on Sundays] has a kind of power. Not economic or political power, but he makes a whole lot of people nervous. I think if someone actually invited him into church, it would provoke a reaction. Maybe one we need to have, because I think we have an assumption that everyone here is 'nice, clean, and well behaved.' Let's add that to the list of assumptions we were generating. This one needs to be challenged, if it is at all accurate."

Finally, one person commented: "Let's not forget how much power we in this room have right now. By virtue of our task, we can do almost anything we need to do within our committee to select and bring a candidate to the church for its vote. That's considerable power."

Although the PNC members were able to generate several trends, the one they settled on that most described Hope Church—at least today—was "we are drifting and have been for several years." This recognition was both frightening and liberating, especially when one said, "This time of pastor search could be a *kairos* moment for us. What we do now will either set us on a new path, or we could really blow it, especially if we move too fast and get too far ahead of the congregation."

As to what will happen if the situation continues as it is, one person offered, "I think we will just gradually get smaller, older, and less relevant to our neighborhood. I don't think it's a crisis yet, but it seems to me that this is the trend, especially with us naming that we are drifting. Maybe we can invite a pastor who will help us look around, pick up our feet, and walk somewhere intentionally."

Just as they were going to head into the Awareness Examen, which they had agreed would tonight be used to notice both the meeting itself and the feelings that had surfaced as they worked individually on the social analysis, one member, who had been rather quiet all evening, said, "I spent a lot of time last week sort of thinking about the question of the vocation of the church, puzzled that we were so puzzled by the question. I think the vocation of the church is to be the concrete location of the people of God. I know that doesn't quite give us our mission, because our mission, it seems to me, has to do with how we are the people of God here, with these people, in this place, with these neighbors, in this city, etc. But I think that is what we are called to do."

## Caveats

As we close the discussion on this phase of the Social Discernment Cycle, some caveats about using social analysis will help us keep it in the perspective of our overall task, discernment. Social analysis breaks a system into its smaller parts, but the smaller parts do not, even if summed, give us the structure, which is more than the sum of the parts. We have already learned in the third chapter that addressing isolated parts of the system will not likely change the system—we need to change the structure itself. Social analysis can leave us feeling overwhelmed, caught in the so-called paralysis of analysis because we now can see just how complex and multilayered the system really is—so where do we start? Why bother anyhow? At this point in the Social Discernment Cycle, people frequently feel worse than they did when they started and are most tempted to jettison the entire project. But don't. Social analysis is only one tool, and by itself it is reductive, abstract, and can sometimes be highly technical. It will need to be balanced with storytelling; simple, concrete descriptions; language that ordinary people can easily understand and use; art, poetry, song, and prayer—also part of the Social Discernment Cycle. Nonetheless, even with these limitations, social analysis is a highly useful tool when we are trying to "get our arms around a structure."[18]

Theologian Eleazar Fernandez offers some words about waiting in hope that may help at this juncture:

> Waiting in hope is not the kind of casual waiting we commonly think of, nor is it an aimless and idle waiting, much less a waiting in dread. The waiting that is generated by a deep sense of hope is an active waiting. Active waiting anticipates that for which one waits. It is a kind of waiting characterized by readiness and anticipation. The activity that is generated by waiting in hope does not kill time but redeems the in-between time or gives significance to the time being. For those who wait in hope, this time being is not to be written off or grimly avoided, but embraced as an occasion for faithful living. The time being is our time, a precious and momentous time, a time to be reclaimed for creative and active living.[19]

May it be so for you.

Chapter 6

# Theological Reflection and Prayer

We've come to the heart of the Social Discernment Cycle, the point at which we put all before God. We have worked hard and intelligently to see what is happening in the structural aspects of our situation, how things came to be this way, what forces make up the structure, and who is involved, directly or indirectly. It's now time to take our hands off of what we have done so far. We stop, we place everything we have learned before God, and we wait. We let God do whatever God wishes to do within us.

On our way to the prayer, we do have one more kind of data to gather, namely, the resources that our religious or spiritual traditions can suggest about the reality we are discerning. To do that, the first of the three exercises in this chapter leads you through a theological reflection on the situation and structure as it now appears to you. Theological reflection is a dialogue between your situation and the distilled wisdom from the past. It provides a way to invite diverse and wide-ranging perspectives on similar situations over time in order to enlarge your view of what is going on. The exercise below also helps distill from everything you have done the most salient aspects, which you will then bring with you into your prayer in the second of the three exercises. After the prayer, we again return to the theological reflection in the third exercise, but this time as it emerges from the context of prayer. I'll comment after each of the practice steps.

I've juxtaposed theological reflection and contemplative prayer in these three exercises. I am asking you to flex between them in the first and second exercises and to integrate them in the third. Theological reflection uses your cognitive faculties once again, with memory, imagining, thinking, and correlating high on the list. The contemplative prayer exercise sets those faculties aside in favor of intuition, silence, resting, and waiting. The third exercise joins both the contemplative and critical moments together in one more prayer. In putting these exercises together, I take my lead from Evagrius

Ponticus (345–99), who wrote: "If you are a theologian, you will pray truly, and if you pray truly you will be a theologian."[1]

If you belong to a religious or spiritual tradition that does not speak in theological terms, you can still proceed through the steps of selecting an experience, describing an experience, and entering an experience. When you come to this new step, look for ways of learning about your experience from some wisdom source outside yourself so that the wisdom perspective enlarges your perspective on the situation. Alternatively, you may be able to find an analogue to theological reflection called something else within your own tradition that encourages such reflecting on and learning from and beyond your experience.

## Theological Reflection on Your Structural Experience

This exercise helps bring the resources of the Christian tradition to bear on the situation and its underlying structure.

1. Renew your desire to understand and follow God's call in this structural aspect of your life that is the focus of your discernment. Ask for the grace to join with God's desires for this structure.
2. Describe briefly the original situation that caused you to select this structure as the focus of discernment. Does your restatement differ from your original understanding of the situation and structure? If so, how?
3. Review all the data you have so far accumulated for your discernment. What stands out, whether positive or negative?
4. Using the results of your social analysis, describe briefly the most salient aspects of the context surrounding the situation and the structure. Did your social analysis turn up anything surprising to you? Is there anything that seems particularly relevant to the situation and its underlying structure?
5. What biblical text (or other sacred text), parable, or metaphor comes to mind that seems to address this situation and structure? How does it invite or challenge you?
6. What theological theme(s) comes to play in the situation or the structure? Examples might include creation, sin, repentance, liberation from bondage, salvation, exile, death and resurrection, ethical living, discipleship, community, justice for the marginalized, grace. How does this theme play out in the situation or structure?

7. What additional guidance from your religious tradition might shed light on this situation?
8. Notice how you are feeling and what you are experiencing, whether positive or negative. Note carefully any movements toward inner freedom and any blocks to it.

As a general category, reflection is the process of critically assessing the content, process, or premises of our efforts in order to interpret and give meaning to our experience. Reflection is integral to thoughtful action.[2] But "theological reflection" may not be a term that you have encountered up to now. What, in fact, is theological reflection? Simply put, theological reflection is a process for helping people to learn to see God in their experience, to "make faith sense" out of it, as Robert Kinast puts it.[3] As *reflection,* its purpose, as I have noted, is to add the wisdom of the tradition to our perspective on the situation and its underlying structure. As *theology,* it is a form of contextual or praxis or experiential theology characterized by its starting and ending points: it starts with specific contexts rather than from general truths or doctrines, and it aims at action rather than at theoretical ideas.[4]

Many methods exist for doing theological reflection, but they all agree on several basic steps: selecting an experience, describing it, entering it, learning from it, and enacting the learning.[5] Since the Social Discernment Cycle also contains these first three steps, we can summarize our earlier reflections rather than starting anew. Thus, the exercise above begins by having you restate the situation and its underlying structure and review both your experience in the structure and your analysis of the underlying structure. But these questions are not *only* restating. They also invite you to notice difference between your earlier statements and your present ones and to ponder what these shifts can teach you. The exercise then refocuses your experience by allowing aspects from the various biblical and theological traditions to dialogue with the situation and structure. It will lead us, eventually, to enacting our learning as we put the results of our discernment into practice.

Our lives are full of meaningful experiences, but we do not always pay sufficient attention to enter them as fully as we might or to see them as theaters of God's action. Theological reflection reminds us to ponder our experience and to find the *theological* meaning it holds. Because God is already in the situation, theological meaning does not need to be imported from outside the experience; it is already in the experience, waiting to be uncovered. But getting from experience to theology and back again is sometimes challenging. Narrating our experience is the usual way to begin the dialogue, enacting Jesuit Anthony de Mello's lovely definition of theology as the art of telling stories about the Divine and also the art of listening to them.[6] Narrative, however, describes the situation from the perspective of the narrator. To move dialogue forward, narrative needs a conversation partner. In theological reflection, the conversation partner is some aspect of one's theological tradition. This dialogue between narrative and theological traditions sets the condition in which a larger meaning may be found, sometimes in the experience, sometimes in the tradition, and sometimes in both.

Unfortunately, too many people have had the experience of theology being played as a trump card that ends the discussion. In theological reflection, however, theology must honor, not erase, the concrete conditions and limitations of any given experience. But that claim does not then mean that experience determines theology or exhausts its meaning. Nor is the dialogue always either simple or smooth. Sometimes it has the character of dialectic, in which experience articulates a critical edge to theology or theology challenges our initial understanding of the experience.[7] The art is to maintain this critical tension.

What aspects of the tradition might we bring to bear on the experience of our structure? A Christian perspective holds that Scripture is a privileged way God speaks to humankind, so we seek biblical texts and themes that might address our situation. Creeds and confessions summarize the experience of our forebears about who God is and how God interacts with us and we with God, so we look for how aspects of creeds and confessions might add to the dialogue. Personal witness, then and now, is also a conversation partner; after all, God is already acting within humans and within the structure we are discerning. Liturgy is also a source of theology as the believing community enacts its worshipful response to God.

Constructive theologian Eleazar Fernandez helps us understand why we need to do theological reflection *on systems*. He reminds us that an entity (a person, an object) is only what it is in relation to the whole—that is, a person is constituted by social relationships. The parts derive their being from the whole even as the parts constitute the whole. Nor is a person simply the sum of family situation, gender, class, race, and socioeconomic status, but a person is himself or herself a *system* constituted by the wholeness manifested in these various attributes in relationship to other persons also so constituted. Being in relationship is also what makes us an image of God, whose very essence is being-in-relationship.[8]

Instead of uniformity as the ideal starting point for theological reflection, Fernandez also insists that diversity is the more basic category. The problems we experience with diversity arise not from diversity itself, but from our attitude to diversity. If we could understand our diversity as an asset,[9] we might arrive at a better understanding of the world. Our reflection would then necessarily be done in community as we seek, from within this community of unique persons and diverse perspectives, a tentative kind of commonality that is always open to revision as other voices join the conversation. In other words, in order to understand the structure, we form ourselves into a reflective community and tentatively and carefully address the structure, seeking to understand what God's desires are for us and for this structure.[10]

Echoing Donal Dorr two decades earlier, Fernandez also wants us to grasp the interconnectedness between the various forms of systemic evils. By systemic evils, Fernandez means evils that pervade the structures of our society and are highly resistant to attempts to relieve them. In what he terms an "exploratory attempt," he describes systemic evils intertwined in class, race, gender, and the ecosystem. As long as we continue to isolate only one of these evils, he claims, or to argue that one dimension is more fundamental than the others, we will fail to understand, let alone dismantle or even alleviate, these structural evils. Nor can a single front suffice at which to attack structural evil; we must mount multiple fronts simultaneously, and this takes a community of reflection and action.[11]

Given the task he set out for himself, Fernandez concentrates on understanding human persons and communities from the perspective of interlocking systemic *evils*. We could just as responsibly focus on systemic *blessings and goods* that come to us embedded in systems. The same observations about discerning communities would hold as we seek to move toward greater systemic good. Consequently, bringing an understanding of systems into our theological reflection can revolutionize how we do our theology as well as how we do our discernment. Our concern here, of course, is not developing a theological method but rather allowing a system perspective to permeate our discernment.

Much theological reflection over the centuries has involved looking at individual people and their actions and then generalizing from individuals to groups. However, such reflection does not necessarily touch the reality of the system as a system. It has also often been assumed that knowledge is "above" the concrete situations of real persons, as if we are minds freed of bodies. Along with disembodied knowingness comes a tendency to universalize from our experience without realizing that these universal statements erase the concrete situatedness of our neighbor. This atomized, disembodied knowing has frequently been the location of theologizing. But such theological metanarratives per se are not the crux of the problem. It's the wedding of these theological metanarratives to power that quickly becomes problematic, because the reflections quickly become universalized. The problem could be stated: Who gets to define what is going on? Who gets to interpret the Sacred for this situation?[12]

Can an individual discerner, then, do theological reflection? Surely, for two reasons. As one brings the wisdom of the tradition to bear on one's system, there is in that wisdom already a community of interpretation. The caution we must keep in mind in all theological reflection is to avoid totalizing theology, or, for that matter, totalizing any single theological voice. So we look in more than one place in the tradition and unpack several texts to see how the various voices illumine our situation and its underlying structure. We enter into a dialogue—actually a trialogue—between the situation, our experience, and the tradition, seeking as our goal a larger view of God's desires in this situation. The second reason is, I recognize, a faith statement: God can illumine your reflection just as surely as the reflection of others. All Christians are invited, by virtue of baptism, to engage in theological reflection, as are all humans by virtue of our shared humanity. No particular technical training is required. The caution here is not to quickly assume that one's take is accurate or even adequate. The remedy: hold your theological reflection lightly and invite other voices into it. Chief among them will be the voice of God as it may be revealed to us in our contemplative prayer—the next exercise.

By what criteria can we evaluate the results of this conversation between theology and experience? One key way will be to assess the fruits that result from the theological reflection and from the Social Discernment Cycle as a whole. We will begin that assessment in chapter 8 as we implement and then evaluate our discerned action.[13]

## Opening to God

This reflection helps you allow the Mystery of God to emerge from the murkiness of your structural existence. Bring yourself, as you are, into prayer.

1. Renew your desire to understand and follow God's call in this structural aspect of your life that is the focus of your discernment. Ask God for the grace to dwell, if only for a moment, in God's own heart for you and for this structure. Make your petition specific to you and your structure.
2. Bring yourself to your time of prayer with all the insights, calmness, or agitation that is stirred up in you. Spend time alone. Be open to

communication from God. You do not have to figure out what you should do, just be present to God in the midst of all the complexity you have discovered.

3. Pause. Allow yourself to become open, as if you are a channel for a river. Spend as much time as you feel able, quietly waiting.

4. Savor the experience. What images came? Metaphors? Imaginative stirrings? Scripture or passages from other sacred writings? Examples of people from the Christian tradition or other wisdom figures? After a while, write down whatever came to you in your time of prayer.

5. Describe the experience of your prayer to someone: pastor, spiritual director, spouse, or friend. How did describing this experience affect you?

6. Pause. Notice any new freedom in you now.

We have come to the contemplative heart of discernment, listening for God. In this practice, once we have set our intention, we stop doing anything. We wait. We give space for God to manifest God's self in us. We seek a deep presence, an opening beyond our habitual ways of making sense. The contemplative moment is one in which we are willing to attempt—and some-times achieve—a letting go of old identities and the need to control and are able to enter into God's desire for ourselves, this system, and all life.[14]

We need not "pray about" the situation during this stage, by which I mean intentionally lifting up the structure or directly asking what our action should be. In fact, we have been praying about the situation since we began. We simply change the form of our praying from an active mode in which we have pondered, meditated about, uncovered, analyzed, and perhaps even agonized over the situation and its underlying structure. Now our prayer turns deliber-ately and intentionally receptive. Contemplation, as I am using the term, is simply receptive openness to the Divine, what Jesuit Walter Burghardt has so helpfully termed "a long, loving look at the real."[15] The key is suspending our assumptions that we have worked so hard to identify. We simply set our intention, to desire what God desires in us and in the structure, and get out of the way. As we do this, we begin to notice our thoughts as products of our own minds, and they begin to have less influence on us.

From the silence may emerge images, metaphors, thoughts, connections, prayers, hunches, or sensibilities (your abilities to sense or be aware of some-thing). Notice them, then go back to the silence. Perhaps there are more. Don't hurry. If you feel led, take more than one time for this spacious prayer. Maybe nothing that you can put your hands on actually comes. Maybe what comes doesn't make sense, appearing unrelated to all that has happened before. Not to worry. Just be there with your whole self, as present as you are able to the Mystery we call God. Sometimes the word of God comes to us later—in the shower, in the moments between waking and sleeping, while engaged in some activity that uses our hands and leaves our minds free to roam. God's word often catches us by surprise when our cognitive guard is relaxed. As Senge and his colleagues put it in their social-science-oriented language, "If we can simply observe without forming conclusions as to what our observations mean and allow ourselves to sit with all the seemingly unrelated bits and pieces of information we see, fresh ways to understand a situation can eventually emerge."[16]

Speaking psychologically, we are inviting intuition to come to the fore. Speaking theologically, we are allowing God to work through all that we are to reveal something of God's own self to us. In terms of discernment, our goal is to come closer to the heart of God for this situation, so in this moment we intentionally open ourselves to the heart of God already working in the situation.

When you come to the savoring moment, collect any offerings that came during the silence—or in the next few days, for that matter. Write them down. They become important foundations for the next exercise. You may only have a general sense of what happened: "I felt peaceful." "It was a relief not to be poking at the structure for clues. I could just be." "It was frustrating after working so hard; at first, it was hard to just be still." "I found myself wanting to take control, it's so deeply ingrained in me to decide and move on. This was new." "I noticed a little energy coming back. Small, but definitely there." Whatever you sensed, write it down, along with any metaphors, images, feelings, ideas, and connections that may also have come to you during this time of prayer.

When you describe the experience as suggested in this and the next exercise, you turn it into a narrative. You also hear yourself say it. The speaking and the hearing deepen what occurred during your time of prayer; you have now added it to the narrative stream of your life and given it life outside you by narrating it to another. Your conversation partner also responds to parts or to the whole of what you related, helping you notice aspects or emphases or connections that might not yet have occurred to you or to which you didn't pay much attention.

The last point in this exercise asks you to notice any spiritual freedom that you are experiencing as you come to the end of the prayer. It could take a variety of feeling tones: energized, nonanxious, peaceful, curious, willing, pleasantly surprised, safe, unencumbered, hopeful, faithful, to name only a few possibilities.

Why do we single out spiritual freedom? Because spiritual freedom allows us to join with God in God's purpose as it gradually comes clear. Thus, any discerned decision should flow from spiritual freedom. Absent it, we return to our prayer, or even to earlier phases of the Social Discernment Cycle. We intentionally try to notice our spiritual freedom here so that we can also notice if it grows or becomes interrupted as we continue through the crucial steps of deciding and implementing. The next exercise begins with spiritual freedom.

---

### Prayer and Theological Reflection, Continued

This exercise helps distill the reverberations of your prayer by comparing them once again to the situation and structure and to your earlier theological reflection.

1. Return to prayer. Recall the freedom that came to you out of your prayer. Dwell in that freedom as you proceed with your reflection.
2. As you stand in this place of freedom, what behaviors in your structure support your freedom or undercut it?
3. What, in Scripture or other sacred texts, do you now connect with your sense of freedom? What texts would help live that out?
4. What images or metaphors now express this experience?
5. What theological truths now express this freedom for you?
6. As you are *now*, look at the structure you have chosen.
   a. Name what is graced and open to God in the structure.
   b. Name what is sinful and turning from God in the structure.
   c. Name the conversion or transformation you notice in your experience so far.
7. Finally, notice how you are feeling as you come to this point in the process.

---

The theological reflection dynamics have returned again with this crucial difference: we are dwelling in a space of spiritual freedom. From that perspective, the Scriptures may shift and different theological themes may surface. In fact, our whole perception of the situation and its underlying structure may change or a direction may build. Spiritual freedom serves as a lodestar against which we touch everything we have done. We are looking for those aspects of the situation that enhance our spiritual freedom (or, by contrast, diminish it). We are trying to see the system from God's perspective. Dense though the system may be, God's freedom is woven into its very fabric like a subtle golden thread that we are now beginning to have eyes to see. As we begin to discern this thread, we let it draw us toward God's heart in the depth of the structure. It will lead us to the first contemplative action that we are to take in response to our structure.

## Unfolding Theological Reflection and Prayer

Sister Joan had been puzzling over the response to Sister Katherine for some weeks before it became apparent that structural discernment could be of assistance in understanding what an appropriate response might be. Personal prayer had been a part of that reflection from the beginning, but she had not paused for any theological reflection. Nor had she given any attention to spiritual freedom. She began there, with several minutes of quiet centering and a spoken prayer asking to become clear, to see as God sees, and to be ready to move when she became aware of her call.

To begin her theological reflection, she recalled Bernard Lonergan's five imperatives: Pay attention. Be intelligent. Be reasonable. Be responsible. Be in love.[17] She did not remember where she had heard or read these imperatives, but they seemed a reasonable way to start. Her social analysis gave her an expanded sense of paying attention, so she reread her notes for that section. What immediately struck her was how she answered the questions on identifying the marginalized and identifying the kinds of power operative within the interpersonal dynamics of the community. She was newly aware that she was an integral part of this dynamic and that whatever the result of her discernment, it was about her, not just about the others. "Be responsible" would, indeed, entail her. She was now holding the question: What is the loving thing to do? As she pondered her answer to the question on who the marginalized are, she realized that this question, too, had unexpected responses. Yes, Sister Katherine was the obviously marginalized person in the group, shut out of the commonly held unconscious assumptions. As the "perceived patient," she was the one who is getting static for not honoring them. But those who were holding the assumptions were also imprisoned in set ways of doing things, limited horizons, and unquestioned assumptions. Everyone, she realized, needed freedom here. Freedom for herself would entail freedom for Sister Katherine; freedom for Sister Katherine would entail freedom for the others. The problem was structural and the solution would also be structural; everyone was implicated.

Sister Joan picked up her Bible and, on an intuition, turned to Isaiah. She realized that the whole book is about God building and upholding a people, a people who have not been faithful much of the time. She also found this passage: "Remember not the former things, nor consider the things of old.

Behold, I am doing a new thing: now it springs forth, do you not perceive it? I will make a way in the wilderness and rivers in the desert" (Isa. 43:18–19 RSV). As she concluded the theological reflection portion, she found this text, and others from Isaiah, both challenging and comforting.

The next day, she began the second exercise inviting her into a contemplative posture with regard to everything she had so far done. As she readied herself for this prayer, she noticed that the tension and frustration that had been present earlier in the process was now gone. The word "nonviolent" surfaced—actually it reappeared, as she remembered it had surfaced earlier in her reflections. This time she noted a cluster of energy around it. She recalled Burghardt's description of contemplation, "a long, loving look at the real," and she allowed her imagination to glance over all the persons involved in the Eastside High School Sisters' Residence, trying to hold each one with a loving inner gaze. Out of the silence the words began to form within her: "You are exactly where I wish you to be. These persons hold a key to your life and growth and you hold a key to theirs. Come close, first in your heart, then in your actions, then in your words." As she related this prayer to her spiritual director later, she noted, "I might think I'd made up these words, so gentle were they, except that I know from experience that God does work that way. That was the highlight of my prayer, which otherwise was uneventful."

Sister Joan waited several days before she moved on to the third part of the prayer and theological reflection. Much of her earlier theological reflection continued to feel relevant, but she began asking herself about gospel values residing in the structure. Her answer was mixed: On the positive side, she believed that together in community is where God works and reveals. Since this living group was her most basic community at this moment, she could expect God to be revealed there, and that God was working and would continue to work in and through this group and these particular people. What undercut this gospel value was the lack of hospitality of some toward Sister Katherine, who was treated as an outsider in her own house. Sister Joan paused here, poised for the next step in the Social Discernment Cycle. As she concluded this third exercise, she was still awaiting clarity about what her concrete response should be.

## The Pastor Nominating Committee's Theological Reflection and Prayer

Hope Church's Pastor Nominating Committee set aside three meetings for this phase of the Social Discernment Cycle. Before they began, they reminded themselves that the goal of these three sessions, and therefore what they would be listening for underneath everything, would be the qualities that should characterize the new pastor. They agreed to compile a weighted list of such qualities and characteristics at the conclusion of the three prayer exercises. This description would constitute the first outcome of their discernment. At the conclusion of the confirmation step, these qualities (or a similar list) would then be embedded in the position description and disseminated through the denomination's call system.

Each committee member worked independently on the theological reflection questions in the first exercise, praying and journaling their responses. As they came together and shared their reflections, they began to see some themes appearing. One of the first things they noted was that their prior assumptions had constrained their imaginations about what kind of pastor should next serve at Hope. They determined actively to pursue candidates who were women or who represented any other underrepresented group. Maybe their next pastor would be farther along in years, too, than their pattern to date—not all pastors need bring spouse and children to the church (though one hastened to say that more children would be good!). Their church demographics, while not surprising, were also a wake-up call when compared to the demographics of the region. What startled them was what was *not* present in their consciousness until they specifically looked: they had maintained a nice cozy island of familiarity while the neighborhood (and world, someone noted) had kept changing. They realized that it was not their role to determine the specifics of what the next pastor should do or be, but it did seem important that this person have skill in uncovering and making space for the disagreements that simmered under "Christian niceness." He or she should also have the interpersonal and group leadership skills—and the desire—to lead the church through a discernment process, first about accurate and operable mission and vision statements, and then about realigning the church's ministries so that they matched their setting's demographics more closely. What new weighting of or possibly new ministries is Hope Church called to? The pastor should facilitate and provide leadership as the congregation answers these questions.

Among the several Scripture passages that came forward in the sharing, the one that seemed to hold the most energy was the early chapters of Acts of the Apostles. "We need to be awakened," said one. "And we need a full measure of the Holy Spirit," echoed another right on the heels of the first. "And we need to speak in such a way that folks can recognize what we are inviting them to, so to speak, 'each in his own language,'" said another. A fourth mused: "We noticed that our youth go away to college, and they don't return.

I wonder if there is any way that they could go empowered and missioned as our ambassadors? If we could figure out how to do that effectively, I bet that some of them would actually come back. And even if they didn't, they'd be spreading the gospel and living it themselves. And instead of thinking of mission as something that takes place out there, which isn't bad, of course, we would be learning to understand our own children in terms of mission. In helping them become our missionaries to their college contexts, we would be setting free the gospel here at home."

Given that conversation, reframing mission and evangelism emerged as one of the theological themes that they coalesced around. One noted, "By assuming that mission is overseas, we've successfully insulated ourselves, beyond mission giving, of course, from taking the responsibility for mission personally. Ironically, that focus—mission is over there—didn't result in making our local community more diverse." "This feels to me like a significant shift," he added softly after a moment's pause. A chorus of nods, and the rejoinder: "As long as we don't go to the other extreme and forget that we belong to a world church."

After their brief Awareness Examen over their sharing, the convener reminded them about praying for spiritual freedom before, during, and after the next exercise. That evoked a question: "How do I know if I have spiritual freedom?" The convener responded: "You may not actually know for sure. If you sense energy and excitement to be about God's work, I think that would be a good signal. But I'm not sure there is any particular way to feel. Sometimes commitment doesn't evoke any particular feelings. And spiritual freedom is a commitment to stay true to this call as we understand it. I guess another way to check for spiritual freedom would be to see what resistances show up inside us, or among us, for that matter. In my case, if I am going kicking and screaming into the prayer, I think I don't have spiritual freedom. Or if the direction that seems to be emerging makes me anxious, I think I should return to the prayer for spiritual freedom. I hope that helps."

Given that Acts of the Apostles evoked so much resonance, the convener decided to close by reading Acts 1:6–8: "So when they had come together, they asked him, 'Lord, is this the time when you will restore the kingdom to Israel?' He replied, 'It is not for you to know the times or periods that the Father has set by his own authority. But you will receive power when the Holy Spirit has come upon you; and you will be my witnesses in Jerusalem, in all Judea and Samaria, and to the ends of the earth.'" The convener concluded, "If we wait on the Holy Spirit this week, I think we will get the measure we need."

Each member of the committee took a week to pray over and ponder the questions in the second of the three exercises. As they assembled to describe the experience of their prayer to another member, as directed in question 5, they quickly realized that their group discernment would be significantly strengthened if each person shared the results of his or her prayer with the whole committee. In order to keep this sharing from sprawling over too much time and providing too much detail, the convener suggested that they pause quietly for a few minutes, look over their prayer journals, and prepare a three-minute synopsis of two points: the significant moments they recorded under question 4, and the quality of their individual experience of freedom at the conclusion of their prayer, as requested in number 6.

The sharing ranged from "I didn't notice anything in particular. I was just there. It wasn't unpleasant, but I'm not sure that I can bring anything from that prayer to help us" to "I had a strong sense that we are on the right track. It doesn't matter that we get the qualities we want in the next pastor perfect, what came to me is that praying our way through this process will bear fruit that we don't even expect. I was encouraged to keep going." A third noted: "I stayed with the Acts of the Apostles, the first couple of chapters. I took a section each day and ended up at the end of the second chapter. I was really pondering how this ragtag group was called together to be the church. If they can do it then, we can do it now with the same Holy Spirit. So I began praying for a new Pentecost for Hope Church." To be sure, one person reported feeling anxious: "I kept thinking how much work we have to do. Sitting there quietly felt like 'Why are we wasting this precious time? Let's get on with it.' I guess I have to go back to the prayer for spiritual freedom!"

The convener picked up on this last comment as he handed out the third prayer exercise. "Uh huh. We all do. I would say, spend more time there than you think you need to. I'll also ask the deacons to hold us in prayer these next couple weeks. I have a sense that us working with a modicum of spiritual freedom is more important than anything particular that comes from the questions."

He continued: "This week I came across this prayer from Ignatius of Loyola. I think it's a good prayer for us now, so I put a copy for you on the back of the prayer exercise sheet for us to use during the week. I'll read it to conclude our time together:

Take, Lord, and receive all my liberty, my memory, my understanding and my entire will—all that I have and possess. You, Lord, have given all that to me. I now give it back to you, O Lord. All of it is yours. Dispose of it according to your will. Give me only the love of you and your grace. That is enough for me.[18]

As the members of the committee assembled around the third exercise for this part of the Social Discernment Cycle, they had a shared sense that these questions were the right ones to use when they are actually selecting the candidate—a while farther into their process. Nonetheless, they reported the highlights of their prayer. They first talked about the quality of their spiritual freedom: some began with the prayer of Ignatius and one spent the first of her reflection times just on this prayer, others used the prayer at the beginning of their reflection time every day, and another decided to make up her own prayer for spiritual freedom each day as she noticed where she was dragging her feet. At that point, someone noted, "You know, this is what we *did,* but I think it will be more important to talk about the result of the prayer for spiritual freedom. I know that praying Ignatius's prayer made it easier to just be open to whatever happened." That comment invited their sharing to move to a new level.

One new metaphor appeared: "Go deeper." It came out of a realization that they had been coasting along, *doing* church, but not really *being* church. Two Scriptures clustered around this metaphor, "Come and see" (John 1:39), and the promise to the church of Laodicea, "If you hear my voice and open the door, I will come in" (Rev. 3:20). The convener encouraged them to stay on the lookout for metaphors and Scripture passages as they continued their work.

The question asking them to name that which is graced and open in the structure and that which is sinful and turning from God, as well as their own conversion through the process, seemed to pull everything together. As they named what is graced and open to God in the structure, it was clear that they and the new pastor alike were called to reinforce these aspects, to go deeper. Likewise, in the three points they identified as turning from God in the structure—talking indirectly and "being nice" instead of being transparent, paying no attention to their neighborhood, and undervaluing their children as persons of faith—lay the seeds of new direction, of going deeper through conversion. The leadership skills to assist the congregation toward lessening these sinful aspects should also appear in the qualities for the new pastor. And one said, in reference to the question about the conversion in their experience so far: "You know, I think we are being church as we go through this process. I know it is calling me to new generosity with God. I keep trying to see how God is calling me and calling us together."

After a break for refreshments, the committee reconvened and within thirty minutes had identified six points to work into the description of the call for the new pastor. They concluded the evening by selecting two of their number to sit with the convener to compose the description of call. Their Awareness Examen this evening noted a definite shift deeper and the ease with which the qualities emerged after the break. It was as if they had been revealing themselves all along.

Chapter 7

# The Decision and Its Confirmation

$G$iven its particular task, Hope Church's Pastor Nominating Committee was able to decide on its first action, developing a list of desired characteristics for a new pastor at the close of its theological reflection and prayer. For many individuals and groups, the first action is not at all obvious. The next exercise is designed to assist discerners in choosing their first contemplative action.

The language "first contemplative action" is deliberate. Behind this simple phrase are several important realities. The first has to do with *contemplative*. By this word, I wish to communicate that the action emerges from earnest prayer to know God's call, coupled with an expectant openness and waiting to allow God's Spirit to work in us, giving us sufficient knowledge and readiness to come closer to God through the resulting action. The exercises in the previous chapter were designed to help us enter that contemplative freedom and prayer. The second reality has to do with *action*. The Social Discernment Cycle, like the Pastoral Circle from which it takes its form, is designed to lead to discerned action. Actions can be interior as well as exterior, as for example: "Every time management does this, I will say to myself, 'In the grand scheme of things it doesn't matter,' and let it go." Prayer is a legitimate action that could result from discernment. A change in one's attitude is also an action, particularly if it is consciously chosen and embraced and practiced. In other words, give the word "action" a broad interpretation.

If an action is well timed and placed at a leverage point in the interlocking forces that compose the system, sometimes a single actor or a single decision can move an entire system. One person can change the direction of a work situation. One person can propose a new ministry that catches a congregation's imagination. One person has sometimes headed off a war. One person can change a system, which in turn changes other systems, forming a network of cascading changes unimaginable from the point of the first contemplative action.

The Quaker John Woolman (1720–72) provides a classic example of what one person can do as the result of a single contemplative choice. On one occasion, "about the twenty-third year of my age," Woolman relates in his journal, while employed as a shopkeeper, his employer instructed him to write the bill of sale for a slave. Despite being troubled by this task, Woolman complied. But once he had done so, he wrote: "I was so afflicted in my mind, that I said before my master and the Friend [who was selling the slave] that I believed slave-keeping to be a practice inconsistent with the Christian religion."[1] Woolman followed this crucial insight with action. He first traveled extensively in Maryland, Virginia, and North Carolina, staying with the local Friends along the way, observing slavery firsthand. Out of this experience, he took a further action: in 1754 and 1763, he wrote the two parts of a treatise against slavery, "Some considerations on the keeping of Negroes," which the Philadelphia Yearly Meeting approved for publication some years later. After the writing came the next action: he resumed his visits to Friends who were slaveholders, but now, as part of his visit, he spoke directly to his hosts about the moral evil of slaveholding. If slaves had prepared the meal, he would leave money on the table for them or find a way to give it to them directly.

Meanwhile, Woolman's basic insight was spreading. By 1755, the Philadelphia Yearly Meeting ordered that members who imported slaves or purchased them locally should be admonished. By 1758, it had banned buying and selling slaves and required members who bought slaves to be removed from positions of authority. By 1784, twelve years after Woolman's death, the Virginia Yearly Meeting officially abolished slavery among its members. There were antislavery advocates among the Quakers prior to Woolman, and he had colleagues supporting and often literally accompanying him in this journey, but he stands out for his courageous yet gracious persistence in pressing the evils of slavery. It was clearly his vocation.[2] But changing the entire system of slavery among Quakers took strategic *collective* action.

"Contemplation" is not a term Woolman would have used, but what he did fits my understanding of the word perfectly: he listened consistently and steadfastly for the still, small voice of God speaking to his heart. Once what he thought that voice was asking of him was clear, he brought this "leading" to his local meeting to consult other Friends. If they also felt that his leading had a divine source, the meeting would send him to perform the action he had discerned. At the individual level, we see Woolman's inner sense of call confirmed by community. But if we look to the actions of the local, Quarterly, and Yearly Meetings, we can also see the cumulative fruit of their contemplative leadings and actions. An individual affected a structure and the structures, in turn, affected wider structures and the individuals within these structures.

At the outset, however, the system may seem impenetrable, with no clear way forward. Nonetheless, we ask to understand the single first action that we are called to implement, small though it may be: speak to one person about what is happening, change one small behavior within the system, shift the power dynamics in one committee, whatever it might be that results from your prayer. Systems, by definition, will adjust to each force acting upon them, so a system that appears immovable still must respond to this single action. *Something* will be different after the action, though the change may be so subtle as not to be perceptible to the discerner. A single action, Woolman's conversations with his dinner hosts, repeated over time, helped convince meeting after meeting to abolish slavery in their midst. The beauty of Woolman's action was that at each point he did the single thing that he felt was required of him—travel, write, visit, have conversations with his hosts, or pay slaves for services—and he then left the outcome beyond that action up to God. Likewise with the Yearly Meeting.

With this introduction, I invite you to prayer once again as you look for the first contemplative action that you are called to enact.

## Deciding on the First Contemplative Action

This exercise assists you in selecting from among the possible actions the one that seems closest to God's call in this structure.

1. Return to last prayer exercise. Remember what happened. Reexperience your moments of freedom. Ask God for strength and courage to move into decision and action.
2. As you do this new phase and you experience freedom, cling to it. It is out of freedom that we determine what to do and how to do it. If you do not experience freedom, do not proceed! Rather, stay in your prayer, repeating the earlier set of exercises. Wait for God to stir up freedom.
3. Describe the freedom as you *now* experience it.
4. Let the freedom deepen. Where does the freedom come from? What does it look like? Smell like? Taste like? Where do you notice it in your body? What images are associated with it?
5. Notice the desire that comes through this freedom. What is it like?
6. Do any concrete responses, that is, actions connected to desire, come to you?

7. What intuitions or nudges about concrete actions came to you during any of the earlier phases?

8. How do these intuitions or nudges look different from the perspective of your freedom?

9. Honoring all your insights and movements, list any other possible concrete actions you could take.

10. Which of these actions (those listed in numbers 6, 7, and 9) is *possible* for you to do at this point in your or your organization's life? Which of these would address the needs of the situation? Which of them would be most effective?

11. Choose one contemplative action to work with or live into now, the one that has the most energy or seems to be calling to you. Write it down.

12. Reflect on what you are currently experiencing. What is the quality of your freedom when you hold it up to the action you have chosen?

This exercise begins where the last one left off, that is, with your experience of spiritual freedom. We come back again and again to this gift of God, freeing us to move however God directs. Our contemplative action should emerge from within this climate. It may be something that occurred to you much earlier in the process, of course, but now it is winnowed by the successive prayer and reflection, and finally it emerges within the context of spiritual freedom.

The exercise's second point deals with what to do if you do not experience spiritual freedom. When the requisite gift of freedom is not (yet) present, wait for it. If it continues to absent itself from your prayer and considerations, take the absence as an indicator that none of the options that have so far surfaced are ones you should select. Perhaps you have framed the issue somewhat inaccurately, perhaps there is a significant aspect of the structure that you have overlooked, perhaps you yet need some conversion, perhaps the timing is not ripe, perhaps God has something else in mind. Whatever may be the cause—and you need not know what the cause is—return to an earlier point in the process and work forward again. Do not automatically assume that this situation is a negative reflection on your generosity or that you have made a wrong turn somewhere along the way. After all, continuing the prayer and reflection and analysis means that you are continuing the spiritual practice of discernment with the intention of continually listening and responding to God. The decision itself is the secondary goal to the spiritual practice, so all the while you are reworking the process, you are continuing with the primary goal. The Quakers have honed to a fine art the practice of waiting to move forward in the absence of a sure conviction; we imitate them in this respect as we wait on the sense of spiritual freedom before moving forward.

The fifth point asks you to name the desires that surface in the context of your spiritual freedom. The source of this direction lies with Ignatius of Loyola. In each of the meditations and contemplations in his *Spiritual Exercises*, he directs retreatants to ask for what they desire. Why? Our desires tell us about our heart, but they can also tutor our hearts and imaginations. When we know our deepest desires, we know something important not only about ourselves, but also about God, because our deepest desires come from and point to God. Desires are also powerful expressions of our passions, and it is passions that move us to action. Thus, when we know our desires, we will also be alerted to the potential for our most powerful actions, be they for good or for ill. When we are attuned to our desires, we notice when they conflict, sending us into an inner struggle and draining energy from other more important issues.[3] Finally, our desires ultimately point us to our vocations — "the place," as Frederick Buechner put it, "where God calls you to is the place where your deep gladness and the world's deep hunger meet."[4] As you notice your desires at this point in the process, check to see if and how they are related to your sense of spiritual freedom, the lodestar for this exercise.[5]

Throughout the course of this exercise, a number of potential actions may surface. As the ninth point directs, collect all these options, including ones that may have surfaced earlier in the process. With that list in front of you, look for one that stands out, that is possible to do, that beckons. This is the one you will tentatively choose as your first contemplative action. Notice that in selecting this action, we don't wait for a thunderbolt from the sky before we choose. We trust that God has been dwelling in our prayer and reflection all along, and our generous cooperation with the process will point to a possible choice with which to begin. Of the several possible choices, we simply select the one that seems the appropriate place to start. We take the responsibility to pick this starting point, knowing that if another action is more appropriate, it will surface as we go forward.

The exercise asks you to write down this selection. By doing so, you are giving it form and concreteness. You will then hold this potential action in prayer and see how it fares as you begin the confirmation process in the next exercise.

### Confirming the Tentative Decision

This exercise invites you bring your tentative decision before God to see if it stands up in the context of various touchstones for discernment gleaned from the long Christian discernment tradition. These touchstones serve as indicators that the Holy Spirit is most likely present in this decision.

1. Return to the experience of the previous prayer. Remember what happened. Reexperience your moments of freedom. Ask God for strength and courage to move into decision and action.
2. Reflect on the contemplative action you have selected. Now notice any signs that this contemplative action is something you should, in fact, choose and implement. Such signs might include greater peace, consolation, energy, courage, sense of "rightness." Other signs might come from outside: others who know you well also confirm it, it fits within your previous commitments and honors them, it falls within the biblical witness, etc.
3. How are the marginalized ones involved in this contemplative action?
4. Notice how power functions in the contemplative action you are called to. Does this action involve service *with* or *for* others? That is, will this action engage you *alongside* others or *on behalf of* others or some other arrangement of power?
5. What are some possible results of this contemplative action (acceptance, hostility, struggle, etc.)? If this reflection elicits some fear or other resistance, touch that fear against your experience of freedom. What happens?
6. Who will join you in implementing this action? How will you select them, invite them, and collaborate with them?
7. What means will be used to evaluate this contemplative action? Name a later date at which you will do this. Name persons who will help you do this review.
8. Continue to pray, dwelling in the freedom experienced, for the strength and courage to move into implementing the decisions and actions that have emerged. However, if significant reservations appear, return to earlier parts of the process and begin again, seeking another contemplative action.

Chief executive officers who know nothing about discernment still know a lot about executive decision making. They know how to discover and refine the issue about which a decision needs to be made, gather all the relevant facts, data, and projections, consult appropriate persons, weigh everything, and make a decision. Wise CEOs may also pay attention to their motives and clarify any biases they might be bringing into the process. They likewise make sure that major decisions are evaluated after the fact and promptly modify the decision if the results indicate the need to do so. The Social Discernment process contains analogues to all these aspects of good decision making.

But typical CEOs probably do not see decision making as a potential spiritual practice, nor do most see God's call in the decision, pray for spiritual freedom, or seek confirmation before finalizing the decision. Business leaders quickly learn that the bottom line is affected by the skill and the speed with which they can analyze, decide, and implement. The received wisdom in the business community is that the faster one can move from decision to implementation, the more successful the outcome is likely to be.[6] In discerned decision making, however, the opposite holds. We have come to one of the most obvious places where the Social Discernment Cycle slows decision making way down—and why in an earlier chapter I somewhat playfully referred to discernment as the "slow food movement" of decision making. I refer specifically to the pause between selecting a first contemplative action and beginning to put this action into practice; this pause provides the opportunity for confirmation, one of the distinctives of discernment.

I base this portion of Social Discernment on Ignatius of Loyola's methods for discerning choices.[7] After detailing rational and imaginative processes to form decisions, he directs further: "When [the decision] has been made, the person who has made it ought with great diligence to go to prayer before God our Lord, to offer him that [decision], and to beg his Divine Majesty to receive and confirm it, provided it is conducive to his greater service and praise."[8]

*The Spiritual Exercises* does not elaborate further what it means that God would receive and confirm the choice that we bring in earnest prayer. Fortunately, however, a small piece of Ignatius's diary survived despite his explicit order that the entire diary be destroyed. Through this snippet, we can follow Ignatius's attempt to confirm a major decision with respect to the future of the Society of Jesus—should the Society have no fixed sources of revenue as part of its practice of poverty? Over successive weeks, he reviewed this tentative choice with its constituent parts and probable outcomes, all the while noticing what happened inside him. He used as his barometer consolation and desolation, assuming that an unbroken period of consolation indicates that God has confirmed and received his decision. But he ran into a major problem with this strategy: he never got the unbroken period of consolation he expected. He restarted his period of confirmation several times until he finally realized that a stretch of unbroken consolation is what *he* wanted, not necessarily what God would use to confirm his decision. Once he came to that realization, he promptly concluded his discernment and implemented his decision.

Besides illustrating confirmation, we can learn several important things from this little section of Ignatius's diary (boring reading though it is!). As when we selected our first contemplative action, we see again that some kind of direct revelation is not the essential ingredient; faithfulness is. We also learn that what we receive during the period of confirmation will not provide absolute certainty. It still takes faith to believe that, as we enact our decision, God goes with us and, indeed, awaits us from within the structure. We also learn something about how long we should give to confirmation: Ignatius's experience suggests that it is only necessary to wait and pray for a reasonable amount of time, taking into account the complexity of the decision and the amount of time that is available. Ignatian scholar Michael Ivens notes, "We pray for confirmation in order to be as sure of doing God's will as it is given us to be; and to counter the tendency in us to opt for hasty closure. . . . Confirmation can be simply that nothing comes up to call our decision into question."[9]

Benedictine Margaret Mary Funk offers a useful overview of what happens at the confirmation point in discernment. A confirming sign has these characteristics:

- It has indications that it will be good for you.
- It comes from outside you. (That is, the confirmation is different from you talking yourself into the decision. Certainly you may consult, but carefully, with spouse or spiritual director or others in a position to know you well and understand that you are listening for God. We are listening for God, not what others want us to do.)
- It is directly linked to the issue at hand.
- It brings the accompanying grace to make the action possible, even if it is difficult and requires some suffering
- It is in proportion to the gravity of the decision. It provides sufficient certainty to move forward, confident that God accompanies us.[10]

Ignatius used his old standby from the Rules for Discernment of Spirits, consolation and desolation, to assess whether God was confirming his tentative decision. But there are other pieces of wisdom in the long Christian tradition that can also assist us in our confirmation. Following Jesus' "You will know them by their fruits" (Matt. 7:16), we can look for the fruit resulting from the decision. Paul helps us at precisely this point by listing typical fruit of the Spirit in Galatians 5:22–23: love, joy, peace, patience, faith, mildness, steadfastness, self-control. This list should not be taken as exhaustive; other virtues could be added from elsewhere in the tradition. The Quakers, for example, held that courage was a sign that the discerner should proceed.[11] Neither should Paul's list be read as only about one's interior; verse 26 reminds us that we are also discerning between ways of being and acting that divide the community, with their poisonous recriminations, versus ways of life that unite the community and center it upon the unifying joy of the Holy Spirit.[12] Galatians 5:1, "For freedom Christ has set us free," provides the basis for holding the tentative decision up to our spiritual freedom, asking if this decision flows from and leads to greater spiritual freedom (question 8 in the previous exercise). Matthew and Luke give us somewhat different lists of Beatitudes (Matt. 5:1–12; Luke 6:20–26); such attitudes as poverty of spirit, hungering and thirsting after justice, and steadfastness in persecution are signs that the Spirit is at work within and among us. Acts of the Apostles portrays the ideal Christian community as one sharing, distributing goods according to need, using each one's gifts for the good of the community, joining in the Eucharist and prayers with joyful hearts (Acts 2:42–47).

The patristic tradition also contributes to the collective wisdom. For example, Origen (ca. 185–254), one of the first Christian commentators to reflect systematically on the role of affections in discernment, taught that when passions and emotions run so high that they cloud personal freedom, a spirit other than the Holy Spirit is at work. Compulsion is a disconfirming sign! To turn this negative statement into a positive point to assist in confirmation, we can ask if our inner liberty is both preserved and grows. In Athanasius's *Life of Antony* (ca. 360), we find that din and confusion cause dejection, grief, remorse, and the like—not what we expect from the Holy Spirit, who comes so quietly and gently that joy, gladness, happiness, and courage arise within.[13] Irenaeus of Lyons (d. ca. 202) famously said, "The glory of God is the human being fully alive."[14] So we ask: Does the decision bring more life? For whom? Do our deep desires point us toward these life-enhancing decisions? John Cassian (ca. 360–435) spoke of humility and openness of heart as characteristic of the Spirit's action.[15] We look back: Have we grown in true humility and genuine openness throughout the process?

All this collective wisdom is behind the second point in this exercise. The "etc." at the end of the point reminds us that these are only examples of the collective wisdom. Look for whatever enhances life, spiritual freedom, and well-being, and be suspicious of whatever depletes life, spiritual freedom, and well-being not only for the discerners, but within the system as a whole. I call these various pieces of wisdom from the tradition "touchstones" because we touch our tentative decision up to them and see what happens. This step is the heart of confirmation.

All the touchstones suggested in the second point can be seen as pointing to our personal condition as discerners: Do we experience greater spiritual freedom, are the fruits within us indicative of the work of the Holy Spirit, do others who know us well confirm that this is the work of the Spirit of God, does it honor our previous commitments? And so on. Points 3 and 4 begin to extend the confirmation process so that it encompasses systems more directly, first in the person of the marginalized and then in evaluating how power shifts in light of the proposed action. We are trying to get a sense about whether the system will better reflect God's desires for it as a result of our action.

Recall from the overview of systems in chapter 3 that, because a noticeable time lag occurs between initiation of an action and the system's response, effects of our actions within systems will only show up after implementing the decision, and sometimes quite a while after. Since we want confirmation within both individual discerners and the systems they are discerning, this time lag suggests developing touchstones that specifically address systems that we check some time after implementing the decision. We shall dwell more extensively in the next chapter on the system analogues to the traditional discerner-oriented touchstones.

At this point, questions naturally arise. What if some of the touchstones don't apply or suggest disconfirmation? We can tell from Ignatius of Loyola's experience that confirmation is an art, not a mechanical checking off of a list of touchstones. If we needn't assume that all the touchstones will apply, how many touchstones should apply before there is sufficient assurance that our tentative decision is confirmed? The answer: the preponderance. However, it won't do simply to count the number of touchstones that suggest going ahead. The touchstones should collectively point toward going ahead, and those doing so should outweigh the touchstones suggesting otherwise.

In the absence of a sufficiently strong and weighty confirmation, it is best to pause longer or return to earlier parts of the process and see if an alternative decision presents itself for confirmation. The tentative decision that receives confirmation may lie among the other suggestions you gathered in the last exercise; to discover if that is the case, simply select the next option that seems right and return again to the confirmation exercises. However, the appropriate decision may yet remain to be discovered. In this case we go farther back in the process, perhaps as far back as reframing the issue and selecting the structure, and redo the process from that point. Again, the need to repeat is not a judgment on the quality of your earlier discernment; it is an act of faith in the desire of God to communicate, guide, and form you through the process of discerning.

The fifth question recognizes that there might be some trepidation or downright fear in the discerners as they approach the moment to enact their decision. Systems push back when the stability of the existing system is threatened, so many, and perhaps most, system actions will exhibit some kind of resistance or outright punishment directed at the perceived source of the change—often the discerner-actor. It is not unrealistic, therefore, to experience some trepidation prior to confirming a decision. Does such fear disconfirm the decision? Not necessarily. Here it is important to observe the quality of the fear, its origin (if possible), and, crucially, what that fear does to one's spiritual freedom. Some fear tells you not to proceed, while some fear results from the natural human need for self-protection that arises even when called to go forward. For example, are you paralyzed with the fear, or is there a quiet courage and sense of call that coexists with the fear, enabling you to proceed in spite of it? It may take time and some discernment to sort out the difference.

At this point the monastic tradition of watching thoughts can help immensely. First we look for the earliest rising of the fear. What triggered it and what is it attached to? What happens if, as soon as we notice ourselves in the grip of fear, we respond with a brief prayer, such as, "O God, come to my assistance, O Lord make haste to help me" or simply "Help!"? What happens if we watch the whole progression of the fear, from beginning to middle to end? If we begin to sense that this fear is a temptation to abandon a good course of action, then we immediately act against it. If we begin to sense the gift of strength and perseverance, we continue ahead despite the fear. In any case, we should anticipate the strength of the fear and seek immediate antidotes so that it doesn't gain strength. The assumption is that we are not the fear itself, and, in fact, we can stand outside of our fear and observe it, and, given what we observe, we can make some decisions accordingly.[16]

In systems work, it is always preferable to have companions, if only for support from afar. The sixth question invites you to ponder who might join you in this decision. Giving some thought to these colleagues before you enact your decision might save you some grief later should you lack support in an action that turns out to be unpopular. In any case, the more actors in the system who join together for one decision, the more likely that the system will move in the direction that the actors initiate. If your discernment has been a solo affair, remember that those who join you may not (at least yet) share your conviction that the action you have singled out is in fact a call from God relative to the system. It may not be necessary to share all the nuances of your discernment, but these colleagues should at least be able to share your conviction about the action taken and be willing to join you in it. If you are discerning in a group, I assume that the discerners are united around the tentative decision and that those who may not be are able to stand aside and allow the others to proceed without hindering or throwing up active opposition. Should opposition exist within the discerning group, it will have some work to do before proceeding. In fact, the group may not have identified the best action and may profit greatly from continued praying and talking until a way appears that all can commit to.

A crucial aspect of any discernment is looking back; in fact, this backward look is one of the best ways to improve the practice of discernment. In working with structures, the review can sometimes suggest a little tweak to the original action that will make its impact reverberate more strongly. As we saw in chapter 3, system changes often precipitate unanticipated outcomes. The carefully discerned action may provoke an unforeseen result that calls the original decision into question, and this review helps you catch and rectify the unintended consequence with dispatch. The seventh question asks you, prior to finalizing the decision, to plan when that review of the process will occur and who will join you in it. This foresight makes it more likely that this last important step in the process will not fall by the wayside in the activity of implementing the decision.

## The Decisions: Sister Joan and the Pastor Nominating Committee

Sister Joan began her prayer by asking again for spiritual freedom, pausing also to remember what it felt like in her earlier exercises. She noted in her journal that her overriding sense at this moment was expectancy: What would surface as a call from God to her in response to these unspoken assumptions in her living group? She reaffirmed her conviction that the call would be to her, not to Sister Katherine or to the other members of the living group. Other than this conviction and her sense of expectancy, she did not sense any other images.

She began to gather the possible responses that came to her earlier in the process or in her prayer at the moment:

- Hold each person, especially those to whom I am not naturally attracted, in contemplative awareness; do this both when irritated and when not.

- Spend conscious time with Sister Katherine on weekends, and help her nourish her vision for ministry and help it become a shared vision.
- Encourage vision for the house quietly and prayerfully.
- Speak nonviolently and nonaccusingly about the assumptions as I notice them.

As she began to list these possible actions, she recognized that some anxiety was rising in her, which she recognized as relevant to her own history. She would do well to collaborate with Sister Katherine in implementing any final decision; this community of two, she recognized, was as much for her as for Sister Katherine. She also noticed a bit of hopelessness: "It'll never change."

As she sat quietly with these four possible actions, the last one began to take on real significance. The statement reframed itself spontaneously in her mind: "If you speak them, they are no longer unspoken." Here, she realized, was her action: to speak to the group, quietly and nonaccusingly, the assumptions as she became aware of them. She didn't have to change any behaviors. She was just to make the unconscious or unspoken assumptions conscious to all by speaking them. Simply that.

Later, as she returned to her prayer, seeking confirmation that this, indeed, was her action, she realized that the simple pattern "come close, act, notice, and speak" had already occurred in her work situation before she connected it to the dynamics of her living situation, as if the Spirit was preparing her to act in the more charged atmosphere of her living group. Next, she realized that the group itself had been able to surface an unspoken assumption recently and had adjusted their collective behavior as a result. Her confidence began to build. Finally, she began to be aware of a contested, but unspoken, assumption about the use of the television in their common living area, as if this might be the first of the assumptions she was invited to name to the group. Her body tensed up. "This isn't going to be easy," she thought, "simple, but not easy." Yet the more she sat with the statement, "If you speak them, they are no longer unspoken," the more she knew she had the action to which she was being called.

Continuing her prayer for confirmation, Joan recognized that she was getting a strong sense of what she was to do but that Sister Katherine was also implicated. As the system's "perceived patient," she could very well be on the receiving end of any pushback from the system. Sister Joan realized clearly how important it would be to let her in on the discernment so that she could be prepared for any fallout directed her way. Reflecting on the power arrangements in the system, Sister Joan noted two things: first, she did have power in this situation, but her power was not "power over," but simply the power of her angle of vision as a relative newcomer to the living group. It would be important, she also realized, to exercise the results of that angle of vision in a nonjudgmental manner.

Sister Joan concluded her discernment the following day, clear about her call and alert to the first occasion in which it appeared she was to name the unspoken dynamics. At her next appointment with her spiritual director, she reviewed the whole course of her discernment. Her director affirmed her sense of call and agreed that the living out of it should be a regular subject of their conversations, especially as the living group's dynamics unfolded.

We rejoin Hope Church's Pastor Nominating Committee some weeks later. Much had happened in the intervening time. Their facilitator submitted the position description and Ministry Information Form to the denominational offices for circulation, and candidate names and their Personal Information Forms began to come in. Committee members considered each one prayerfully, posing the question, Is this person a viable candidate for becoming our pastor, given what we have discerned are God's leadings for our congregation? Each committee member filled out a worksheet that contained the following headings:

- Name of candidate
- Background information
- Education
- Prior ministry service
- Reasons for continuing this candidate in the search process
- Reasons against continuing this candidate in the search process

Then, at regularly scheduled meetings, they prayed and talked through each candidate. Some candidates were eliminated relatively quickly as not presenting enough of the desired qualities. Other names were kept in the "continuing consideration" category. Given that there were dozens of applications for the position, this process continued for a number of meetings after the close of the application process.

Next, the committee set itself the task of paring the pool to a manageable size. They agreed to go back through the two dozen candidates remaining in the "possible candidate" group and weight each candidate application, with three representing "has most of the characteristics and qualities" and one "has few of the characteristics and qualities." Each committee member again committed to a time of personal prayer during which he or she weighted each candidate's dossier and prepared a statement about why this candidate received the weighting. Their next several meetings were some of their hardest, as they tried to come to consensus on no more than five candidates. The meeting at which they accomplished this goal concluded with a prayer of gratitude, and they immediately began to pray specifically for each of these five possible candidates and for the next steps in the discernment process itself, that it would yield the person best fitted by God to next lead the congregation.

The committee continued winnowing and distilling the candidates, always trying to bathe their processes in prayer, listening carefully both to their hearts and to one another. At their next meeting, they narrowed their list to two candidates. At this point, they brought both candidates and their spouses to the area in order to hear them preach in a nearby neutral pulpit and to answer the same set of questions that they had crafted out of their earlier discernment. Since this was the committee's first chance to meet the candidates, they carefully attended to what was said, how it was said, the questions the candidates asked, and what was not said. While they were in the area, each candidate also met with the Committee on Ministry. At the conclusion of these interviews, the Committee on Ministry chair relayed through the member common to both committees that each candidate was appropriate for this church and for membership in the presbytery. These steps completed, the nominating committee next set out to check the references for each candidate.

Finally, reference checks and interviews completed, the PNC assembled for its final discernment on the candidate to recommend to the congregation. For this final step, each of the remaining two candidates was considered separately, using the question: "Given what our research and the interviews have surfaced, is candidate A (or B) being called to pastor Hope Church?" In the first round, each person commented on any reason against, and on the second round, on reasons for. Returning to a time of personal prayer, each PNC member was asked which candidate he or she would select to be the next pastor and the most weighty reasons for this choice. Candidate B began to gather the energy and imagination of the PNC members and seemed to be the choice of the committee. After several rounds of consensus building, the convener posed the final discernment question, to which each member was asked to speak: Do you assent to calling candidate B as Hope Church's next pastor? When all had assented, though one or two with less enthusiasm than the others, the convener tested the consensus. He checked with the two members who expressed qualified enthusiasm: Are you able to support this candidate when we bring her before the congregation? Upon receiving affirmative statements from each, the convener concluded the proceedings with the statement: "We have our call. It is candidate B."

Confirmation of their discernment was still in front of the PNC. Their convener suggested: "Let's sleep on this name for the rest of this week. After worship, let's meet briefly and check to see how we feel at that point about our candidate. After that check, if the signs still suggest we go ahead, I'll contact candidate B with the result of our discernment. We can then set up the congregational meeting to present candidate B for vote. This final step can serve us as further confirmation of our discernment."

As had been their practice, the PNC members concluded this final part of the discernment with a brief examen over the process. Some of their comments after this last session were: "I'm tired but satisfied that we have done the best we could to surface the best candidate for us right now." "I was surprised that, once we had done all our homework, this last meeting was quiet and prayerful, as if that calm was itself an affirmation." "I think we did a very careful and prayerful process. I trust the congregation will receive this nominee in the same spirit as we offer her to them." "I'm satisfied." "We did a good job and we did it together." "If something happens farther along in the process, I will still know that our process was as good as we could humanly make it."

Chapter 8

# Implementation and Evaluation

*T*he long journey through the Social Discernment Cycle is almost complete. We have one more step, which we might be sorely tempted to skip, having spent so much energy to get to this point. But it is a crucial part of the confirmation process that we began in chapter 7. Here we review the discernment process itself, seeing what we can learn, about ourselves or the process, as we look back. Then, after we have begun to implement our first contemplative action, we look at the system's response, using system analogues to the touchstones we considered in the last chapter.

The next exercise might well be divided into two parts. The first three questions can most profitably be done very close to the discernment process itself, while the various steps are still vivid. The final eight may better be taken up somewhat later, after the system has time to respond to the initial action. In any major structural change, periodic evaluations can carry the fruits of the original discernment into the future. If you do divide the exercise, remember to begin each with the prayer for freedom, that is, with numbers 1–2. Spiritual freedom continues to anchor even this final step.

## Looking Back in Order to Learn

This exercise helps you review your entire discernment, including what has happened since you implemented your contemplative action. It may suggest some adjustments to your contemplative action, or it may prepare the way to discern the next contemplative action. Be open to noticing what you might do differently in your next discernment.

1. Begin your review by remembering the spiritual freedom within which you chose your contemplative action. Dwell again in spiritual freedom

as you begin this review. It may feel similar, or it may have a new quality to it.

2. Ask for the grace to see clearly the fruits of your contemplative action upon the system.

3. Look back over your entire Social Discernment *process*.

a. Can you recall any juncture where you experienced serious resistance, lack of freedom, discouragement, disinclination to proceed? Did (how did) those inner states shift?

b. Likewise, pay attention to the places where you experienced clarity, consolation, energy to proceed. What can you learn from these moments?

c. What, if anything, will you do differently in your next Social Discernment process?

4. Now shift your attention to the *contemplative action* you have begun to implement. Look for the fruits of the action in the wider system. Does the system now better promote, for example, unity, security, justice, meaningful work, sustainable progress, meaningful relationships, cultural roots, hope, inclusiveness, flexibility, and greater care for creation?

5. What has happened to the people who are involved in carrying out the contemplative action you chose? To the people who experience the effects of this action?

6. In particular, how have the marginalized ones actually fared as a result of this contemplative action?

7. Notice how power functions as a result of your contemplative action. Who now holds power? What kind of power? Who pays?

8. How has (has not) the action been received into the system?

9. Does this review suggest any adjustments to the contemplative action you originally chose? What changes seem appropriate? Hold these potential adjustments in prayer for some sense of confirmation prior to making changes.

10. Continue to pray for strength and courage as you implement the decision(s).

11. Express gratitude for all you have experienced throughout the Social Discernment Cycle.

We've done a long and careful process. Why pray again over what we have done? Because in this looking back we have an excellent opportunity to grow in our understanding of discernment, and also because we might spot a flaw in our process that affects the decision we are beginning to implement. That is, the quality of our discernment process is part of the confirmation step. Discernment can only be learned by experience, and experience means a certain amount of learning by trial and error. It is one thing to read about discernment, but quite another to do it for oneself, and still another to become proficient in discerning.

Once again, we can find an example in Ignatius of Loyola. In dictating his autobiographical notes toward the end of his life, one of Ignatius's goals was to illustrate the long process he went through in learning to listen for the call of God in the various circumstances of his life. His initial attempts, while he was recovering from a serious leg wound, centered around noticing that he felt quite different interiorly after reading spiritual books, the only ones in his sister's house, than he had when reading chivalric novels. By continually looking at what was happening interiorly and its effect on his life, he worked out the basics of the Rules for Discernment of Spirits by the time he had fully recuperated. Yet he had much to learn, which caused him to live for the next eleven months within walking distance of the Benedictine Abbey at Montserrat. There he was able to receive some instruction in discernment of spirits and the basics of the Christian life and prayer.

He kept trying out what he was learning through instruction and reading. He gradually realized, for example, that his ascetical extremes, done with the intention of serving God, were not actually enabling him to do God's work effectively, so he stopped them. He learned that he needed to be transparent with someone outside himself to relieve the scruples that sorely afflicted him during this period. He learned to pay attention to how other people were affected, sometimes negatively, by his fervor and to moderate it accordingly. He pondered becoming a member of the Carthusian Order but realized this way of life was not for him—he was going to Jerusalem to convert Muslims! But when he got to Jerusalem, the Franciscan in charge of the Holy Land wisely realized it would not be a good idea to allow Ignatius free rein to proselytize, so he sent him packing on the next ship. A major discernment and a lot of time that didn't turn out at all as Ignatius had imagined! Over time, we see him discerning his next step over and over based on his reflections over his past discernment and as new circumstances developed.

He summarized his experiential learning in the Rules for Discernment of Spirits. There he added an important point: we should examine the whole train of our thoughts, beginning, middle, and end, and if all parts are wholly good, it is a sign of the good angel. And the contrary, if we see a place that is not wholly good, we should suspect that the evil one has had a hand in it. In that case we should carefully go back and examine every part of the process to see where we got off track. "Thus," he says, "the person, by understanding this experience and taking note of it, can be on guard in the future against these characteristic snares."[1] We might appropriate this wisdom, given that it is stated in Ignatius's medieval worldview, by saying that it doesn't matter if you get off track at the beginning of the thought process, the middle, or the end; once you get off track, you won't reach the desired goal. So we look back to see if there was any point at which we got deflected from the goal, which we will most likely know by reading what happens inside us. As for major choices, he tells us that if we've made one in a way that turns out upon investigation not to be rightly ordered, it would be profitable to make it anew in a proper way.[2] Clearly, Ignatius fully expects discernment to consist in two steps forward and one step back, but as long as our desire is the glory of God and we are learning from our experience, that seems to be fine with him.

In question 3, spiritual freedom is the lens for your review of the discernment process. Where did it grow, where did it fade, where (if anywhere) did you individually or collectively ignore your lack of spiritual freedom and go ahead anyhow? Since spiritual freedom is a gift given to us by God, following its ebb and flow gives us some clues about how God might have been at work within and among us as we proceeded through the discernment process. The crucial moment is the decision: Was it made in spiritual freedom? If not, go back and remake the decision out of spiritual freedom. But spiritual freedom does come and go (recall the ebb and flow of consolation and desolation while Ignatius was trying to confirm an important decision), so the fact that spiritual freedom might have faded at other points in the process need not derail the decision if the actions taken at that point do not also call into question the outcome of the discernment. Meanwhile, we see what we can learn from this investigation that will help us in future discernments.

The next several questions invite us to look at the decision we have now begun to implement in order to see what fruits are appearing in the system itself. The touchstones that we examined in the last chapter do not work so well here. How could the system love more, be more patient, show more faith? We need system analogues to the discerner-oriented touchstones that thread through the long Christian tradition. The key to finding such structural touchstones is, I believe, in the statement: *As love is in the personal and interpersonal levels, justice is in the structural level.* While we can't easily speak of an institution loving, we can speak of a system exhibiting justice. Taking justice as the linchpin of structural discernment, then, we can find touchstones for structures by looking at how justice appears and grows in the system as a result of our action.

Just as there are many virtues that cluster around love and bring out its various facets, there are also structural virtues that cluster around justice and bring out its various facets. Theologian Donal Dorr set out to examine the kinds of values that would permeate just systems. He calls them "Kingdom values" or "values for the ideal future." What he intends to identify are the deepest longings of the human spirit.[3] He identifies five such values that just institutions manifest: unity, security, justice, meaningful work, and progress.

*Unity:* A deep interdependence that binds persons and communities and promotes their well-being. Our global world reveals the arbitrariness of our political boundaries, which often have no relationship to the cultural identities of those within the boundaries. More significantly, we now are recognizing how utterly dependent we are upon all other peoples in the world for the surviving, let alone the thriving, of all of us. Technology and the global economic system have unified the world, but they have not united it, says Dorr. A truly united world would be one where the people of its different parts would benefit in a fairly equitable way, and everyone would be better for their joint collaboration. People are searching for a unity in which all are respected, and where there is mutual support rather than the exploitation of the weak by the strong. Unity, however, doesn't mean uniformity. How ironic when uniformity is touted as the way to unity, as rigorous uniformity ignores cultures and traditions different from the dominant one.[4] Roman Catholic social teaching[5] might describe this value as "the common good" or "solidarity."

*Security:* Well-being that grows in a climate of trust throughout the institutions of the society, where all are perceived to benefit from the social organization. In our contemporary world we have seen the increasing occurrence of a dehumanizing trade-off when moving toward democracy also brings anarchy, as seems to have occurred in Afghanistan. Security, the ability to be safe as one goes about one's ordinary life, is indeed a deep human need. In some places that deep human need for security has evolved into a near fetish, fostering increasingly intrusive spying, security, and militarization, even to repression, denial of fundamental rights, and torture. The basis on which the Kingdom value of security is based, however, is far different from the militarized and violent ways that are used to justify this latter view of security. It is based on trust and respect fostered by the whole society in its political, economic, social, cultural, and religious manifestations. The best foundation for this kind of security, says Dorr, is social justice throughout all aspects of the society.[6]

*Justice:* Giving all persons their due or, more expansively put, "deep right-relatedness with all others."[7] By listing justice as a Kingdom value, Dorr helps validate my original thesis that the structural analogue to love is justice.

He believes that the issues with respect to social justice are best articulated in terms of basic human rights, political rights, and the right to be free of arbitrary arrest, to be sure, but also the right to work, a living wage, schooling, access to markets and fair prices for goods, decent housing, technology, one's culture, one's choice of religion. Absent any of these, persons do not thrive.[8] Catholic social teaching would speak of the preferential option for persons who are poor when developing or evaluating structures. We might expand that statement to the preferential option for anyone marginalized.

*Work:* Right livelihood through meaningful labor. Observing those who cannot find work quickly shows how corrosive lack of work is to the human spirit. But this work is not the endless toil of sweatshops and subsistence living found in so much of the world, not the grinding poverty of much of the world's lowest economic classes, and certainly not the "work" of sex trafficking and child labor that feed off desperation and greed. Work is a Kingdom value when it taps the human capacity for creativity, inventing, shaping, cooperating with others to create something useful and beautiful for enhancing human community.[9] Catholic social teaching likewise holds the principle of the dignity of work.

*Progress:* Sustainable advances in living conditions, intellectual and cultural capital, means of livelihood, health care for all. Dorr here is referring to the belief that local communities, and the world as a whole, can change for the better, can experience lasting improvements that enhance human living as well as preserve the earth for future generations—not the kind of progress sought as elites strive to capture a greater and greater share of the world's resources for their enrichment.[10]

As I have been reflecting on structural touchstones, I have isolated several more values I would add to Dorr's list that can also serve as structural touchstones: inclusiveness, flexibility, and care of creation.

*Inclusiveness:* Welcoming otherness into the group; including all voices at the table; sharing power widely. We have only to look at the power of gangs in urban areas to verify the need that humans have for inclusion. What a contrast to the Benedictine value of hospitality, which welcomes the stranger as Christ.[11] An inclusive institution doesn't make decisions about the life of other members of the community when no one like them is represented at the decision-making table. Letting everyone in requires a radical trust that God will provide for all and that our task is to open our arms and hearts to others as we have been welcomed by God.

*Flexibility:* Responding appropriately to needs and challenges in the environment, learning from and honoring the past but not being imprisoned by it. Rigid structures break sooner or later, and before they do, they often break their less powerful constituents. For example, a penal system that allows judges no flexibility in sentencing can result in such obvious injustices as life imprisonment for stealing a bicycle. Flexibility as a Kingdom value, however, doesn't mean that all tradition goes out the window. Just the opposite: tradition is honored for its wisdom, but it is not ossified into a set of rules to be applied no matter what. Systems that are "flex-able" can absorb many stresses and incorporate the valuable aspects of the stresses into the ongoing life of the structure.

*Care of creation:* The nonhuman creation is also a focus of justice and right relationships. This value takes the long view that we are all in this together, humans along with all of creation. Care for these nonhuman others is part of the calculus in all decisions.[12]

What happens to humans in structures that exhibit these "values for the future"? The effect of just systems on humans and other creatures can also suggest touchstones for our structural discernment. Among other outcomes, deep relationships can form, sometimes across enormous cultural or social or religious gaps. People honor their cultural, ethnic, and religious roots, and society becomes naturally more diverse. Diversity is not seen as something to fear but a sign of a healthy community. Harmony grows, despite differences, though not without struggle and hard work. People have hope for the future and for their children's future. They care for and cherish the natural world.[13]

How do we move from these touchstones to the structure about which we made a decision? Basically, in our prayer, we pose the structural touchstones to the structure as we posed the personal touchstones to the discerner. As before, we look for a preponderance of touchstones pointing toward the action of the Spirit within the structure. Let me give you an example at the level of an academic institution. If I want to test the fruit of a discerned decision in my own rather small freestanding graduate institution, I might look for a healthy representation of the following concrete manifestations of the more abstract structural touchstones:

- Social exchange up and down the institution (unity, flexibility, inclusiveness)
- Care for the facilities and grounds, tools, and machines (work, care of creation)
- Frugality in the use of resources, recycling (care of creation)
- Honesty in accounting (justice)
- Transparency in personal exchanges, lack of secrecy (unity, security, inclusiveness)

- Enhanced communication between arms of the institution (unity, inclusiveness)
- Mutual support and respect (unity, security, justice)
- Good morale, people feeling valued (security, work)
- Just wages and safe working conditions (security, work, progress)
- Balanced budget (justice, progress)
- Attention to the voices of those with least power (justice, inclusiveness)
- Culture of service and hospitality (justice, flexibility, inclusiveness)
- Subsidiarity or decentralized decision making (flexibility, unity, work)
- Ministry to the surrounding community (unity, justice)
- Appropriate loyalty to the institution (unity)
- Great celebrations (unity, inclusiveness)

If the structure I am focusing on is a subset of the entire institution—the faculty, for example—I might concentrate on enhanced communication, talking directly to one another rather than in cliques, good morale, people feeling valued, subsidiarity, participation of all in the shared work, and the enjoyment we take in each other (which might be embodied in our parties). You may need to use a bit of imagination to find concrete manifestations of the structural touchstones that most effectively illumine your structure.

Questions 5 through 8 help you focus concretely on your particular structure. Question 5 asks you to look at specific people involved with you in the decision, not the "people in general" of the abstract touchstones. Are *these* people thriving? Suffering more? Why? As we saw earlier, those who are marginalized in the structure function as the canary in the coal mine; what is their condition now, after the structural change is implemented? Does their situation alert you that all may not be well? Do you need to change the action or any part of its implementation to improve their situation? Likewise, tracing the kinds of power and how it now flows within the structure provides important information on whether the structure has moved closer toward its vocation. Is power concentrated in such a way that more or different persons are disempowered? Has power shifted from power over to greater empowerment? Whose speech now holds sway, and how is that speech being used? What authority is being invoked to justify the new power arrangements? Since power is neither good nor bad in the abstract, we look to see how the power affects the structure and whether the power points to and assists the structure to more deeply live out its divine call.

Question 8 points to how the action has been received, or "accepted," as Olsen and Morseth put it.[14] Has it worked its way into the life of the structure? Or are the people in the structure widely resisting the action? What is the quality of the rejection? Is it simply the difficulty of changing a long-standing habit or the inevitable grinding of gears as the structure shifts and rebalances itself? Or is the resistance more basic, a way of saying without saying, perhaps unconsciously, "This isn't us!" If the action has been accepted, what is the quality of the acceptance? There is a huge difference between apathy or fear of upsetting the power structure or losing one's job and the sense "Yes! This is us!" This quality may not be revealed for a long time, perhaps generations, so acceptance/rejection needs to be tentatively held, as do other touchstones. Each touchstone is a pointer, but each may also suggest further discernment.

The crucial judgment comes in question 9. As we prayerfully hold both the process and the decision in the light of our prayer, is there sufficient sense that we should continue? Do we sense, in the power of the Spirit of God, that all is in line to proceed? Or do we sense that something is not right or not timely? If the latter, stop implementing and return to prayer. Perhaps we need to shift the decision or the implementation a little so that something that appeared during this reflection can be attended to. What would that shift look like? And does it withstand its own prayer for confirmation? With Ignatius of Loyola, have we prayerfully waited a sufficient amount of time so that God could get a word in edgewise?

When we have favorably passed through the confirmation period, we conclude this prayer and this cycle of Social Discernment. We know there will be another cycle on this or another structural issue. But for now we continue our prayer for strength, courage, and energy for implementation and express our gratitude for all that has happened through this extended cycle of discernment.

## The Cases Brought Full Circle

Sister Joan began, carefully and after much prayer, to speak unspoken assumptions. Not surprisingly, the system pushed back. It took the form of long and sometimes contentious house meetings. Sensing less than full support for her ministry, Sister Katherine began to look for another living arrangement once her initial commitment to programming near Eastside Catholic Sisters' Residence had been fulfilled. By the end of her second year at Eastside, she had made arrangements to create a new household with two other members of her religious congregation about thirty miles away. Sister Joan continued trying to name unspoken assumptions, but without Sister Katherine to serve as the "perceived patient," it was harder to notice the unconscious assumptions. However, her own ministry situation was also shifting. Within a year of Sister Katherine's departure, she too announced her intention to move on from Eastside's residence.

Several years later, I asked Sister Joan, "Reflecting back on that long process, would you expend the energy to complete a Social Discernment again if the circumstances arose?" "Oh, yes," she said, "in fact, I have used Social Discernment any number of times since then. I learned that systems can be unpacked and that I am not powerless in the face of even big and complicated structures. Sometimes dealing with a structure is the only or the best way to follow God's call in my life. I have also *begun* to learn that I am only responsible for my own careful discernment and for acting on what comes from it. God is responsible for changing the system. For me that is the greatest grace of all."

The Pastor Nominating Committee's major discernment complete, they began the initial process of evaluating all they had done. Just after the congregational meeting in which the assembled members of Hope Church voted to call candidate B, they convened again. They had two agenda items: evaluating their discernment process and setting up a subset of the Pastor Nominating Committee to serve as a transitional support group for the new pastor and her family. This latter item was quickly disposed of, and the bulk of their time together was given to reviewing the process. All members had brought whatever notes they took, including the records they had made of their own prayer times. A time of quiet allowed each member to range back over the process, notes in hand. Then each person responded to question 3a. Far from finding this review of their resistances discouraging and depressing, the general consensus, expressed with a bit of surprise, was that the resistances and frustrations were an essential part of arriving at the outcome. As they worked through them, their direction became clearer. That left them with a new understanding not only of the inevitability of such resistances— "desolations," Ignatius of Loyola would have called them—but also of the fact that the Spirit of God can bring clarity despite and even because of them! Once they had cleared the desolations off their collective plate, the consolations suggested in question 3b only added to their energy.

What would they do differently in their next discernment? "Know more about discernment before we start" came up clearly, and they tended to agree until someone observed that what they really needed to know about discernment could only be learned in the process. But, they agreed, once through the process, it had made discernment real, and all but one agreed they would serve in another discernment group if their personal circumstances would allow the time commitment. They asked their Committee on Ministry liaison to recommend that some training in discernment be given to the committee members and also to those of the Committee on Preparation for Ministry, since they deal with vocational discernment of candidates preparing for ministry.

In terms of the structural touchstones, they looked at the comments and the votes from the congregational meeting and the candidate's approval by the presbytery as a first pass at structural confirmations. They agreed to meet just prior to the new pastor's first review to reflect on her first months, returning to the structural touchstones to see how the wider structure, the church community, the presbytery, and the neighborhood had been impacted through this call. Since they had been in the mode of examen most of the evening, they concluded this session with spontaneous prayers offered by the members of the committee and ritualized their conclusion by shredding all the confidential material generated throughout their process.

### Bird's Eye View of the Social Discernment Cycle

As we complete the confirmation, with its look back over the entire course of the Social Discernment Cycle, taking a long-range perspective on the cycle itself ideally will pull all the threads together as well as deepen the theoretical grounding for this method of discernment. In this final section, I will illustrate how the Social Discernment Cycle actually contains all the steps for discerned decision making while pointing out some limitations to the process.

In the first chapter, I named the necessary elements in discerned decision making, basing that list on a survey of various discernment processes over the course of the history of Christian spiritual practice. These elements, as I see them, are:

- Seek spiritual freedom, the inner disposition often called "indifference," upon which discernment rests and that creates the climate for discernment.
- Discover and focus the options open to decision.
- Gather and evaluate appropriate information relevant to these options.
- Pray in the light of all the information, seeking in the light of faith the better way forward among the options.
- Formulate a tentative decision through an appropriate process.
- Seek confirmation that this option is God's call in this moment.
- Finalize the decision, putting it into action and assessing the result.

Does the Social Discernment Cycle, as we have undertaken it and as laid out throughout this book, actually contain these seven elements? The seven elements are indeed present, though the way the chapters are divided may obscure the way that the Social Discernment Cycle maps onto the elements of discerned decision making. Let me make these connections explicit.

Before we can actually begin the discernment process itself, there are several key preliminaries: We need to understand what discernment is, treated in chapter 1. We also need to prepare ourselves for discernment by seeking the inner disposition for discernment, variously called indifference or, as I have preferred to call it, spiritual freedom, begun in chapter 2. The first of the seven elements of discerned decision making speaks of "indifference," language from the Ignatian tradition,[15] and names a disposition of willingness to hold God above any other created thing. In terms of decision making, indifference could be framed as a willingness to follow God's call above any other call or commitment. Shifting the language from indifference to spiritual freedom assumes that spiritual freedom is the fruit of indifference and that the language of spiritual freedom addresses a structural reality more directly and positively than the intrapersonally oriented term "indifference." Spiritual freedom, I have reiterated throughout the process, is God's gift. It is also ephemeral, so we will need to renew our prayer for spiritual freedom again and again. The complexity of the Social Discernment Cycle and the usual difficulties in maintaining a stance of openness to the call of God are compounded in group discernment, making it even more important that the discerning group also consciously return to the prayer for spiritual freedom. Hence, each phase of the social discernment process begins here.

Chapter 2 also treats the formation of the discerning group. This, we saw, is an intentional process of faith or value sharing, gaining conversation skills, trust-building, and commitment to a common project, namely, seeking the action(s) that will help the target structure live into its vocation more deeply. To put this common project in more overtly religious language, the discernment group is seeking the initial contemplative action that will lead toward greater actualizing of the call that God has for the structure in this moment in its history. At its best, the discernment group becomes a container for the deep listening and vulnerability necessary for shedding preconceived notions of what is and what might be and for allowing a new vision of the structure to take shape in their imaginations, such that a first step in that direction becomes obvious.[16]

In chapters 2–4, we tackled the second element of discerned decision making, framing the structure and focusing the matter for discernment. In all discernment, discerners must clarify what it is that they are discerning about, a task complicated when the object of discernment is a structure or an institution. In order to unpack the structural elements, we need both to conceive of the discerning group as a system, addressed in chapter 2, and also to grasp the way systems function in general, addressed in chapter 3. The Social Discernment Cycle embeds system analysis in the description and information-gathering phases of the discernment, helping us notice the linkages that form the structure. We take a focused look at the linkages that form the structure through social analysis, treated in chapter 5.

It is not always immediately clear, however, at what level of the structure the discernment should focus, so what looks straightforward when we record it as an element of discerned decision making is often a process of discovery in practice. Sometimes it is useful to move from a broad structure to a more focused aspect of the system, either because the discerners have direct personal experience at the more contained size or an action may have a more immediate impact in that size structure. In this simplifying move, we follow Donal Dorr's wisdom that we concentrate, as far as possible, on our own structure rather than one we are more "looking at" than operating within. An upshot of our early system analysis is that we may shift the target system to one that is more to the scale of our direct participation and (collective) action—or, conversely, we may broaden our scope to investigate a system more likely to affect the appropriate scale of change. Chapter 4 introduced us to these aspects of the current situation, especially the essential connection to the direct experience of the discerner or discerning group. Ignatian commentator Joseph Veale notes trenchantly: "There is a place for description and analysis. It is indispensable. But it cuts no ice until some other level of experience is stirred and attended to. Then the subsequent analysis can bear fruit."[17]

The next element of discerned decision making, gathering the necessary information, also happens at various places in the Social Discernment Cycle. It begins in chapter 4 with the description of what is going on and how the discerners are responding to the situation. But the primary locus of data gathering in terms of structures comes through social analysis, introduced in chapter 5. Here the strength of the Social Discernment Cycle for discerning structures comes to the fore and brings into the heart of discernment a task that ordinarily has no connection to discernment. As the linkages that compose the structure are uncovered, what appeared to be impermeable is actually revealed to contain junctures, or soft spots, as we have sometimes called them, points at which the structure is more amenable to leverage, which is crucial information to be brought to prayer and theological reflection. The kind of analysis that is appropriate is dictated by the particular system that is the focus of the discernment, and the complexity and sophistication of the analysis should reflect the complexity of the system. A common mistake at the other extreme is to get lost in complex analysis—studying a system is easier than deciding on an action and implementing it! Sometimes simple analyses are the most useful and appropriate.

Experience is a valuable teacher at this point. Participants struggle, sometimes mightily, with the analysis, which reveals hitherto unforeseen complexity. The result is that the structure appears *more* complex and resistant to change than at the beginning of the process. Nor does this phase "feel spiritual." It requires hard, critical work. Unless the discerners have the faith perspective to see critical analysis as part of the prayer and as a spiritual practice in its own right, they can feel disoriented and discouraged at its conclusion. At this point, discerners are, in fact, in the midst of the shift from focusing on the parts as a way to affect the "old" whole, to looking at the parts from a vision of the "new" whole, a critical but disorienting shift that sets the condition for an action that actually emerges from what the system "wants to become" through the agency of the discerners.[18] On the other hand, for some persons, social analysis will be easier and the spiritual work of prayer will feel disorienting. Prayer as a way of working, being together, and getting things done is a radical notion, even for many Christians.

Just as the data gathering so crucial to discernment is spread over various chapters, so too is the fourth element of discerned decision making, prayer, integrated throughout the Social Discernment Cycle. It begins with the prayer and faith sharing that help form a group of individuals into a discerning group. It continues through the repeated prayer for the gift of spiritual freedom to permeate the process, and particularly the critical judgment leading to action that concretizes the act of discernment. Chapter 6 is dedicated to this phase of the Social Discernment Cycle, which we have dubbed "Theological Reflection and Prayer" precisely to highlight this distinctive. It likewise permeates the time of confirmation, which we discussed in chapter 7, and continues as we look back over the discernment process and the fruits of our discerned action, addressed in the present chapter.

Hearkening back to the Pastoral Circle as originally presented by Holland and Henriot, we pause at this point for theological reflection. We begin chapter 6 with a straightforward form of theological reflection, in which memory, imagination, and critical thinking help connect this situation and structure to the richness of the tradition. I write from within the Christian tradition, but discerning groups could also glean from other wisdom traditions suitable to the discerners, the situation, and the structure.

The original form of the Social Discernment Cycle collapsed theological reflection, its own step in the Pastoral Circle, into the prayer exercise. I pulled it back out and gave it its own distinct exercise. Discernment, like theological reflection, is a praxis process; that is, the theory is embodied by practice.

In theological reflection, the reflection surfaces an action, through which the wisdom of the tradition is brought to bear. In Social Discernment, the praxis is an appropriate action that will occur at the conclusion of the process. By means of theological reflection, both theology and Social Discernment have a better chance of being realistic and grounded in the practical wisdom of the discerning community.

In order to move from the Pastoral Circle's planning mode to discernment, it is necessary to dwell specifically and intentionally in a space of unknowing that allows God to move in us. Hence the Social Discernment Cycle intentionally inserts an extended time of contemplative prayer, in which the discerners are invited simply to wait before God for any way that God might choose to move. After this period of contemplation, we return to the theological reflection, now winnowed through contemplative prayer. Only in light of this prayerful openness to God are we poised to identify the first contemplative action in response to the situation and its underlying structure. I didn't at first see the radicality of this shift toward contemplative prayer, since such prayer would be natural to discernment. But early in our work with the Social Discernment Cycle, I presented it in a class in which there was a Jesuit student who was used to both Ignatian group discernment and the Pastoral Circle planning process. He spontaneously burst out, "We Jesuits have been using the Pastoral Circle for years and nothing much has changed, but you are asking us to *pray* the Pastoral Circle. That makes all the difference." I knew that he had intuitively grasped the similarities and the distinctive difference between the Pastoral Circle and the Social Discernment Cycle, between pastoral planning and discernment.[19]

Chapter 7 leads us through the next of the distinctives in discerned decision making, namely, formulating a tentative decision through some method. The Social Discernment Cycle has relied heavily on social analysis and theological reflection to prepare us for choosing this action, but other processes will be useful as well—indeed, nonrational aspects of decision making take center stage at the point of our contemplative prayer. Using memory and imagination, consulting our feelings, paying attention to wisdom held in the body, weighing pros and cons of specific actions, all might be braided into the Social Discernment Cycle, depending on the discerners and the structure being discerned.[20] This chapter also begins the next distinctive of discerned decision making, namely, seeking confirmation that this option is God's call in this moment. We can certainly use traditional "touchstones" from the Christian tradition as we do in chapter 7, but reflecting on system analogues to these classical touchstones, as in this chapter, proves particularly useful when our discernment is about a system action and change in the system as a system.

Finally, in this chapter, came finalizing the decision and some thought and prayer about the how and when and who of the implementation. Evaluating discerned decision making is at least as crucial as it is in secular decision making. Not only do we want to see if our decision brought the kind of system change that we had hoped (and systems frequently surprise us at precisely this point), but also we want to discover where our discernment practice can grow in the future. Learning discernment by looking back is a time-honored discernment practice, embedded, for example, in the processes for making a choice in Ignatius of Loyola;[21] we simply adapt the practice in our system's context.

It's appropriate to list some of the limitations of the Social Discernment Cycle, since I have been trumpeting its strengths throughout the book. I call attention to five.[22]

First, Filipino theologian José de Mesa points up a limitation in the Pastoral Circle that also dogs the Social Discernment Cycle. He argues that for the Pastoral Circle to continue to develop as a theological method, the theological reflection must deepen to match the depth of the social analysis.[23] We need access both to experience and, at a sufficiently sophisticated level, to the tradition in order to ground our discernment adequately. Although developing a theological method is not the purpose of the Social Discernment Cycle, shallow theological reflection can likewise weaken our discernment. For a number of years, I have taught a seminary course, Interdisciplinary Theological Reflection, in which the students present cases from their ministry. Inevitably, even students with good systematic theology background struggled to do their theologizing from a concrete ministry event, as we need to do in discernment. The difficulties may occur at three points: being able to locate oneself in experience, being able to access the theological constants to guide the theologizing, and being able to link the two starting points in the same reflection. Practitioners excel in the first, and theologians in the second, but discernment needs to integrate both sensibilities.

Second, the Social Discernment Cycle is long and can be very complex. It can daunt even a discerner of goodwill who has yet to develop patience and trust to let the process do its work. But once you grasp the central aspects of discernment and the fourfold dynamic of experience, analysis, theological reflection/prayer, and action, you can simplify (or expand) the process to the degree that your situation permits (or requires). Again, it is not the particular reflection questions that matter, but the underlying dynamic that spawned the questions. Appendix 1 provides a synopsis of the entire process that can assist you in developing a process suited to the scale and complexity of your situation.

Third, it is not particularly productive to hand people several sheets of questions and expect them to make their way through the process on their own. This reality is both a difficulty and an opportunity. Social Discernment calls out for community. Creating a discerning community is ideal, but at the least, solo discerners need someone to provide a good ear to attend their processing, to help them maintain their stance of spiritual freedom, and to encourage them when the structure looks hopelessly impenetrable. They often need companions with whom to enact their decision. Discernment groups, if they have developed sufficient trust, can often perform these services for each other and can themselves become the implementing group. In other words, social discernment becomes the occasion for developing communities of action.

We can be tempted to take a shortcut and omit one or more of the phases. Without attending clearly to the situation or structure that is being discerned, we can get hopelessly sidetracked in what turn out to be rabbit trails. We can skip directly to the prayer and theological reflection, thus avoiding the hard work of analysis, or we can mix value judgments into the analysis to the degree that we miss the illumination that social analysis can bring to discernment. We can skip from analysis to action and omit the crucial moment of contemplative openness to being transformed from within by God's grace. We can omit the action and leave the entire process without its final fruit. All the steps of the Social Discernment Cycle are essential to the transforming dynamic. Individual questions are expendable; none of the steps are.

Finally, the Social Discernment Cycle does not address the sometimes substantial issues involved in actually changing systems, particularly at the level of increasingly interconnected and hugely complex global systems. Here the Social Discernment Cycle needs to be combined with other resources.

The key to the transformative nature of Social Discernment lies in the indifference that leads to spiritual freedom. No decision is made outside this spiritual freedom. Thus, our experience has revealed, even a small response to an enormous structure or complex problem can be suffused with a sense of grace, bringing great satisfaction and the courage to go on to the next small, contemplative action. Out of such small faithful responses, whole systems can change.

I pray for you a sense of accomplishment, gratitude, and humility as you reach this point. I pray also that your structure, and you as well, have been transformed by God's grace in the doing of this Social Discernment Cycle.

# Appendix 1

# Social Discernment Cycle:
# A Condensed Form*

### Phase 1: Focus for discernment

Pray for spiritual freedom.
Prayerfully select the system or clarify the aspect of the system that will
be the focus of the discernment.

### Phase 2: Current Situation

Pray for spiritual freedom.
Describe concrete instances of the roles, behaviors, environment, and
events in this structure, paying particular attention to the situation of
the marginalized.
Note how you are responding physically, intellectually, emotionally,
and spiritually.

### Phase 3: Social Analysis

Pray for spiritual freedom.
Identify the history, mission, traditions, and cultures of this system.
Describe assumptions made by people in this structure, their social rela-
tionships, and the flow of power.
Note how you are feeling at this point.

---

*An earlier version of this condensed form appeared in Elizabeth Liebert, "Discernment for Our
Times: A Practice with Postmodern Implications," in *Studies in Spirituality* 18 (2008): 347–48.

## Phase 4: Prayer and Theological Reflection

Pray for spiritual freedom.

Spend some time in quiet prayer, just being present to God and to your structure; notice any new freedom in you.

What Scriptures connect to your sense of freedom?

What theological truths express this freedom?

Name what is graced and sinful in the structure, and the transformation in you so far.

Note how you are feeling at this point.

## Phase 5: The Decision and Inner Confirmation

Reexperience the freedom from phase 4. If you do not experience freedom, repeat phase 4. What desires flow from your freedom?

Surface possible concrete responses you could make, and touch them against your spiritual freedom. Discard those that do not continue or strengthen your spiritual freedom.

Choose a response that you will implement first, and again touch it against your spiritual freedom.

Name the people who will be involved in carrying out the action.

What means will be used to evaluate it? When?

Carry out the action, noting the changes, both within you and within the structure, that happen as a result.

## Phase 6: Review and Structural Confirmation

Return to your experience of spiritual freedom.

Look back over the entire discernment process for places where you experienced significant resistance, discouragement, or disinclination to proceed. How did these shift?

Conversely, look for places where you experienced clarity, consolation, energy to proceed. What can you learn from these shifts?

Look for indicators that the structure is moving Godward, such as greater justice, security, meaningful work, sustainable progress, cultural roots, unity, meaningful relationships, diversity, flexibility, and so on.

Notice how your action has affected the marginalized, how power functions, and some possible results. Do these indicators suggest. continuing?

If yes, conclude your discernment. If no, adjust your action accordingly or return to earlier phases of the discernment process.

Express gratitude for all that has transpired.

Appendix 2

# The Dynamic Pattern of Christian Discernment

*T*heologian Mark McIntosh offers a useful overview of the notion of spiritual discernment within the Christian tradition, in which he synthesizes into five aspects the rich and varied senses in which discernment has appeared within Christian history, theology, and practice:

> *1. Discernment as faith:* spiritual discernment as grounded in a loving and trusting relationship with God; 2. *Discernment as distinguishing between good and evil impulses that move people;* 3. *Discernment as discretion, practical wisdom, moderation, and generally good sense about what to do in given practical situations;* 4. *Discernment as sensitivity to and desire to pursue God's will in all things;* and 5. *Discernment as illumination, contemplative wisdom, a noetic relationship with God that irradiates and facilitates knowledge of every kind of truth.*[1]

How does the Social Discernment Cycle pick up on these five aspects? Clearly, this process is a concrete expression of the fourth of these phases of discernment. It contributes freshly to this dynamic by extending "all things" through its careful attention to systems and system dynamics. Its goal is to determine and implement a series of actions flowing from a desire to incarnate God's will in the structural aspects of our existence. Rather than speaking of God's will, however, I have chosen to speak of God's call, basing my choice of language on the assumption that God is already present and acting not only in persons but also in systems, actively sustaining systems in existence and inviting us to collaborate in calling them to their fullest potential for manifesting God's own creative life.

It participates in other of McIntosh's phases as well. We don't begin such an intentional process as the Social Discernment Cycle without being grounded, at least to a certain extent, in a loving and trusting relationship with God, the first aspect that McIntosh notes. Why would we bother? There are many useful processes for constructive engagement with systems.[2] But it is also the case that as we practice discernment we grow in our faith, so the process and its faith underpinning actually feed each other. The more I look for God's action, the more I will gain the eyes to see how God is at work in the world. The more I see God at work in the world, the more faith I bring to the particular situation that I am discerning.

In terms of the second of McIntosh's aspects, "distinguishing between good and evil impulses that move people," the Social Discernment Cycle presupposes that we are seeking either to decrease the negative aspects of a system or to increase the potential for positive aspects of a system, where "positive" and "negative" relate to how effectively this system lives its God-given vocation. Structural confirmation looks for how and to what degree this move has occurred. The Social Discernment Cycle implicitly attends to the good and evil impulses within individual persons, focused as it is on how these personal realities become magnified and embedded in systems that perpetuate them far beyond the actions of individual people. Being able to move toward the good without exacerbating the evil is precisely the intention of attending carefully to the experience of the marginalized. Yet Social Discernment does require that the discerner is sufficiently free of inner pulls and attachments as to sense and then follow God's call for the structure. At this point, discernment of spirits clearly comes to the fore. In the time of confirmation, in particular, discerners review the quality of their inner movements as and after they discern, asking, What has been the fruit in me as this process unfolded?

Discernment as discretion, practical wisdom, moderation, and common sense about what to do in practical situations, McIntosh's third cluster of meanings for discernment, is also addressed. Systems, however, often confound common sense. Being able to grasp how the system actually functions develops a new sophistication in common sense; it becomes a kind of "common system sense." Frequently, the outcome of the discernment process is highly commonsensical once the system dynamics are clear. In the example of Eastside Sisters' Residence developed in the body of the book, it took some processing for Sister Joan to realize that the issue at hand was the unspoken assumptions about how the sisters lived together. But within that analysis of the structure, the inspiration that came to her during the contemplative prayer time, "if you speak them, they are no longer unspoken," was completely obvious and commonsensical.

Finally, McIntosh addresses discernment as "illumination, contemplative wisdom, a noetic relationship with God that irradiates and facilitates knowledge of every kind of truth." I am convinced that Social Discernment, faithfully practiced over time, brings not only the ability to understand system dynamics and to see systems whole, but also confidence in the power of God at work in systems. Discerners can relax in this reality, even in the face of complex and apparently intractable systems, knowing that ultimately it is God who sustains, upholds, and invites discerners into systems and the systems themselves into their vocations. The Spirit of God, God's power at work in systems, enables discerners to move forward with courage and confidence amid complexity and, indeed, the crushing dynamics that systems too frequently manifest when they have become displaced from their God-given vocations.

"What in the world is God doing?" asks theologian Lee Snook. He replies to his own question: "God is not doing everything, but God is doing what only God can do within and among all creatures to cajole, persuade, lure, entice and inspire them to use the power of their God given freedom for the sake of justice to the end that the kingdom of God come on earth."[3]

Appendix 3

# Discerners as Reflective Practitioners

$S$ocial Discernment can be employed in major institutional processes that involve lots of personnel, economic resources, and time, resulting, for example, in a five-year strategic plan. But to limit the Social Discernment Cycle to these mammoth projects would be to miss a good deal of its power. Social Discernment also functions beautifully as a lens helping individuals respond to everyday system dynamics: Your child reports being bullied by kids at school; what's going on, and which of the possible responses is the one to which you are called? What about the clique at work whose penchant for gossip is making the workplace unpleasant? The neighborhood is changing; what role should we take with respect to that change? Donald Schön's classic work on reflective practitioners provides a way to think about the discerner's increasing capacity to perceive and respond discerningly to systems large and small.

Reflective practitioners, Schön demonstrates, respond, often intuitively, to the concrete situation presented them, but they learn to reflect on their practice so that they are increasingly able to articulate why they do what they do. They see each situation before them as a case of one, unique in its own right, not as an illustration of some ideal type. They use their experience as a kind of base against which they touch the new situation, always assuming that the new case will present something novel. On the basis of their bank of experience, they respond to the novel situation with a sort of mini-experiment. An experiment is "successful" if it explains the situation in a way that makes sense to the practitioner, whether or not another experimenter would achieve the same results. If an experiment results in something surprising, either positively or negatively, the practitioner responds with curiosity: What does that mean? The response to one mini-experiment and subsequent reflection sets the conditions of the next mini-experiment/reflection, and the next.[1]

In discernment, each situation is unique because we don't know in advance how God may call. Each discerned action forms a mini-experiment: Does the structure move forward more fruitfully? And when the result is surprising, we either give thanks or adjust our discernment accordingly. Also, each completed discernment process results in an action addressing the structure, which inevitably changes the structure, however subtly. The structure after the action is a different structure, potentially calling for a new discernment. We speak of Social Discernment as a *cycle* and illustrate it with a helix precisely to highlight this continually moving action-reflection process.

Setting up a problem is not the same as solving the same problem. But until the issue is clear, it is not possible to determine the direction to move to increase the probability of a positive outcome or decrease the probability of a negative outcome. Reflective practitioners are artists at setting up the problem, used as they are to working with cases of one. Similarly in the early stages of the Social Discernment Cycle, discerners must set the contours of the problem, here understood as the question or issue to be discerned and the scope of the structure that maintains the situation. The actual framing of the discernment question and selecting the scope of the structure happens in a similar series of little experiments until it is judged by the discerner to be right—that is, manageable and useful. Another discerner may define the scope of the discernment differently.

In reflective practice, an overarching theory does not provide a rule that can be applied to predict or control a particular event.[2] Likewise, each discernment, open to God's movement, must be a case of one, as the discerners, the configuration of the structure, and the presence of the ever-creative God within both the structure and the discerners come together in a fluid and ever-changing configuration. The bank of experience that one uses to judge the discernment experiment is not only from one's own experience, but also draws on the accumulated wisdom of the discernment tradition—the touchstones, as I have called them. This reservoir of wisdom undergirds and confirms discerners' initial sense of the rightness of the decision in what is a unique and unrepeatable discernment.

Finally, Schön reminds us that reflective practitioners practice repertory-building research for accumulating and describing exemplars in ways that are useful for their particular communities. In this repertory building, they trace the evolution of the practice, not simply the results, which is the key to the kind of double learning of both content and practice that characterizes reflective practice.[3] In our practice of discernment, we regularly trace the evolution of our practice; indeed, this is exactly the intent of the Awareness Examen that begins and ends our times of discernment—and our days—to notice how

God is continually at work in us and in the system. Over time, the promise of this spiritual practice is that we become ever more skillful at noticing and responding, that we become reflective practitioners of discernment within our own communities.

Schön has, in fact, carefully described and given respectable epistemological status to the action-reflection method that characterizes repeated cycles of Social Discernment. Reflective practitioners are inside the situation they are experimenting with, attempting to affect the situation by actually changing it—exactly the case with the discerner in a structure prayerfully seeking the first contemplative action, taking that action, and then reflecting on what happened, all from within the structure.[4]

# Appendix 4

# Social Discernment as an Exemplar
# of Change Theory

*P*aul Watzlawick, John Weakland, and Richard Fisch's treatment of the principles of problem formation and resolution, introduced in chapter 3, where we cited their eminently useful distinction between first- and second-order change, also provides another rubric to understand the Social Discernment Cycle. At the conclusion of their treatment of change, they propose a four-step procedure summarizing their method of practicing and promoting change:

- A clear definition of the problem in concrete terms
- An investigation of the solutions attempted so far
- A clear definition of the concrete change to be achieved
- The formulation and implementation of a plan to produce this change[1]

With the caveat that the Social Discernment Cycle is about much more than solving problems, but about unleashing the power of the Spirit in institutions, it is still instructive to see how it fits within this change scheme.

We begin our system work by identifying an issue and the structure that holds it. Doing so also involves identifying both the structure and the scope of the structure that will be most effective in helping us see the issue, imagine an action appropriate to this situation, and plan for its implementation once discerned. This process is organic, cycling through several of the steps, and is determined by reflecting on and adjusting the question and its scope as many times as helpful until it fits the situation and the discerners.

Gathering the history of the structure illumines the "solutions attempted so far" as it describes the trajectory that brought the system to its present configuration. We name the significant players in this system, past and present. As we move into the social analysis, we begin to see how the players inform the structure and also how the structure constrains the players as it maintains the status quo.

The Social Discernment Cycle departs somewhat from the change scheme at its third point. We may not be able to formulate all the steps to the concrete change to be achieved, especially in complex systems. The Social Discernment Cycle is based on the premise that each change opens a new moment for discernment and action. Thus the ultimate outcome of a series of discerned changes may, in fact, be quite different than originally imagined and therefore can't be precisely planned for in advance, though the Social Discernment Cycle certainly does not categorically rule out planning. If the outcome is to be truly novel, however, planning can only be done after the qualitatively new aspect, idea, or structure has appeared. In this case, planning too early prevents the truly novel and creative from emerging. What the Social Discernment Cycle is committed to is discerning the first contemplative action that we are being called to in response to the situation and its history. And then we discern the next step, and the next. Each discernment cycle begins with openness to understanding how God calls in this new moment. We also hold a vision of the qualities of God-informed institutions—the structural touchstones—and we use those touchstones to evaluate our steps along the way.

Finally, we plan for the implementation of our first contemplative action. We ponder who our colleagues will be along the way and imagine the difficulties that might be thrown in our path. But we don't begin the implementation until our plan has once again been submitted to prayer. We don't want to move unless we are as humanly certain as it is given us to be that God invites us to this action. Once the implementation begins, we pause for yet another review, checking to see that the fruits of our action continue to reflect the touchstones we have come to associate with God's action in systems. With appropriate adjustments required by the theological underpinnings of discernment, clearly the Social Discernment Cycle exemplifies change theory as summarized in this scheme.

# Social Discernment
# and Transformational Learning

*I*f the Social Discernment Cycle exemplifies the major characteristics of change, at least in the system advocated by Watzlawick and his colleagues, can the same be said for transformation of the discerner? Adult learning specialist Jack Mezirow sets up the conditions for this examination. Mezirow holds that "significant learning, involving personal transformations, is a social process with significant implications for social action,"[1] exactly what we hope for as a result of the Social Discernment Cycle. Ideal learning conditions include these:

- [Sufficiently] accurate and complete information
- Freedom from coercion and distorting self-deception
- Openness to alternative points of view: empathy and concern about how others think and feel
- The ability to weigh evidence and assess arguments objectively
- [Growing] awareness of the context of ideas and, more critically, reflectiveness o[n] assumptions, including their own
- An equal opportunity to participate in the various roles of discourse
- Willingness to seek understanding and agreement and to accept a resulting best judgment as a test of validity until new perspectives, evidence, or arguments are encountered and validated through discourse as yielding a better judgment[2]

With Mezirow, we acknowledge that there is hardly ever a perfect situation for transformational learning,[3] yet the Social Discernment Cycle sets up many of the conditions. Social analysis helps provide sufficiently accurate and complete information. Our information will be as good as the particular combination of input and analysis, but the opportunity for accurate and complete information is certainly an aspect of the Social Discernment Cycle. The analysis of the information, particularly its structural aspects, is also a fruit of the social analysis phase of Social Discernment. The critical thinking advocated at this part of the process relies on the ability to weigh evidence and evaluate arguments. While the whole discernment process need not disintegrate if one or more members of the discernment group lacks these abilities, it will be more difficult for the group to reap the best outcome from the social analysis in that case.

The fruit of continual prayer for spiritual freedom threaded throughout the Social Discernment Cycle is intended to help us move away from limited, distorted, or self-centered perceptions, that is, away from self-deception. It also helps us set aside our well-known worldviews in order to be prepared to see something new emerging. In addition, the egalitarian ethos of the discerning group minimizes the possibility of coercion. To the degree that individual discerners are able to approach spiritual freedom, they will be able to speak their sense of the issue after prayerfully weighing the options without undue concern for what other discerners are saying. They understand that differing perspectives are part of finding a better "way through" the complexities and are patient with the process of moving back and forth between the perspectives of individual discerners. They are able to offer their piece of the wisdom and then stand back and let the discernment process proceed.

The constant reminder to include the perspective of the marginalized ones and to track the flow of power helps the Social Discernment Cycle equalize the opportunities for participation, as does wide consultation, to the extent that the discerners build it into the data-gathering and confirmation aspects of the process.

What might need more comment is the point "ability to weigh evidence and assess arguments objectively." Good hard, critical thinking and reflection is a characteristic of the Social Discernment Cycle, particularly at the social analysis phase. But, as Mezirow himself asserts, learning through metaphors is an important complement to rational discourse.[4] Metaphors often form a key aspect of decision making, seeking as we are to "enflesh" the metaphor of "God's call" in the system. Do I mean, then, that God's call is *only* metaphorical? No, but I do mean that we can grasp the mystery of God, who is beyond all thought, only through metaphors. Likewise, with Mezirow, we can also approach the unknown through imagination and intuition—intuition can suggest metaphors and analogues and directions. Indeed, the more reflective and open we are to the perspectives of others the richer our imagination of alternative contexts for understanding.[5] Intuition and imagination are frequently the primary modes of thinking when discerners move from critical reflection to contemplative prayer. Critical rationality, intuition, and imagination all have a place in the Social Discernment Cycle.

Mezirow is clear about the importance of review after action because, he says, we need to find out whether our initial prioritizing of needs has been adequate and to examine the gains in our transformative learning.[6] Hence, we can add another reason for the final look back that completes each iteration of the Social Discernment Cycle. But Mezirow also offers a justification for the importance of faith-based touchstones that we use to gauge the adequacy of our discernment: "Meaning perspectives provide us with criteria for judgment or evaluating right and wrong, bad and good, beautiful and ugly, true and false, appropriate and inappropriate."[7] Our touchstones become trustworthy insofar as they also enshrine the wisdom of experiences far beyond our individual discernment process.

Clearly, if discerners enter the Social Discernment process with goodwill, participate wholeheartedly in all the steps, and wrestle with the complexity presented by the systems, their discernment colleagues, and their own emotional responses, they can expect to be engaged in transformational learning. Indeed, discerners often spontaneously report how much they have been transformed in the process, whether or not they can see much transformation in the system about which they have been discerning.

# Appendix 6

# Social Discernment and Theory U:
# A Case of Simultaneity?

*I*n the Social Discernment Cycle, the term "simultaneity' has a somewhat technical meaning: the concurrent existence of several dimensions of the human person that together constitute the human person.[1] In using "simultaneity" in this heading, I am extending this meaning to suggest that the Social Discernment Cycle and Theory U share a simultaneous reality that constitutes the same whole but is described in somewhat different ways and on somewhat different scales. Why do I make this claim?

First, a bit of history. As I mentioned in the introduction, my first exposure to what we now call the Social Discernment Cycle came in 1992, when my institution, San Francisco Theological Seminary, invited its neighbor, Mercy Center, Burlingame, to cosponsor a workshop in spirituality and justice under the leadership of Brother John Mostyn, CFC. Several of our staff participated in this workshop, learning the process from the inside out. When it came time to plan a new credit-bearing program to prepare persons for the ministry of spiritual direction, we realized that issues of structure needed to be embedded in this new curriculum so that we didn't simply replicate a privatized understanding of spiritual direction in an institution in which justice issues were key to its identity and mission. We asked Jack Mostyn to facilitate our yearlong planning process, and he chose to base our planning on Social Discernment.[2] Eventually, after numerous conversations and a rather significant test of faith that we would actually produce a program philosophy, design, curriculum, and delivery system, we did, in fact, reach our goal. The Certificate in the Art of Spiritual Direction, as it was then called, got under way in January 1994, and Jack became the lead faculty person for our course "Discernment with Systems and Structures." As we watched the impact of the Social Discernment Cycle in the spiritual direction certificate, we soon began to offer Social Discernment in a semester-long format to master of divinity students as part of their preparation for ministry. In fact, we quickly claimed Social Discernment as distinctive in the SFTS spirituality curricula, highlighting the uniqueness in our institution's preparation for both spiritual direction and pastoral ministry and setting it off from the literally dozens of similar programs that sprang up in the next two decades.

Fast-forward to 2013. After a stint in academic administration, I finally had the leisure to write up the Social Discernment Cycle, completing the two-part project that began with *The Way of Discernment: Spiritual Practices for Decision Making*. As part of this writing project (this book), I began to research the foundations of the Social Discernment process, including the more recent writing of or about the figures influential in the original development of the Social Discernment Cycle, among them Joe Holland, Peter Henriot, Jack Mostyn, Walter Wink, Donal Dorr, and Peter Senge. Senge had completed his seminal work, *The Fifth Discipline*, in 1990, and his name and perspective threaded through our original exposure to the Social Discernment process and through Jack's own doctoral work. Senge's later collaboration with C. Otto Scharmer eventually led me to Theory U, so named from the U-shaped diagram illustrating the dynamics of the movement of this "social technology" designed to help individuals and groups learn from the future as it emerges.[3] Beginning on the left side of the U, one "descends" through and embracing the new ("presencing") to "ascend" the other side of the U into increasingly deep ways of seeing ("sensing") to a critical point of letting go old ways of seeing effective ways of transforming action ("realizing").

It was nothing short of startling, after two decades of tweaking, teaching, and practicing a method of discernment based on a pastoral planning method, to find striking parallels in this theory developed in management circles during the same decades. Let me give but one example. Depending on what aspect of Theory U's dynamic movement is being highlighted, various iterations of the U have been produced. Lifting up different iterations reveals a variety of parallels between Theory U and Social Discernment. Using cocreating as the highlighted rubric, Theory U demonstrates the U movement as follows: Descending the U, we see a movement from coinitiating (building commitment to stop and listen both to others and to oneself and to how life is calling) to cosensing (increasingly deeper observing, going to the places of most potential and listening with both mind and heart) to presencing at the bottom of the U (in silence, connecting to the source of inspiration and will, allowing the inner knowing beyond one's mind to emerge) to ascending the other side of the U by cocreating (generating prototypes or mini-experiments to begin to embody the new), and finally to coevolving (embodying the new in ecosystems that facilitate seeing and acting from the whole).[4]

The Social Discernment Cycle uses a helix to signify the repeated iterations of a similar dynamic over time, in contrast to Theory U's U-shaped diagram. In the Social Discernment Cycle's first movement, Looking at the Current Situation, we look ("gaze contemplatively" is the language I usually use) at what life is throwing us through the system we are examining. We look first with our descriptive eyes, noticing what is going on and how it is affecting us and other players in the system. We continue to deepen our observing as we "descend" around the circle to the second moment, Social Analysis. Here we are trying to see the system in its parts *in order to see the system whole,* also a key development as one proceeds down the U. Next, we come to the critical moment in Social Discernment, the moment of contemplative prayer. Here we call on the long Christian contemplative tradition for practices about which Theory U is almost completely mute. (The authors of *Presence* and Scharmer himself do cite Jesus' teaching Matt. 19:23–24, about how difficult it is for a camel to go through the eye of the needle, for a convenient image for the process of letting go of the old before the new can emerge, but their writings do not evidence much understanding of the wider meaning and interpretation of Christian Scriptures.) As Social Discernment moves around to the "up side" of the cycle, we allow an action, which we have sometimes called "the single first contemplative action," to emerge, and we try it on, as in Theory U's prototype. But—and this would be a distinctive taken from the discernment tradition—Social Discernment asks the discerner to check to see if this action is indeed coming from the call emerging in that deep place of letting go that we have called spiritual freedom, where Theory U emphasizes moving quickly to setting up implementing prototypes. Only after this period of confirmation does the Social Discernment Cycle begin the implementation, adjusting, and evaluating, with further adjusting as necessary.

I could give many more examples, but I have pointed out a number of resonances between these two processes in the notes throughout the text. Here it is sufficient to observe that the two processes actually complement each other in striking ways. From Theory U I take a renewed commitment to the contemplative heart of the Social Discernment. Instead of watering down this part of the process for those unused to or uncomfortable with contemplative prayer, Theory U teaches me that, however this contemplative moment is described, it is crucial to the process. So rather than soften this step, the challenge is to invite participants to enter it in a variety of ways so that those uncomfortable with a Christian practice can find another way in to the same transformative letting-go. Theory U likewise reminds me that all the effort put into developing what I have called the contemplative listening skills of the discerning group is also key to the transforming potential of the Social Discernment Cycle and is not just some nice way to be together. It is actually part of the dynamic of learning *together* to see the new whole out of the old way of thinking. Theory U also offers a good deal more detail on the action (ascending) side of the U, and, indeed, Scharmer's latest book, *Leading from the Emerging Future*, spends as much space describing the action side of the U as it does describing the problem and the deconstructing of unworkable thought process on the descending side of the U. Thus, Theory U can provide very useful detail on bringing a discerned action into implementation in such a way that it changes not only the structure, but the discerners themselves.[5] Theory U has been generated through cross-disciplinary conversations around the world, suggesting that the underlying reality that is captured in the Social Discernment Cycle will likewise serve in multiple cultures, taking suitable care to adapt to local culture.

But Social Discernment also has some things to offer to Theory U, most notably in redressing its serious lack of theory and practice from the Christian tradition. A bit of dialogue from *Presence* reveals the paucity of the authors' knowledge of Christian resources for doing exactly what they want to do with Theory U: "So what the major Western religions conceive as a transcendent, exterior God, the Eastern religions conceive of as immanent," said Otto. "Right." [replied Senge?][6]

Unfortunately, no one in this conversation (Senge, Scharmer, Jaworski, and Flowers) seems to know the Christian teaching about the indwelling of the Holy Spirit, in which the Christian believer would understand that the source of life and wisdom is already within (but not reduced to) all of creation, including the believer's own self and the system that is under consideration. Furthermore, the Christian doctrine of the Trinity suggests systems and structures as we experience them are faint images of God who, in the Christian understanding, is simultaneously both three and one (triune). The "parts," in the case of the triune God,[7] are called persons, and named in the tradition as Father (whose primary manifestation is as Creator), Son (whose primary manifestation is to have taken on human existence and serves as Redeemer), and Holy Spirit (who brings life, wholeness, and wisdom, and so is experienced as Lifegiver, Advocate, Teacher). See John 14:17; 15:26; 16:13, for example. These persons, though distinct, do not act on their own but always in unity: "The Father and I are one" (John 10:30). Although the tensions inherent in describing the triune nature of God cannot be resolved logically, as Christians have affirmed over two millennia, the very assumptions about God as Tri-Unity ground the processes for discerning and acting in all other created systems within God's own nature.

Perhaps the deeper issue is that Senge, Scharmer, Jaworski, and Flowers, and Scharmer in his later work, have been unable to break out of the box that the Enlightenment has drawn around religion and spirituality, and hence such categories as soul, spirit, contemplation, and prayer, the very expressions of spirituality, cannot be admitted as valid categories in their Western scholarship. So when it comes to the moment of presencing, which is essentially a spiritual task, they are forced to grasp for analogues from Eastern religious perspectives that have been partially domesticated and secularized as useful "technologies" as they moved into the West.[8]

But Christian "technologies" (that is, contemplative practices) also exist, and they can provide the disciplined practice that Senge and Scharmer recognize as key to accessing that presence.[9] The Social Discernment Cycle repeatedly insists on spiritual freedom, which highlights the ongoing nature of the spiritual practice and the inner condition out of which one allows the new action to emerge. Awareness Examen gives a relatively simple and flexible practice to assist individuals in developing their inner observer and to help discernment groups in becoming aware of the quality of their presence to themselves and to each other, a quality of presence that the authors of Theory U repeatedly call for.[10] Contemplative listening and responding and dialogue, as described in chapter 2, mirror Scharmer's description of listening as making a place for the other within oneself.[11] But because the authors of Theory U are unable to access the richness of the Christian tradition and practice at the critical point in the U process, they inadvertently resort to a stereotype of the Christian tradition as they set up their (minimal) discussion of Eastern practices. They rely on Taoism, Confucianism, and, in Scharmer's more recent work, *Leading from the Emerging Future,*[12] Buddhism, and vague concepts such as Sacred Mind to supply the necessary spiritual practice. The Social Discernment Cycle can fill in a huge lacuna at this transformative juncture in the Theory U dynamic.

Because of this lacuna, some Christian persons may be unable to readily relate to Theory U, seeing it as based on a somewhat diffuse New Age spirituality or solely upon Eastern religious and philosophical systems. For this Christian population, the Social Discernment Cycle can supply the critical theological and spiritual and practice elements based in the Christian tradition that they need to access the dynamic movement precisely as a spiritual practice. Theory U, on the other hand, offers suggestions for non-Christian or nonreligious language, should such language be more accessible to other practitioners.[13] A strikingly similar underlying dynamic, but employing somewhat different languages related to their chronologically parallel origins, the differences in context and goals of those who developed the processes, and the scope of their inquiries— this is what I mean by simultaneity.

# Notes

## NOTES TO INTRODUCTION

1. Elizabeth Liebert, *The Way of Discernment: Spiritual Practices for Decision Making* (Louisville, KY: Westminster John Knox Press, 2008).

2. Peter Senge, C. Otto Scharmer, Joseph Jaworski, and Betty Sue Flowers, *Presence: Human Purpose and the Field of the Future* (Cambridge, MA: Society for Organizational Learning, 2004), 6.

3. Sister Margaret Carney, "Trusteeship as Ministry," interview by Christa Klein, *In Trust* 25, no. 1 (Autumn 2013): 23.

4. Nancy Bedford, "Little Moves against Destructiveness: Theology and the Practice of Discernment," in *Practicing Theology: Beliefs and Practice in Christian Life,* ed. Miroslav Volf and Dorothy Bass (Grand Rapids: Eerdmans, 2002), 157–81.

5. Joe Holland and Peter Henriot, *Social Analysis: Linking Faith and Justice* (Maryknoll, NY: Orbis Books, 1980). This book is currently in the twentieth printing of the revised edition (1983) and translated into seven languages, attesting to its impact. The roots of the Pastoral Circle are described in Joe Holland, "The Roots of the Pastoral Circle in Personal Experiences and Catholic Social Tradition," in *The Pastoral Circle Revisited: A Critical Quest for Truth and Transformation,* ed. Frans Wijsen, Peter Henriot, and Rodrigo Mejía (Maryknoll, NY: Orbis Books, 2005), 1–12.

6. This evolution is described by Elinor Shea in "Spiritual Direction and Social Consciousness," *The Way Supplement* 54 (Autumn 1985): 30–42.

7. Holland and Henriot, *Social Analysis*, 7–9.

8. Juan José Luna, "The Pastoral Circle: A Strategy for Justice and Peace," in *The Pastoral Circle Revisited,* ed. Frans Wijsen, Peter Henriot, and Rodrigo Mejía (Maryknoll, NY: Orbis Books, 2005), 38.

9. Eastside High School Sisters' Residence and the names of its residents are fictitious. The situation, however, actually occurred some years ago.

10. This Hope Presbyterian Church does not exist in real life, and any resemblance to an existing Hope Presbyterian Church is purely coincidental. The situation, however, is not unique; many churches face a situation not unlike Hope's, though the specifics of the polity may differ. For further discussion, suggestions, and examples for discerning new church leaders within a variety of church polities, see Charles M. Olsen and Ellen Morseth, *Selecting Church Leaders: A Practice in Spiritual Discernment* (Nashville: Upper Room Books, 2002).

Olsen and Morseth devote chapters to the particular issues raised by inclusivity and to the candidate's side of the discernment process, which I have not addressed. Like Olsen and Morseth, I subscribe to the position that discernment, in many instances, does not need to replace existing forms of polity. Rather, discernment can transform existing polity into an intentional listening for the call of God within the parameters of that polity. That commitment appears in this case, which presumes the polity in place within the Presbyterian Church (U.S.A.) at the time of this writing.

11. Liebert, *Way of Discernment*, 15–19.

12. This ability to cocreate is sometimes called tertiary creation or subcreation. See, for example, Jordan J. Ballor, *Get Your Hands Dirty: Essays on Christian Social Thought (and Action)* (Eugene, OR: Wipf & Stock, 2013), 68.

13. A recent symposium in *Pastoral Psychology* discusses how the reductiveness inherent in the unexamined and unchallenged assumption of metaphysical naturalism severely limits the social sciences from dealing with the rich, messy complexity of life as it is lived by real human beings. Such an unexamined assumption obviously also rules out of bounds any appeal or even reference to the sacred, even a sacred conceived as immanent in the created order. See Brent D. Slife and Frank C. Richardson, "Naturalism, Psychology, and Religious Experience: An Introduction to the Special Section on Psychology and Transcendence," *Pastoral Psychology* 63 (2014): 319–22.

14. Lee E. Snook, *What in the World Is God Doing? Re-Imagining Spirit and Power* (Minneapolis: Fortress Press, 1999), introduction, esp. 5–9. Much rich theologizing on the Holy Spirit has occurred recently. See Veli-Matti Kärkkäinen, *The Holy Spirit: A Guide to Theology* (Louisville, KY: Westminster John Knox Press, 2012), chap. 6, for an overview of the major twentieth-century voices.

## NOTES TO CHAPTER 1: DISCERNMENT IN AN AGE OF COMPLEXITY

1. Ruth Haley Barton, *Pursuing God's Will Together: A Discernment Practice for Leadership Groups* (Downers Grove, IL: IVP Books, 2012), 10.

2. John 14:17 and 16:13, among other texts, illumine the New Testament beginnings of an understanding of the Holy Spirit.

3. Greg Boyle, founder of Homeboy Industries in Los Angeles, offers a delightful metaphor that makes this very point: "We try to find a way to hold our fingertips gently to the pulse of God. We watch as our hearts begin to beat as one with the One who delights in our being. Then what do we do? We exhale that same spirit of delight into the world and hope for poetry." Discernment, this image suggests, does not have to be grim, but can be like poetry that comes from breathing out God's delight in us. See *Tattoos on the Heart: The Power of Boundless Compassion* (New York: Free Press, 2010), 147.

4. I have gathered many practices for personal discernment in *The Way of Discernment: Spiritual Practices for Decision Making* (Louisville, KY: Westminster John Knox Press, 2008). Any practices that improve skill in contemplative prayer, contemplative listening, and prayerful decision making can enhance the ability to discern.

5. Ignatius of Loyola, *The Spiritual Exercises*, particularly nos. 10, 313–36, and C. S. Lewis, *The Screwtape Letters: Annotated Edition* (New York: HarperCollins, 2013; original copyright, 1942). These authors and their very different treatments of "the enemy of human nature," as Ignatius calls him, or the panoply of major and minor devils that Lewis brilliantly depicts, raise the question about whether the understandings of discernment can make any sense at all for Christians who do not believe in a literal devil or for persons who are not

Christians. Interestingly, in the preface to the Macmillan 1962 edition of *Screwtape Letters*, Lewis answers the question "do I believe in devils?" in the affirmative, adding: "I believe this not in the sense that it is part of my creed, but in the sense that it is one of my opinions. My religion would not be in ruins if this opinion were shown to be false. Till that happens—and proofs of a negative are hard to come by—I shall retain it" (viii).

According to the New Testament, notes biblical scholar Sandra Schneiders, the personal agent in the complex network of destructive forces at work in New Testament times and that we see around us today is Satan, "the final enemy of God and Jesus, bent on the destruction of the world which is God's good Creation, including the human race called to divine filiation. But Satan does not operate in the open and has so hidden his persona that most people in the Western world have trouble believing that this is such an agent, much less recognizing him where he is operative. Satan's vision and agenda are incarnated in the systems of domination in all areas of human experience." See *Buying the Field: Catholic Religious Life in Mission to the World* (New York: Paulist Press, 2013), 46–47.

In the next chapter, we will encounter the work of Walter Wink, who also recognizes the extreme difficulty that persons embedded in Western materialism have in admitting any reality to angels, demons, or Satan. But Wink believes that if we demythologize angels and demons out of existence, we do so at our own peril. The key is whether, without Satan to symbolize evil's presence, we can still actually experience and confront evil in and around us. Based on careful exegesis of numerous New Testament passages, Wink speaks of demonic systems as the inner spirituality of systems gone astray. In Wink's hypothesis, Satan and demons are the symbolic language that the ancients used to point to the working out of evil in individuals and communities. They do not have separate personal existence; they are always incarnated inside humans and human systems, carried forward both by the systems themselves and by the individuals who are formed by and operate within the systems. In the first chapter of *Unmasking the Powers*, he says, "Whether one 'believes' in Satan, then, is not nearly as important as recognizing the satanic function as part and parcel of every decision." See *Walter Wink: Collected Readings*, ed. Henry French (Minneapolis: Fortress Press, 2013), 97.

Since the notion of a personal tempter has been consistently present in Christian theology and discernment tradition, the question about what happens to the sense of discernment if we do not hold that the source of evil is a supranatural personal being naturally arises. In my experience, holding that the source of evil is literally and only a personal being is not essential to the practice of discernment. I say this because I have watched many persons who hold such understandings of evil work comfortably in discernment. Understanding evil in its systemic manifestations actually makes great sense in a systemic perspective on discernment such as we are developing here. I am not denying the long Christian teaching on personal beings as a source of evil, simply noting that its nature is unresolved in contemporary theological discussions. However one settles the ontic nature of evil, its reality is everywhere attested.

6. The following several paragraphs rely on my earlier work, *Way of Discernment*, 17–18. For a discussion of call as vocational choice integral to our identity, see Suzanne Farnham, Joseph P. Gill, R. Taylor McLean, and Susan M. Ward, *Listening Hearts: Discerning Call in Community,* rev. ed. (Harrisburg, PA: Morehouse Publishing, 2011), 7–16.

7. Douglas J. Schuurman, among others, critiques this position. See *Vocation: Discerning Our Callings in Life* (Grand Rapids: Eerdmans, 2004), 125–30.

8. In fact, says Edward Hahnenberg, following Karl Barth, God has created humans precisely *with* limitations. Rather than something to be lamented, these limitations actually provide the platform for vocational choice. Vocation emerges from what am I to do with this life

that I have been granted, in all its particularities. "We can be obedient to this summons only from within our own humanity," he claims, including all the determinisms and limitations of one's concrete situation. In choosing a vocation, we must ask ourselves two questions: "What are the needs of my historical situation?" and "What are my own gifts and dispositions?" See *Awakening Vocation: A Theology of Call* (Collegeville, MN: Liturgical Press, 2010), 118–22. See Schuurman, *Vocation*, 53–56, for a treatment of dependence as both a gift and a task.

9.  Hahnenberg, *Awakening Vocation*, 206, also unpacks the turn toward history in Salvadoran theologian Ignacio Ellacuría's work: "There are not two histories, a history of God and a history of humanity. 'Rather there is a single historical reality in which both God and human beings intervene, so that God's intervention does not occur without some form of human participation, and human intervention does not occur without God's presence in some form.'" The quote from Ellacuría is from "The Historicity of Christian Salvation," trans. Margaret D. Wilde, in *Mysterium Liberationis: Fundamental Concepts of Liberation Theology*, ed. Ignacio Ellacuría and Jon Sobrino (Maryknoll, NY: Orbis Books, 1993), 254. See Schuurman, *Vocation*, 37–47, for a biblical perspective refracted through the Reformed tradition.

10.  For a brief but substantial treatment of the theological underpinnings of discernment, see Edward Collins Vacek, "Discernment within a Mutual Love Relationship with God: A New Theological Foundation," *Theological Studies* 74 (2013): 683–710, in particular, 686–89.

11.  For a rich discussion of this process, along with prior discernments leading up to the gathering in Jerusalem, see Luke T. Johnson, *Scripture and Discernment: Decision Making in the Church* (Nashville: Abingdon, 1983), esp. chap. 5, and Pieter G. P. de Villiers, "Communal Discernment in the Early Church," *Acta Theologica* Supplement 17 (2013): 132–55 (http://dx.doi.org/10.4314/actat.v32i2S.8).

12.  Joseph Lienhard, "On 'Discernment of Spirits' in the Early Church," *Theological Studies* 41 (Spring 1980): 505–29. In Athanasius's *Life of Antony* (ca. 357), a text immensely influential in the development of monasticism in the West, a slight shift began to occur. Instead of distinguishing between good and evil spirits, this text focuses on recognizing various kinds of *evil* spirits. Over the next hundred years, the understanding of spirits became depersonalized; eventually "spirits" referred to various capital sins (such as gluttony, pride, anger, and revenge). We see this shift developing in John Cassian's *Conferences* (ca. 420). As it took place, "discernment of spirits" began to be shortened to "discernment" and eventually came to mean balance between extremes. Discernment of spirits had metamorphosed into the virtue of *discretion*.

13.  The account of what has come to be called the "Deliberations of the First Fathers" can be found at John Predmore, SJ, http://predmore.blogspot.com/2010/04/spirituality-text-of-deliberations-of.html. See also Ladislaw Orsy, "Towards a Theological Evaluation of Communal Discernment," *Studies in the Spirituality of Jesuits* 5, no. 5 (1973): 139–86.

14.  One more development in this period helps set the stage for a Lutheran contribution to communal discernment. A highly influential Lutheran treatise on soul care is Philipp Jakob Spener's *Pia Desideria* (1675); this book is often regarded as the foundation book of the Pietist movement. Spener wanted to encourage deep and rich personal spirituality with a strong emphasis upon communion and the mutual priesthood of all believers, and upon an emotional commitment to the gospel. About 1670, he began to hold conferences for mutual edification in his study in Frankfurt. These conferences employed discussion materials from the Bible and from a wide variety of devotional books. This pattern of mutual soul care became widely practiced beyond Lutheranism, indeed throughout much of Protestantism. The

formation of a group that expects to grow in the understanding of the spiritual life is fertile ground for communal discernment.

15.   The theory and practice of Clearness Committee has been discussed in both Quaker and non-Quaker sources. See, for example, Parker Palmer, "Clearness Committee: A Way of Discernment," *Weavings* 3 (July–August 1988): 37–40 and more extensively in *A Hidden Wholeness: The Journey Toward an Undivided Life* (San Francisco: Jossey-Bass, 2004); Farnham et al., *Listening Hearts;* and Patricia Loring, "Spiritual Discernment," Pendle Hill Pamphlet 305, 1992.

16.   David Lowes Watson, *Covenant Discipleship: Christian Formation through Mutual Accountability* (Nashville: Discipleship Resources, 1991), 38. For an extensive discussion of Methodist class and band meetings and their contemporary revival in North American Methodism, see also the two companion volumes to Watson's *Covenant Discipleship,* both published in Nashville by Discipleship Resources in 1991: *Forming Christian Disciples: The Role of Covenant Discipleship and Class Leaders in the Congregation* and *Class Leaders: Recovering a Tradition.*

17.   Both texts are available from Christian Classics Ethereal Library. *Religious Affections:* http://www.ccel.org/ccel/edwards/affections.html. *Distinguishing Marks of a Work of the Spirit of God:* http://www.ccel.org/ccel/edwards/works2.html.

18.   Evan Howard, *Affirming the Touch of God: A Cognitive and Philosophical Exploration of the Role of Affectivity in Christian Discernment* (Lanham, MD: University Press of America, 2000), 129–30.

19.   Elizabeth Liebert, "Discernment for Our Times: A Practice with Postmodern Implications," *Studies in Spirituality* 18 (2008): 345. See also Liebert, *Way of Discernment,* 19–21.

20.   See Ignatius of Loyola, *Spiritual Exercises,* nos. 178–83. For a similar set of steps gleaned from the monastic tradition, see Margaret Mary Funk, *Discernment Matters: Listening with the Ear of the Heart* (Collegeville, MN: Liturgical Press, 2013), 133–39.

21.   Javier Melloni, *The Exercises of St Ignatius Loyola in the Western Tradition* (Herefordshire: Gracewing, 2000), 50.

22.   Suzanne Farnham, Stephanie Hull, and R. Taylor McLean, *Grounded in God: Listening Hearts Discernment for Group Deliberations* (Harrisburg, PA: Morehouse Publishing, 1996), 74. For another take on the essential elements of communal discernment, see James Borbely, Marita Carew, John English, John Haley, Judith Roemer, and George Schemel, *Focusing Group Energies: Common Ground for Leadership, Organization, Spirituality,* vol. 1 (Scranton, PA: University of Scranton, 1992), 131–32.

23.   See, for example: Mary Benet McKinney, OSB, *Sharing Wisdom: A Process for Group Decision Making* (Allen, TX: Tabor Publishing, 1987). Assuming a homogeneous Roman Catholic audience, McKinney understands the issues in bringing a group together to discern (though she does not use this language until an appendix). Her exercises offer solid options in addition to those suggested in this work. Danny Morris and Charles Olsen, *Discerning God's Will Together: A Spiritual Practice for the Church* (Nashville: Upper Room Books, 1997) is designed for a largely Protestant audience that would frequently be using parliamentary procedure and Robert's Rules of Order for their decision making. Morris and Olsen structure their step-by-step process around church traditions and biblical examples of decision making. Farnham et al., *Listening Hearts,* is based on the Quaker Clearness Committee but adapted for use in contemporary mainline congregations, particularly the Episcopal Church. An extension of the *Listening Hearts* process, Farnham, Hull, and McLean, *Grounded in God,* provides contemplatively paced reflections with an appendix of practical suggestions

for use with groups. Gil Rendle and Alice Mann, *Holy Conversations: Strategic Planning as a Spiritual Practice for Congregations* (Bethesda, MD: Alban Institute, 2003), explores the place of group spiritual discernment in pastoral planning but does not offer a specific method for discerning, since pastoral planning is their central concern. Lon Fendall, Jan Wood, and Bruce Bishop, *Practicing Discernment Together: Finding God's Way Forward in Decision Making* (Newberg, OR: Barclay Press, 2007), reflects the authors' Quaker background and offers sections on cultivating the personal skills and faith perspective that make discernment possible and the individual's role in group discernment. Finally, Barton, *Pursuing God's Will Together,* reflects the fact that communal discernment has made its way into evangelically oriented church communities. All of these excellent resources assume that the group members have a common spirit, are willing to seek God together, are willing to become spiritually vulnerable to each other, and can work face-to-face with each other over time.

24.  Meditation 17, *Devotions on Emergent Occasions.* Cited at http://web.cs.dal.ca/~johnston/poetry/island.html.

25.  It is also instructive to think of your "self" as a system made up of conflicting loyalties, competing values and interests, preferences, aspirations, and fears. In this sense, we are not simply one self but many selves, all of which affect behaviors and decisions. Understanding self as system helps address the sometimes puzzling behaviors that appear at the time of decision making. For an extensive treatment of self as system, stressing its implications for leadership, see Ronald Heifetz, Alexander Grashow, and Marty Linsky, *The Practice of Adaptive Leadership: Tools and Tactics for Changing Your Organization and the World* (Cambridge, MA: Cambridge Leadership Associates, 2009), part 4.

26.  This assertion raises an interesting question: Is it possible to do structural discernment across space and time when the discerners are not physically present to one another? At this point in the development of the practice (and perhaps at the point in the development in the discerning community as a system), it appears possible only when the discerning group has already been formed and its members understand and already practice discernment.

27.  Predmore, "Spirituality: Text of the Deliberations of the First Fathers (one of five)," http://predmore.blogspot.com/2010/04/spirituality-text-of-deliberations-of.html.

28.  For an analysis of decision making as practiced by Quakers, see Michael Sheeran, *Beyond Majority Rule: Voteless Decisions in the Religious Society of Friends* (Philadelphia: Philadelphia Yearly Meeting, 1983).

29.  Rose Mary Dougherty, SSND, *Discernment: A Path to Spiritual Awakening* (Mahwah, NJ: Paulist Press, 2009), 63–64.

30.  The dynamics inherent in building a discernment group bear a striking resemblance to the processes necessary in building shared vision in any group, but the ultimate goal or purpose of a discernment group is discovering and acting on the call of God for this group at this time. See Peter M. Senge, *The Fifth Discipline: The Art and Practice of the Learning Organization* (New York: Doubleday/Currency, 1990), esp. chap. 11.

31.  "Examen" appears to be a technical term, but it is simply Spanish for "examine," Spanish being the original language of the *Spiritual Exercises* of Ignatius of Loyola from which this process is adapted. As a widely used spiritual practice, the Awareness Examen, also called Consciousness Examen, can be traced to a 1972 article by George Aschenbrenner, SJ, titled "Consciousness Examen," reprinted at http://www.ignatianspirituality.com/ignatian-prayer/the-examen/consciousness-examen/. The version used here is adapted from Timothy Gallagher, OMV, *The Examen Prayer: Ignatian Wisdom for Our Lives Today* (New York: Crossroad, 2006), 25.

32.  As Vacek puts it: "In the ordinary course of a day, we can connect any event to God in a way that makes it part of our shared world. We may experience each new thing as God's way of communicating with us" ("Discernment within a Mutual Love Relationship," 700).

33.  For one such adaptation see Borbely et al., *Focusing Group Energies*, 187

34.  Peter Senge, C. Otto Scharmer, Joseph Jaworski, and Betty Sue Flowers, *Presence: Human Purpose and the Field of the Future* (Cambridge, MA: Society for Organizational Learning, 2004), 48–49: "You can learn to pay attention to the 'external' dynamics of the meeting as well as to your own thoughts and feelings. When the meeting is over, look at an incident that engaged you emotionally. Using your imagination, take time to re-create how you felt and what you thought as the incident played out. It can be helpful to talk through your experiences with a colleague, or perhaps to write them down.

"If you do this carefully for several incidents, you'll learn a lot about yourself and your organization. You'll see where you felt safe and where you felt threatened. . . . As you practice this, you'll be able to engage your imagination more actively to 'see' the details of your experience."

## NOTES TO CHAPTER 2: DISCERNERS: WHO ARE YOU?

1    Peter Senge, *The Fifth Discipline: The Art and Practice of the Learning Organization* (New York: Doubleday/Currency, 1990), chap. 11, "Shared Vision," and chap. 18, "The Leader's New Work," describe several such leaders.

2.  A useful synopsis of Wink's larger corpus can be found in *The Powers That Be: Theology for a New Millennium* (New York: Doubleday, 1998). See also *Walter Wink: Collected Readings*, ed. Henry French (Minneapolis: Fortress Press, 2013).

3.  How Wink came to this synthesis is illumined by his 1994 essay, "Write What You See." This essay is reprinted in *Walter Wink*, xxi–xxxii.

4.  *Walter Wink*, 33–34. Excerpted from the introduction to Walter Wink, *Naming the Powers: The Language of Power in the New Testament* (Minneapolis: Fortress Press, 1994).

5.  Douglas J. Schuurman, *Vocation: Discerning our Callings in Life* (Grand Rapids: Eerdmans, 2004), 29: "If the duties and obligations of these spheres serve the neighbor, they should be fulfilled 'as to the Lord.' . . . If the duties and obligations of these spheres harm the neighbor, they should be rejected. . . . These spheres should be transformed, if at all possible, so that they issue in actions that serve the neighbor." See also 36, 39, 45, and elsewhere.

6.  In addition to *Naming the Powers,* the other two volumes in the trilogy are *Unmasking the Powers: The Invisible Powers That Determine Human Existence* (Minneapolis: Fortress Press, 1986) and *Engaging the Powers: Discernment and Resistance in a World of Domination* (Minneapolis: Fortress Press, 1992).

7.  For a detailed theological study of the concept of vocation, see Edward P. Hahnenberg, *Awakening Vocation: A Theology of Christian Call* (Collegeville, MN: Liturgical Press, 2010). Hahnenberg's primary focus is to create a substantial theological foundation for discerning personal call, but I also find intriguing parallels with structures.

8.  "Kingdom values" is Donal Dorr's term. See *Spirituality and Justice* (Maryknoll, NY: Orbis Books, 1984), 102–4. Michael Crosby interprets Kingdom for today as "governance of the Trinity" in *Repair My House: Becoming a "Kingdom" Catholic* (Maryknoll, NY: Orbis Books, 2012), particularly parts 2 and 3.

9.  Eleazar Fernandez, *Reimagining the Human: Theological Anthropology in Response to Systemic Evil* (St. Louis: Chalice Press, 2004), 56.

10.  Ibid., 69. The 1971 Synod of Bishops statement is relevant here: "Action on behalf of justice and participation in the transformation of the world fully appear to us as a constitutive dimension of the preaching of the Gospel, or in other words, of the Church's mission for the redemption of the human race and its liberation from every oppressive situation." See "Justice in the World," the document of this synod, no. 6. Available at http://www.shc.edu/theolibrary/resources/synodjw.htm.

11.  Mark Graves, *Mind, Brain and the Elusive Soul: Human Systems of Cognitive Science and Religion* (Burlington VT: Ashgate Publishing, 2008), 144–47, quote 147.

12.  Ibid., 150.

13.  Mark Graves, *Insight to Heal: Co-Creating Beauty amidst Human Suffering* (Eugene, OR: Wipf & Stock/Cascade Books, 2013), 111.

14.  "Annual Sleep in America Poll Exploring Connections with Communications Technology Use and Sleep," National Sleep Foundation, March 7, 2011, http://www.sleepfoundation .org/article/press-release/annual-sleep-america-poll-exploring-connections-communications -technology-use-.

15.  The Rev. Trey Hammond, speaking to the 2013 Evangelism and Church Growth Conference, St. Pete Beach, Florida, as quoted by Jerry L. Van Marter, Presbyterian News Service, September 19, 2013. Hammond believes that what he calls "Individual Relational Meetings," a structured way to enter into another's story, are the most important tool to establish relationships at the level that will lead to the ability to act as a group.

16.  James Borbely, Marita Carew, John English, John Haley, Judith Roemer, and George Schemel, *Focusing Group Energies: Common Ground for Leadership, Organization, Spirituality,* vol. 1 (Scranton, PA: University of Scranton, 1992). This was first published as *Ignatian Spiritual Exercises for the Corporate Person.*

17.  John English, *Spiritual Intimacy and Community: An Ignatian View of the Small Faith Community* (New York: Paulist Press, 1992), 59–62, quote 62. In an extensive interview shortly after his election, Pope Francis commented: "Only in narrative form do you discern, not in philosophical or theological explanation, which allows you rather to discuss. Discernment, of course, presupposes discussion, but the mystical dimension of discernment never defines its edges and completes its boundaries." For the full text of the interview, see www .americamagazine.org/pope-interview.

18.  Werner Heisenberg, *Physics and Beyond: Encounters and Conversations,* cited in Senge, *Fifth Discipline,* 238.

19.  David Bohm, as cited in Senge, *Fifth Discipline*, 239–241, quote 239.

20.  C. Otto Scharmer, *Theory U: Leading from the Future as It Emerges; The Social Technology of Presencing* (Cambridge, MA: Society for Organizational Learning, 2007), chap. 17, building on Bohm's work, presents more detailed description of various kinds of conversation. Downloading, or responding to ideas from one's preconceived notions of what is being said, is the least helpful. Debate surfaces other opinions, but the goal in debate is to win over the other position. Dialogue allows for reflective inquiry together. Presencing, or speaking from the generative flow, actually invites something new to arrive from the future.

21.  Margaret J. Wheatley, *Turning to One Another: Simple Conversations to Restore Hope to the Future* (San Francisco: Berrett-Koehler, 2002), 29–37. Wheatley also claims that listening is one of the most healing acts we can do, because listening creates relationship. See, for example, 89.

22.  Nelle Morton, *The Journey Is Home* (Boston: Beacon Press, 1985), 127–29.

23.    Elements of these points are found in Suzanne G. Farnham, Stephanie A. Hull, and R. Taylor McLean, *Grounded in God: Listening Hearts for Group Deliberations* (Harrisburg, PA: Morehouse Publishing, 1999), 55. Their guidelines are designed to be given to groups learning conversation skills for discernment.

24.    Adam Kahane, *Solving Tough Problems: An Open Way of Talking, Listening, and Creating New Realities* (San Francisco: Berrett-Koehler, 2004), 37.

25.    David Cooperrider and Diana Whitney, *Appreciative Inquiry: A Positive Revolution in Change* (San Francisco: Berrett-Koehler, 2005), 1, 3.

26.    Sue Annis Hammond, *The Thin Book of Appreciative Inquiry,* 3rd ed. (Bend, OR: Thin Book Publishing, 2013), 19. In the 5D model of Appreciative Inquiry, the group moves through five phases: Define, Discover, Dream, Design, and Deliver; the cycle is then repeated regularly. There are interesting parallels between the 5D model of Appreciative Inquiry and the Social Discernment Cycle as presented in the introduction. In Appreciative Inquiry, the group first defines what it is looking for and creates the discover questions; in Social Discernment, the group selects the structure and focuses it at a level such that it can grasp the whole structure. They use the suggested questions, amending them as appropriate for the group. In the AI Discover step, the group identifies the best of what is; in the Social Analysis step of Social Discernment, the group attempts to uncover the significant linkages in the structure. In AI's Dream step, the group imagines what might be; in the SDC Reflection and Theological Reflection step, the group tries to envision God's call for the structure. In the AI Design step, the group imagines a future and creates "provocative propositions" to stimulate imagination and action. In the SDC Implementation step, the group plans the actions that will move toward God's call for the organization. In AI's Deliver stage, the group performs actions consonant with the provocative propositions; in the Implementation stage of the Social Discernment Cycle, the group implements and looks back, seeking indications that confirm the decision and action as God's call. Significantly, AI does not have a step that parallels the moment of confirmation, in which the group pauses to pray about and await some inner and exterior signs that they have, indeed, chosen something consonant with living into God's call for the structure, confirming my judgment that confirmation, along with the inner attitude of spiritual freedom, is a distinctive moment in discernment.

27.    Cooperrider and Whitney, *Appreciative Inquiry,* 55–60.

28.    Mancur Olson Jr., *The Logic of Collective Action: Public Goods and the Theory of Groups* (Cambridge, MA: Harvard University Press, 1965), 54.

29.    Ruth Haley Barton, *Pursuing God's Will Together: A Discernment Practice for Leadership Groups* (Downers Grove, IL: IVP Books, 2012), 146–47.

30.    Olson, *Logic of Collective Action,* 64.

31.    Barton, *Pursuing God's Will,* 156.

32.    Joan S. Gray, *Spiritual Leadership for Church Officers: A Handbook* (Louisville, KY: Geneva Press, 2009), 23.

33.    Ignatius of Loyola introduces the concept of indifference in *The Spiritual Exercises,* no. 23. For a contemporary treatment of the necessity of conversion in coming to personal vocation, of which indifference is a synonym, see Hahnenberg, *Awakening Vocation,* 159–61. For a discussion of spiritual freedom, see Edwards Collins Vacek, "Discernment within a Mutual Love Relationship with God: A New Theological Foundation," *Theological Studies* 74 (2013): 704–6. Robert E. Doud, "Ignatian Indifference and Today's Spirituality," *The Way* 52, no. 4 (October 2013): 94–105, illustrates one way to connect Ignatian indifference to spiritual freedom.

34. Ignatian indifference might be described as a readiness to hear a new call from God and respond to that call in freedom. See Doud, "Ignatian Indifference," 99.

35. Fernandez, *Reimagining the Human,* 191–94.

36. The practice, Seeking Spiritual Freedom, is from Elizabeth Liebert, *The Way of Discernment: Spiritual Practices for Decision Making* (Louisville, KY: Westminster John Knox Press, 2008), 32–33.

37. For further reflection on spiritual freedom for discerning groups, see English, *Spiritual Intimacy and Community,* 90–108.

## NOTES TO CHAPTER 3: SYSTEMS AND STRUCTURES: WHAT ARE THEY?

1. Paul Watzlawick, John H. Weakland, and Richard Fisch, *Change: Principles of Problem Formation and Problem Resolution* (New York: W. W. Norton, 1974), 2.

2. Peter M. Senge, *The Fifth Discipline: The Art and Practice of the Learning Organization* (New York: Doubleday/Currency, 1990), 68, 75, 114, 127–28.

3. Developers of these theories include William Perry, Lawrence Kohlberg, Jane Loevinger, Carol Gilligan, Robert Kegan, Ken Wilber, and Susanne Cook-Greuter. Although not claiming to follow Piagetian principles, Mary Belenky, Blythe Clinchy Nancy Goldberger and Jill Tarule, *Women's Ways of Knowing* (New York: Basic Books, Inc., 1986) also could be classed as a structural theory.

4. Robert Kegan, *The Evolving Self: Problem and Process in Human Development* (Cambridge, MA: Harvard University Press, 1982).

5. http://www.merriam-webster.com/dictionary/system.

6. *Oxford Dictionaries.com,* s.v. "structure," http://www.oxforddictionaries.com/definition/english/structure.

7. *Merriam-Webster.com,* s.v. "structure," http://www.merriam-webster.com/dictionary/structure.

8. Donella H. Meadows, *Thinking in Systems: A Primer,* ed. Diana Wright (White River Junction, VT: Chelsea Green Publishing, 2008), 188.

9. Eleazar Fernandez, *Reimagining the Human: Theological Anthropology in Response to Systemic Evil* (St. Louis: Chalice Press, 2004), 65.

10. Meadows, *Thinking in Systems,* 76–78.

11. M. Mitchell Waldrop, *Complexity: The Emerging Science at the Edge of Order and Chaos* (New York: Simon & Schuster, 1992), 11–12, 230–34, 278–80. Recognizing that these four qualities of dynamic systems are by no means intuitively obvious, Waldrop masterfully tells the stories of ten scientists trying to puzzle out the patterns in all this complexity.

12. Meadows, *Thinking in Systems,* 3–4. Meadows's goal in this book is to make system behavior clear to nonspecialists. I particularly recommend the appendixes "Summary of Systems Principles," "Springing the System Traps," "Places to Intervene in Systems," and "Guidelines for Living in a World of Systems," 188–95, for additional guidance on systems and how to understand and affect them in discernment processes.

13. Ibid., 13. Fritjof Capra brings together the insights of physics, chemistry, and biology to identify three basic characteristics of living systems: "they create themselves ('autopoeisis'); they generate new patterns of organizing, or 'self-organize,' in ways that could not be predicted from their past ('emergence'); and they're aware, in the sense of interacting effectively with their environment ('cognition')." Fritjof Capra, *The Hidden Connections: Integrating the Biological, Cognitive and Social Dimensions of Life into a Science of Sustainability* (New York: Doubleday, 2002), xvi–xvii, cited in Peter Senge, C. Otto Scharmer, Joseph Jaworski,

and Betty Sue Flowers, *Presence: Human Purpose and the Field of the Future* (Cambridge, MA: Society for Organizational Learning, 2004), 204.

14. Meadows, *Thinking in Systems,* 16.

15. Ibid., 23.

16. Ibid., 189.

17. Ibid., 189–91.

18. Senge, *Fifth Discipline,* 57–67. By "there is no blame," Senge means that it is fruitless to look outside the system for a culprit, for someone or something else that "did this to us." As he says, "Systems thinking shows us that there is no outside; that you and the cause of your problems are part of a single system. The cure lies in your relationship to your 'enemy'" (67). Notice the similarity to Walter Wink's position that the demonic is the inner and outer manifestations of a system itself gone astray.

19. Meadows, *Thinking in Systems,* 190.

20. Ibid., 191–94.

21. Watzlawick, Weakland, and Fisch, *Change,* 77–91.

22. Waldrop, *Complexity,* 82.

23. Watzlawick, Weakland, and Fisch, *Change,* 83.

24. Waldrop, *Complexity,* 280–318, quote 291.

25. Peter Block, *Community: The Structure of Belonging* (San Francisco: Berrett-Koehler, 2009), 24–27.

26. Senge et al., *Presence,* 234.

27. "'Mental models' are deeply ingrained assumptions, generalizations, or even pictures or images, that influence how we understand the world and how we take action. Very often we are not consciously aware of our mental models or the effects they have on our behavior" (Senge, *Fifth Discipline,* 8). Mental models are often why new insights never get put into practice—our deeply ingrained mental models unconsciously limit us to familiar ways of thinking and acting. For example, when an employee discovered that a company rule had been applied unfairly to him, he hesitated to bring it to the attention of the human resources department. When his supervisor later asked why he hadn't immediately gone to HR, the employee replied, "Once you take something to HR, you get a reputation for being a troublemaker." His mental model prevented him from getting relief and prevented HR from doing its appropriate function effectively.

Senge suggests that we first begin to unearth our own mental models, bringing them to light. But in an institution or group that has learned to trust each member and desires to learn together, the group can bring out the unstated (and sometimes unconscious) mental models that operate in their system and in the players within the system. Once mental models are uncovered, they may be owned or modified so that they correspond more readily to reality. See *Fifth Discipline,* chap. 10, for individual and group strategies for unearthing mental models and turning the resulting insights into learnings that promote change toward the desired goal.

Prayerfully working through the steps of the Social Discernment Cycle often has the result that individuals discover mental models that they are holding, such as "I am powerless in this system," and begin, through prayer and consultation, the process of adopting more effective mental models ("I do have the ability to act in this system").

28. Watzlawick, Weakland, and Fisch, *Change,* 92–109. The King Christian example is related on 107, though these authors do not acknowledge that the story is unfounded.

29. Senge, *Fifth Discipline,* 40.

30.   C. Otto Scharmer calls these points of high leverage "Archemedian points." See *Theory U: Leading from the Future as It Emerges; The Social Technology of Presencing* (Cambridge, MA: Society for Organizational Learning, 2007), 463.

31.   Block, *Community*, 30, 42–43, 47.

## NOTES TO CHAPTER 4: THE SITUATION AND THE SYSTEM

1.   Joe Holland and Peter Henriot, SJ, *Social Analysis: Linking Faith and Justice* (Maryknoll, NY: Orbis Books, 1980), 8.

2.   Peter Henriot, "Social Discernment and the Pastoral Circle," in *The Pastoral Circle Revisited: A Critical Quest for Truth and Transformation*, ed. Frans Wijsen, Peter Henriot, and Rodrigo Mejía (Maryknoll, NY: Orbis Books, 2005), 20.

3.   Henriot, "Social Discernment," 17.

4.   James Hug, "Redeeming Social Analysis: Recovering the Hidden Religious Dimensions of Social Change," in *The Pastoral Circle Revisited*, ed. Frans Wijsen, Peter Henriot, and Rodrigo Mejía (Maryknoll, NY: Orbis Books, 2005), 196–210.

5.   A particular challenge when working with systems is to avoid the pitfall of abstraction, in which we detach ourselves or abstract away from everyday experience of reality and fall into perceiving events and our own experiences and actions as separate components of formal, impersonal systems that are perceived as rational, controllable, and predictable. To counteract this tendency to abstraction, we return again and again to the concrete, unpredictable, and messy dimensions of the system. See Frank C. Richardson, "Investigating Psychology and Transcendence," *Pastoral Psychology* 63 (2014): 357.

6.   Peter Senge, *The Fifth Discipline: The Art and Practice of the Learning Organization* (New York: Doubleday/Currency, 1990), 21.

7.   Edward P. Hahnenberg, *Awakening Vocation: A Theology of Christian Call* (Collegeville, MN: Liturgical Press, 2010), 193–229.

8.   Seasonal affective disorder is a type of depression that occurs annually, in either the winter or the summer, often triggered when the season changes.

9.   For a thoughtful discussion on designing physical space so that it supports community, see Peter Block, *Community: The Structure of Belonging* (San Francisco: Berrett-Koehler, 2009), 131–62.

10.   Holland and Henriot, *Social Analysis*, 96.

11.   Jon Sobrino, "Faith, Justice and Injustice," in *The Pastoral Circle Revisited*, ed. Frans Wijsen, Peter Henriot, and Rodrigo Mejía (Maryknoll, NY: Orbis Books, 2005), ix–xvii, quote at x.

12.   Patricia Loring, "Spiritual Discernment: The Context and Goal of Clearness Committees," Pendle Hill Pamphlet 305 (1992), 22, and Parker Palmer, "The Clearness Committee: A Way of Discernment," *Weavings*, July–August 1998, 27–30.

13.   See, for example, Caroline Stephen (1839–1909), *Quaker Strongholds*, excerpted in *Quaker Spirituality: Selected Writings*, ed. Douglas V. Steere (New York: Paulist Press, 1984), 243–58, particularly 246, par. 20: "The one corner-stone of belief upon which the Society of Friends is built is the conviction that God does indeed communicate with each one of the spirits he has made, in a direct and living inbreathing of some measure of the breath of his own life."

14.   Holland and Henriot offer a questionnaire to guide an analysis of the context. See *Social Analysis*, 106–9. A number of services available online provide recent demographic data

for purposes of ministry planning. See, for example, Percept (www.perceptgroup.com) and MissionInsite (http://missioninsite.com).

## NOTES TO CHAPTER 5: SOCIAL ANALYSIS

1. Joe Holland and Peter Henriot, *Social Analysis: Linking Faith and Justice* (Maryknoll, NY: Orbis Books, 1980), 8, 13, 14, quote 13.

2. Joseph Elsener, "Pitfalls in the Use of the Pastoral Circle," in *The Pastoral Circle Revisited: A Critical Quest for Truth and Transformation*, ed. Frans Wijsen, Peter Henriot, and Rodrigo Mejía (Maryknoll, NY: Orbis Books, 2005), 40–55, particularly 48.

3. For our purposes, I treat feelings and emotions as synonymous, though technically there is a difference.

4. C. Otto Scharmer, *Theory U: Leading for the Future as It Emerges; The Social Technology of Presencing* (Cambridge, MA: Society for Organizational Learning, 2007), 422, notes that the "new" shows up in our minds first as unspecified feeling, which then morphs into a sense of what the new significant idea might be, then how the idea is related to the problem or challenge that we have been working with, and finally the rational provides the "what" and the "where."

5. Holland and Henriot, *Social Analysis*, 21–22.

6. Walter Wink, *Naming the Powers: The Language of Power in the New Testament* (Minneapolis: Fortress Press, 1984), 5, cited in Ted Grimsrud, "Engaging Walter Wink," in *Transforming the Powers: Peace, Justice, and the Domination System*, ed. Ray Gingerich and Ted Grimsrud, 1–13 (Minneapolis: Fortress Press, 2006), 2.

7. Walter Wink, *Engaging the Powers: Discernment and Resistance in a World of Domination* (Minneapolis: Fortress Press, 1992), 10.

8. On his way to developing the Powers metaphor, Wink looked at uses of the term "power" in the New Testament, but he also examined other words, such as "rulers," "kings," "authorities," "elders," "angels and principalities," "authority," "commission," "law," and "lawyers and keepers of the law." He determined that each of these terms also has, in some sense, inner and outer aspects. See Grimsrud, "Engaging Walter Wink," 2.

9. Donal Dorr, *Spirituality and Justice* (Maryknoll, NY: Orbis Books, 1984), 55–56.

10. Ibid., 56–58.

11. Ibid., 80–81.

12. Ibid., 217–35. See also Edward Hahnenberg, *Awakening Vocation: A Theology of Christian Call* (Collegeville, MN: Liturgical Press, 2010), 193–229.

13. Valerie Saiving Goldstein set in motion this line of thinking in her 1960 critique of Reinhold Niebuhr: "The Human Situation, a Feminine View," *Journal of Religion* 40 (April 1960): 100–112.

14. James Borbely, Marita Carew, John English, John Haley, Judith Roemer, and George Schemel, *Focusing Group Energies: Common Ground for Leadership, Organization, Spirituality*, vol. 1 (Scranton, PA: University of Scranton, 1992), 49–50. This was first published as *Ignatian Spiritual Exercises for the Corporate Person*.

15. Lee E. Snook, *What in the World is God Doing? Re-Imagining Spirit and Power* (Minneapolis: Fortress Press, 1999), 120–25.

16. Scharmer, Senge, and colleagues speak of "acupressure points," trying to get at the same system reality. See, for example, Otto Scharmer and Katrin Kaufer, *Leading from the Emerging Future: From Ego-System to Eco-System Economies; Applying Theory U to Transforming Business, Society, and Self* (San Francisco: Berrett-Koehler, 2013), 240–41, where

they list eight acupressure points for closing the feedback loop between mind and economy and ecology.

17.   Based on Peter Henriot, "Social Analysis: A Practical Methodology," in Holland and Henriot, *Social Analysis*, 102.

18.   Holland and Henriot are quite candid about the limits of social analysis. See *Social Analysis*, 15–18, 89–93.

19.   Eleazar Fernandez, *Reimagining the Human: Theological Anthropology in Response to Systemic Evil* (St. Louis: Chalice Press, 2004), 218.

## NOTES TO CHAPTER 6: THEOLOGICAL REFLECTION AND PRAYER

1.   Evagrius Ponticus, cited with no further attribution in Kathleen Norris, *Acedia and Me: A Marriage, Monks, and a Writer's Life* (New York: Penguin Group/Riverhead Books, 2008), 262–63.

2.   Jack Mezirow, *Transformative Dimensions of Adult Learning* (San Francisco: Jossey-Bass, 1991), 104–7.

3.   Robert Kinast, *Making Faith Sense: Theological Reflection in Everyday Life* (Collegeville, MN: Liturgical Press, 1999). See also Patricia O'Connell Killen and John de Beer, *The Art of Theological Reflection* (New York: Crossroad, 1994) for a variety of methods as well as a substantial and accessible introduction to theological reflection. For an adaptation of theological reflection that is potentially more useful to those of other traditions, see Edward Foley, "Reflective Believing: Reimagining Theological Reflection in an Age of Diversity," *Reflective Practice* 34 (2014): 60–75, available at http://journals.sfu.ca/rpfs/index.php/rpfs/article/viewFile/325/319.

4.   Robert Kinast, *What Are They Saying about Theological Reflection?* (New York: Paulist Press, 2000), 1.

5.   Robert Kinast, *Let Ministry Teach: A Guide to Theological Reflection* (Collegeville, MN: Liturgical Press, 1996), x–xi.

6.   Anthony de Mello, *The Song of the Bird* (New York: Doubleday, 1982), xvi. Cited in Christopher Pramuk, *Hope Sings, So Beautiful: Graced Encounters across the Color Line* (Collegeville, MN: Liturgical Press, 2013), 165.

7.   Kinast, *What Are They Saying*, 66–68. Reflecting on the Pastoral Circle as a site for theological reflection, Rodrigo Mejía, a Colombian Jesuit working in Ethiopia, also insists that experience be the starting point for reflection, not something added after the fact to illustrate theological themes or apply them to some human situation: "The starting point is . . . real questions touching human life. Moreover, it is not enough that the theologian starts with a question, even if real, if it is a theoretical question with which the theologian has no direct experience." See "The Impact of the Pastoral Circle in Teaching Pastoral Theology," in *The Pastoral Circle Revisited: A Critical Quest for Truth and Transformation*, ed. Frans Wijsen, Peter Henriot, and Rodrigo Mejía (Maryknoll, NY: Orbis Books, 2005), 127–136, quote on 128.

8.   Eleazar Fernandez, *Reimagining the Human: Theological Anthropology in Response to Systemic Evil* (St. Louis: Chalice Press, 2004), 185–208, esp. 188.

9.   Alex Pentland, author of *Social Physics: How Good Ideas Spread* (New York: Penguin, 2014), comments that diverse groups earn 30 percent more than homogeneous groups because the diversity spurs creativity in the group. Sound quantitative and qualitative research clearly suggests that diversity is an asset, though our siloing behavior often directly contradicts these findings. Public lecture, Dominican University of California, February 5, 2014.

10.   Fernandez, *Reimagining the Human*, 13–30.

11.   Ibid., 31–52. The heart of Fernandez's book provides rich fodder for theological reflection in turn on class, race, gender, the environment.

12.   Ibid., 11–17.

13.   Kinast, *What Are They Saying*, 68–69. Indian Jesuit Michael Amaladoss points toward action as the end of theological reflection: "Today, theology starts and ends with life. Its aim is not faith seeking understanding, but faith transforming life. Correlation between experience and the traditions of the faith is a process of mutual hermeneutics, in which faith enlightens and guides life, while life grasps and expresses the faith in new and creative ways. Theological reflection is systematic, but it does not create an abstract, objective system." See "A Cycle Open to Pluralism," in *The Pastoral Circle Revisited*, ed. Frans Wijsen, Peter Henriot, and Rodrigo Mejía (Maryknoll, NY: Orbis Books, 2005), 169–82, quote 179. Thus, we can look to the fruit of our praxis to judge the adequacy of our theological reflection.

14.   Senge et al. describe this contemplative stance as Presence, noting that spiritual traditions around the world have recognized the shift from oneself to a larger field of knowing. They puzzle that so little has been written about this shift as a collective phenomenon. See Peter Senge, C. Otto Scharmer, Joseph Jaworski, and Betty Sue Flowers, *Presence: Human Purpose and the Field of the Future* (Cambridge, MA: Society for Organizational Learning, 2004), 11–12.

15.   Walter Burghardt, "Contemplation: A Long Loving Look at the Real," *Church,* Winter 1989, 14–18. Reprinted in *An Ignatian Spirituality Reader: Contemporary Writings on St. Ignatius of Loyola, the Spiritual Exercise, Discernment and More,* ed. George W. Traub, SJ (Chicago: Loyola Press, 2008), 89–98.

16.   Senge et al., *Presence*, 31.

17.   The works in theological method and hermeneutics of Canadian Jesuit theologian and philosopher Bernard Lonergan (1904–84) have been widely influential in Roman Catholic theological circles. A brief discussion of his imperatives can be found in Denise Lardner Carmody, "Lonergan's Transcendental Precepts and the Foundations of Christian Feminist Ethics," in *Lonergan and Feminism,* ed. Cynthia S. Crysdale (Toronto: University of Toronto Press, 1994), 134–48.

18.   Slightly adapted from the translation of George Ganss in *Ignatius of Loyola: Spiritual Exercises and Selected Works,* ed. George E. Ganss (New York: Paulist Press, 1991), no. 234.

## NOTES TO CHAPTER 7: THE DECISION AND ITS CONFIRMATION

1.   John Woolman, *Journal* (Christian Classics Ethereal Library, http://www.ccel.org/ccel/woolman/journal.i.ii.html). This citation comes at the close of chap. 1.

2.   Ann Moore Mueller, "John Woolman," http://trilogy.brynmawr.edu/speccoll/quakersandslavery/commentary/people/woolman.php. See John Greenleaf Whittier, "An Appreciation" (1871), published at the head of Woolman's *Journal* by Christian Classics Ethereal Library, http://www.ccel.org/ccel/woolman/journal.i.i.i.html, for more detail on the progress of Woolman's original action among the various Yearly Meetings in the United States.

3.   The progression of our desires was well observed in the ancient monastic tradition. An accessible treatment of desires in this tradition can be found in Mary Margaret Funk, *Thoughts Matter: Discovering the Spiritual Journey* (Collegeville, MN: Liturgical Press, 2013). The sequence and content of thoughts has a direct connection to desire: "Thoughts . . . rise in the mind. They come in a sequence, a train of thoughts. We are not our thoughts. Thoughts come and thoughts go. Unaccompanied thoughts pass quickly. Thoughts that are

thought about become desires. Desires that are thought about become passions. Good thoughts become virtues. Bad thoughts become bad desires; bad passions or habits of action become sins. . . . We can redirect our thoughts. We do this by noticing our thoughts rather than thinking our thoughts. . . . First thoughts beget second thoughts, which become intentions. Intentions constitute motivations and indicate where the heart resides. Motivation moves us to decide and act on the thought. Decisions give voice to the choices we intend to act upon" (7–8).

4. Frederick Buechner, *Wishful Thinking: A Theological ABC* (New York: Harper & Row, 1973), 95. Buechner introduces this well-known quotation as follows: "By and large a good rule for finding out [what our vocation is] is this. The kind of work God usually calls you to is the kind of work (a) that you need most to do and (b) that the world most needs to have done. If you really get a kick out of your work, you've presumably met requirement (a) but if your work is writing TV deodorant commercials, the chances are that you've missed requirement (b). On the other hand, if your work is being a doctor in a leper colony, you have probably met requirement (b), but if most of the time you're bored and depressed by it, the chances are that you have not only bypassed (a) but probably aren't helping your patients much either."

For a more extensive treatment of the place of desires in discernment, see Gil Rendel and Alice Mann, *Holy Conversations: Strategic Planning as a Spiritual Practice for Congregations* (Herndon, VA: Alban Institute, 2003), chap. 11, and Elizabeth Liebert, *The Way of Discernment: Spiritual Practices for Decision Making* (Louisville, KY: Westminster John Knox Press, 2008), chap. 2, upon which I have based this paragraph. For a treatment of desires within our biology and physiology and how they can lead us to connect with each other and the divine, see Nancy K. Morrison and Sally K. Severino, *Sacred Desire: Growing in Compassionate Living* (West Conshohocken, PA: Templeton Foundation Press, 2009). C. Otto Scharmer avoids desire language altogether; see *Theory U: Leading from the Future as It Emerges; The Social Technology of Presencing* (Cambridge, MA: Society for Organizational Learning, 2007), 407–10.

5. When "desire" tends to be collapsed into "sexual desire," as happens in some traditions, paying attention to one's desires is often more complicated. In this situation, desires can become something we either try to flee or put a tight cap on. Alternately, our desires become unconscious, at which point we don't have to deal with them directly. But Ignatius of Loyola did not see desires in this limited way. Philip Sheldrake reminds us that Ignatius and other spiritual masters understood desire as a central metaphor for our quest for God. Only by paying attention to our desires are we able to reach into our deepest selves where our deepest desires dwell and there meet the living God. See *Befriending our Desires* (Ottawa, Canada: Novalis, 2001), 9.

6. A notable exception, and I am sure there are others, is Peter Senge, who describes effective managers as persons who spend a lot of quality time living with big decisions, regularly delegating routine decisions. See *The Fifth Discipline: The Art and Practice of the Learning Organization* (New York: Doubleday/Currency, 1990), chap. 15.

7. See also parallels in the monastic tradition as summarized by Mary Margaret Funk, *Discernment Matters: Listening with the Ear of the Heart* (Collegeville, MN: Liturgical Press, 2013), 135–37.

8. Any translation will illustrate the point. I am using George Ganss, ed., *Ignatius of Loyola: Spiritual Exercises and Selected Works* (New York: Paulist Press, 1991), no. 183.

9. Michael Ivens, *Understanding the Spiritual Exercises: Text and Commentary; A Handbook for Retreat Directors* (Herefordshire, England: Gracewing, 1998), 141.

10. Funk, *Discernment Matters,* 136–37.

11.   The Quakers also add an interesting nuance to peace as a touchstone in discernment. Many interpretations, including those of numerous Quakers, see the presence of peace as a sign confirming the particular action to implement. But Quaker testimonies and diaries also sometimes indicate that some internal nudge described in the language of conviction, not peace, propels them to action. As long as the conviction is present, the action is to continue. When the conviction ceases and peace settles over one's spirit, it is a sign that one's work is done, and one may cease with the action. Woolman provides excellent illustrations of the latter. For example, in a journal entry dated "5th, 5th month, 1768," he details the meetings he has just visited on one of his itinerant journeys, which he had attended "under the humbling hand of the Lord," and with a certificate from his meeting. At the conclusion he reports, "It was a journey of much inward waiting, and as my eye was to the Lord, way was several times opened to my humbling admiration when things had appeared very difficult. In my return I felt a relief of mind very comfortable to me, having through divine help labored in much plainness, both with Friends selected and in the more public meetings, so that I trust the pure witness in many minds was reached." See *Quaker Spirituality: Selected Writings*, ed. Douglas V. Steere (New York: Paulist Press, 1984), 161–237, quotation 218.

12.   Mark McIntosh, *Discernment and Truth: A Spirituality and Theology of Knowledge* (New York: Crossroad/Herder, 2004), 15.

13.   The references to both Origen and Athanasius are found in Mark McIntosh, *Discernment and Truth*, 93. Ignatius of Loyola picked up on Athanasius's distinction eleven hundred years later with his metaphor of water dripping on a sponge and on a stone; using this metaphor, Ignatius insists that we will always be able to tell the difference, however subtle, between the actions of the good and evil spirit. See *Spiritual Exercises*, no. 335. For a detailed development of the concept of discernment in Origen, see P. B. Decock, "Discernment in Origen of Alexandria," *Acta Theologica* Supplementum 17 (2013): 189–208 (http://www.ajol.info/index.php/actat/article/view/96161).

14.   Irenaeus, *Adversus haereses* 4.20.7, "For the glory of God is a living man; and the life of man consists in beholding God." Translation from New Advent, http://www.newadvent.org/fathers/0103.htm.

15.   Gustave Bardy, "The Patristic Period," in *Discernment of Spirits*, trans. Innocentia Richards (Collegeville, MN: Liturgical Press, 1970), 60. This is a translation of the article "Discernement des Esprits" from *Dictionnaire de Spiritualité Ascetique et Mystique* (Paris: Beauchesne, 1957), vol. 3, cols. 1222–91.

16.   Funk, *Discernment Matters*, 64–66; Funk, *Thoughts Matter*, 8–12.

## NOTES TO CHAPTER 8: IMPLEMENTATION AND EVALUATION

1.   See Ignatius of Loyola, *Spiritual Exercises*, nos. 333–34.

2.   Ibid., no. 174.

3.   Donal Dorr, *Spirituality and Justice* (Maryknoll, NY: Orbis Books, 1984), 102–4.

4.   Ibid., 105–7. See also Nancy K. Morrison and Sally K. Severino, *Sacred Desire: Growing in Compassionate Living* (West Conshohocken, PA: Templeton Foundation Press, 2009), chap. 10, for a discussion on living globally with compassion as a direct connection to the Divine.

5.   Roman Catholic social teaching developed from roots reaching back to the Hebrew prophets and Jewish law. It took contemporary form beginning in the nineteenth century with the development of modern industrial society that in turn gave birth to new concepts of society, the state, and the means of production, labor, and ownership. I call attention to it because

I myself belong to this tradition, and because it is one of the most clearly articulated forms of social critique developed by the Christian churches. For articulations of Catholic social teaching, see Daniel G. Groody, *Globalization, Spirituality and Justice* (Maryknoll, NY: Orbis Books, 2007), chap. 4, particularly 102–18, where Groody articulates the acronym A GOD OF LIFE as a way to quickly summarize the major tenets of Catholic social teaching: A: Analysis of social reality; G: Gratuity of God; O: Ordering society to the common good; D: Dignity of the human person; O: Option for the poor; F: Freedom as rights and responsibilities; L: Life as a sacred gift; I: Involvement of all people in creation of a new social order; F: Family of blood and family of humankind; E: Environment and ecological stewardship. See also *The Catechism of the Catholic Church*, United States Catholic Conference, nos. 2419–49. For an extensive list of themes and links to key documents, see "Compendium of the Social Doctrine of the Church" at http://www.vatican.va/roman_curia/pontifical_councils/justpeace/documents/rc_pc_justpeace_doc_20060526_compendio-dott-soc_en.html. For a one-page summary of the major themes, see http://www.cctwincities.org/document.doc?id=13.

6. Dorr, *Spirituality and Justice*, 107–10.

7. This expansive statement is adapted from Luisa M. Saffiotti, "Life-long Formation for Living in Right-Relationship: 'Only this: act justly, love kindness and walk humbly with your God,'" seminar presentation for the Religious Formation Conference, 2009, privately printed, 11. See also: *InFormation* 19 (Summer 2010): 2–6. Available at http://www.csasisters.org/RFC%20Information%20Spring%202010.pdf.

8. Dorr, *Spirituality and Justice*, 110–13.

9. Ibid., 113–15.

10. Ibid., 115–18.

11. Timothy Fry, OSB, *The Rule of Benedict in English* (Collegeville, MN: Liturgical Press, 1982), chap. 53, including the following admonition designed to level social-cultural differences: "Great care and concern are to be shown in receiving poor people and pilgrims, because in them more particularly Christ is received; our very awe of the rich guarantees them special respect."

12. I list care of creation among the signs that the Holy Spirit is at work in an institution for theological reasons of justice, where the subject of justice is other than human beings. Senge, Scharmer, Jaworski, and Flowers raised the stakes when they took seriously the fact that humans have all the means to destroy themselves and realized it's possible that we will. This realization propelled them to investigate what it would take so that humans might break through their denial and first imagine and then create a different kind of world where both humans and the rest of the earth's creatures might all thrive together. See *Presence: Human Purpose and the Field of the Future* (Cambridge, MA: Society for Organizational Learning, 2004), 22.

Care of creation has a pragmatic outcome as well. A study of businesses that made changes toward ecological health, by Heather Dixon-Fowler, Alan Ellstrand, Jon Johnson, Dan Slater, and Andrea Romi, found that there is a modest but positive correlation between some indicator of financial performance and an indicator of environmental performance. This result was found whether the environmental action was proactive or reactive, whether the company was large or small, whether the entity was public or private, whether it was U.S.-based or international, and whether the entity was among the worst offenders or a nonimpact company. In other words, care of creation is not only just but is good for the bottom line. For a nontechnical summary, see Matt McGowan, "When Does it Pay to Be Green?" *University of Arkansas Research Frontiers* (Fall–Winter 2013–14): 12–17.

13. Dorr, *Spirituality and Justice,* 119–30.

14. Charles M. Olsen and Ellen Morseth, *Selecting Church Leaders: A Practice in Spiritual Discernment* (Nashville: Upper Room Books, 2002), 154. The technical theological term for acceptance or rejection in matters of faith is *sensus fidelium* or "sense of the faithful." The Second Vatican Council document *Lumen Gentium,* par. 12, brought this dynamic reality to the fore a half century ago. More recently, addressing a group of theologians in December 2013, Pope Francis said, "By the gift of the Holy Spirit, the members of the Church possess a 'sense of faith.' This is a kind of 'spiritual instinct' that makes us *sentire cum Ecclesia* [think with the mind of the Church] and to discern that which is in conformity with the apostolic faith and is in the spirit of the Gospel. Of course, the *sensus fidelium* [sense of the faithful] cannot be confused with the sociological reality of a majority opinion." Cited in Catherine Harmon, "Francis to Theologians: Don't Confuse 'Sensus Fidelium' with Majority Opinion," *The Catholic World Report,* CWR blog, December 09, 2013, http://www.catholicworldreport .com/Blog/2774/francis_to_theologians_dont_confuse_sensus_fidelium_with_majority_opinion .aspx#.UzZ-xvl_uSo.

I am not, however, using acceptance/rejection in this technical theological sense. I am merely suggesting that the amount and quality of acceptance or rejection as revealed in the behavior of the collection of players in the structure can serve as a structural touchstone, since it involves the response of the whole body of persons rather than the response of a single actor.

15. *Spiritual Exercises,* par. 23.

16. C. Otto Scharmer stresses the importance of such a container for the emergence of genuinely novel and creative new structures; see *Theory U: Leading from the Future as It Emerges; The Social Technology of Presencing* (Cambridge, MA: Society for Organizational Learning, 2007), 410–12, 430–34.

17. Joseph Veale, SJ, "The Silence," in *Manifold Gifts: Ignatian Essays on Spirituality* (Oxford: The Way Publications, 2006), 232.

18. See Senge et al., *Presence,* chap. 3, for a more extended discussion of seeing from the whole.

19. Although the social technology theorists Senge, Scharmer, Jaworski, and Flowers are relatively speechless on Christian "technologies" to assist in bringing forth emerging structures, they are absolutely clear about the need for laying aside our preconceived ways of doing things and opening ourselves to the new that is waiting to be born. See, for example, Scharmer, *Theory U,* chap. 4.

20. In *The Way of Discernment: Spiritual Practices for Decision Making* (Louisville, KY: Westminster John Knox Press, 2008), I have provided exercises for seven "entry points" to discerned decision making, all of which could be adapted to group discernment. Ruth Haley Barton proposes a sound and prayerful method of group discernment in *Pursuing God's Will Together: A Discernment Practice for Leadership Groups* (Downers Grove, IL: IVP Books, 2012), as do Suzanne Farnham and colleagues, *Grounded in God: Listening Hearts for Group Deliberations* (Harrisburg, PA: Morehouse Publishing, 1996); Danny Morris and Charles Olsen, *Discerning God's Will Together: A Spiritual Practice for the Church* (Nashville: Upper Room Books, 1997); Lon Fendall, Jan Wood, and Bruce Bishop, *Practicing Discernment Together: Finding God's Way Forward in Decision Making* (Newberg, OR: Barclay Press, 2007); and Jules Toner, *What is Your Will, O God? A Casebook for Studying Discernment of God's Will* (St. Louis: Institute of Jesuit Sources, 1995).

21. *Spiritual Exercises,* par. 170–89.

22. The first four critiques were originally published in Elizabeth Liebert, "Discernment for Our Times: A Practice with Postmodern Implications," *Studies in Spirituality* 18 (2008): 333–55.

23. José de Mesa, "Theological Constants and Theological Reflections," in *The Pastoral Circle Revisited: A Critical Quest for Truth and Transformation*, ed. Frans Wijsen, Peter Henriot, and Rodrigo Mejía (Maryknoll, NY: Orbis Books, 2005), 89–107.

## NOTES TO APPENDIX 2: THE DYNAMIC PATTERN OF CHRISTIAN DISCERNMENT

1. Mark A. McIntosh, *Discernment and Truth: The Spirituality and Theology of Knowledge* (New York: Crossroad Publishing, 2004), 5. Italics in the original.
2. See Peggy Holman, Tom Devane, and Steven Cady, eds., *The Change Handbook: The Definitive Resource on Today's Best Methods for Engaging Whole Systems* (San Francisco: Berrett-Koehler, 2007), for both in-depth and thumbnail descriptions of more than sixty systemic change processes. Future development of the theory and practice of Social Discernment can benefit from research on which among these processes can challenge and strengthen discernment with systems or assist leaders of such structures.
3. Lee E. Snook, *What in the World is God Doing? Re-Imagining Spirit and Power* (Minneapolis: Fortress Press, 1999), 74.

## NOTES TO APPENDIX 3: DISCERNERS AS REFLECTIVE PRACTITIONERS

1. Donald Schön, *The Reflective Practitioner: How Professionals Think in Action* (New York: Basic Books, 1983), 129–45.
2. Ibid., 273.
3. Ibid., 317.
4. Ibid., 151.

## NOTES TO APPENDIX 4: SOCIAL DISCERNMENT AS AN EXEMPLAR OF CHANGE THEORY

1. Paul Watzlawick, John H. Weakland, and Richard Fisch, *Change: Principles of Problem Formation and Problem Resolution* (New York: W. W. Norton, 1974), 110.

## NOTES TO APPENDIX 5: SOCIAL DISCERNMENT AND TRANSFORMATIONAL LEARNING

1. Jack Mezirow, *Transformative Dimensions of Adult Learning* (San Francisco: Jossey-Bass, 1991), 208.
2. Jack Mezirow, "Learning to Think Like an Adult: Core Concepts of Transformation Theory," in *Learning as Transformation: Critical Perspectives on a Theory in Progress*, ed. Jack Mezirow (San Francisco: Jossey-Bass, 2000), 3–33; list of ideal conditions on 13–14.
3. Mezirow, *Transformative Dimensions*, 207.
4. Ibid., 80.
5. Ibid., 82–83.
6. Ibid., 215.
7. Ibid., 44.

## NOTES TO APPENDIX 6: SOCIAL DISCERNMENT AND THEORY U: A CASE OF SIMULTANEITY

1. The term "simultaneity" came to the Social Discernment Cycle through Peter Henriot's work on the Pastoral Circle, further undergirded by the theological perspective of Karl Rahner. See, in particular, Peter Henriot, "Spiritual Direction and Social Consciousness," in

*Soundings* (Washington, DC: Center of Concern, 1973), 13. John Mostyn, CFC, writes extensively about the process of coming to "see" simultaneity operative in the spiritual direction process and defines simultaneity as "the existential connection within the person of the grace that occurs in any arenas [of experience]. Once grace occurs in one arena, it is present in all." See John H. Mostyn, "The Reforming Spirit of God Simultaneously Shaping Person and Society: Implications for Training Spiritual Directors" (dissertation/project in partial fulfillment of DMin requirements, San Francisco Theological Seminary, 1996), 182. The creators of Theory U, following Carl Jung, use the term "synchronicity" to refer to the simultaneous occurrence of the same phenomenon in different places at the same time, apparently unconnected to each other. Simultaneity and synchronicity share the notion of "existing at the same time."

2.  See John H. Mostyn, "Transforming Institutions: God's Call—A Director's Response," in *Tending the Holy: Spiritual Direction across Traditions*, ed. Norveen Vest (Harrisburg, PA: Morehouse Publishing, 2003), 148–69, for Jack's description of this process.

3.  For a concise summary of Theory U, see C. Otto Scharmer, *Theory U: Leading from the Future as It Emerges; The Social Technology of Presencing* (Cambridge, MA: Society for Organizational Learning, 2007), chap. 15. For numerous illustrations of the Theory U dynamic, search for "Theory U" at https://images.google.com/,

4.  See Ana Cristina Campos Marques, "Theory U — Part 2," at http://sustainabilitythinking.wordpress.com/2011/10/08/theory-u-part-2/ and elsewhere for this diagram.

5.  See, for example, Scharmer, *Theory U*, chaps. 12–14 and 21, where he discusses such strategies as prototyping, crystallizing, forming focus groups, and engaging in rapid cycle learning.

6.  Peter Senge, C. Otto Scharmer, Joseph Jaworski, and Betty Sue Flowers, *Presence: Human Purpose and the Field of the Future* (Cambridge, MA: Society for Organizational Learning, 2004), 236.

7.  The reference to parts is based on Donella Meadows's distinction between a system and "a bunch of stuff." A system exhibits at least the first three of the following four points: "Can you identify parts? *and* Do the parts affect each other? *and* Do the parts together produce an effect that is different from the effect of each part on its own? *and perhaps* Does the effect, the behavior over time, persist in a variety of circumstances?" See *Thinking in Systems: A Primer*, ed. Diana Wright (White River Junction, VT: Chelsea Green Publishing, 2008), 13 (italics added).

8.  Lee E. Snook, *What in the World is God Doing? Re-Imagining Spirit and Power* (Minneapolis: Fortress Press, 1999), describes this perspectival issue as a failure of imagination. See, in particular, chap. 1.

9.  Compare Scharmer's religiously neutral practice in *Theory U*, 403.

10.  Ibid., 380, 424.

11.  Ibid., 391, 395, 397.

12.  Otto Scharmer and Katrin Kaufer, *Leading from the Emerging Future: From Ego-System to Eco-System Economies; Applying Theory U to Transforming Business, Society and Self* (San Francisco: Berrett-Koehler, 2013), chap. 4.

13.  See, for example, the Theory U analogue faith sharing groups in Scharmer, *Theory U*, 412.

# Further Reading

## PERSONAL AND GROUP DISCERNMENT

Au, Wilkie, and Noreen Cannon Au. *The Discerning Heart: Exploring the Christian Path* New York: Paulist Press, 2006.

Barton, Ruth Haley. *Pursuing God's Will Together: A Discernment Practice for Leadership Groups*. Downers Grove, IL.: IVP Books, 2012.

Bieber, Nancy L. *Decision Making and Spiritual Discernment: The Sacred Art of Finding Your Way*. Woodstock, VT: Skylight Paths, 2012.

Brackley, Dean. *The Call to Discernment in Troubled Times. New Perspectives on the Transformative Wisdom of Ignatius of Loyola*. New York: Crossroad Publishing, 2004.

Dougherty, Rose Mary. *Discernment: A Path to Spiritual Awakening*. Mahwah, NJ: Paulist Press, 2009.

Farnham, Suzanne G., Joseph Gill, R. Taylor McLean, and Susan Ward. *Listening Hearts: Discerning Call in Community*. Rev. ed. Harrisburg, PA: Morehouse Publishing, 1991.

Farrington, Debra. *Hearing with the Heart: A Gentle Guide to Discerning God's Will for Your Life*. San Francisco: Jossey-Bass, 2003.

Funk, Mary Margaret. *Discernment Matters: Listening with the Ear of the Heart*. Collegeville, MN: Liturgical Press, 2013.

Gallagher, Timothy. *Discernment of Spirits: An Ignatian Guide for Everyday Living*. New York: Crossroad Publishing, 2005.

_____. *Spiritual Consolation: An Ignatian Guide for the Greater Discernment of Spirits*. New York: Crossroad Publishing, 2007.

Libanio, J. B. *Spiritual Discernment and Politics: Guidelines for Religious Communities*. Maryknoll, NY: Orbis Books, 1977. Reprint, Eugene, OR: Wipf & Stock Publishers, 2003.

Liebert, Elizabeth. *The Way of Discernment: Spiritual Practices for Decision Making*. Louisville, KY: Westminster John Knox Press, 2008.

Morris, Danny E., and Charles Olsen. *Discerning God's Will Together: A Spiritual Practice for the Church*. Nashville: Upper Room Books, 1997.

Nouwen, Henri. *Discernment: Reading the Signs of Daily Life*. Edited by Michael J. Christensen and Rebecca J. Laird. San Francisco: Harper One, 2013.

Palmer, Parker. *Let Your Life Speak: Listening for the Voice of Vocation*. San Francisco: Jossey-Bass, 2000.

Smith, Gordon T. *Listening to God in Times of Choice: The Art of Discerning God's Will.* Downers Grove, IL: InterVarsity Press, 1997.

Wolff, Pierre. *Discernment: The Art of Choosing Well; Based on Ignatian Spirituality.* Liguori, MO: Triumph Books, 1993. Rev. ed. 2003.

## THEOLOGICAL FOUNDATIONS

Dorr, Donal. *Spirituality and Justice.* Maryknoll, NY: Orbis Books, 1984.

Fernandez, Eleazar. *Reimagining the Human: Theological Anthropology in Response to Systemic Evil.* St. Louis: Chalice Press, 2004.

Groody, Daniel G. *Globalization, Spirituality, and Justice: Navigating a Path to Peace.* Maryknoll, NY: Orbis Books, 2007.

Hahnenberg, Edward P. *Awakening Vocation: A Theology of Christian Call.* Collegeville, MN: Liturgical Press, 2010.

McIntosh, Mark A. *Discernment and Truth: The Spirituality of Knowledge.* New York: Crossroad, 2004.

_____. *Mystical Theology.* Malden, MA: Blackwell, 1998.

Snook, Lee E. *What in the World is God Doing? Re-Imagining Spirit and Power.* Minneapolis: Fortress, 1999.

Waaijman, Kees. *Spirituality: Forms, Foundations, Methods.* Dudley, MA: Peeters, 2002.

Wink, Walter. *The Powers That Be: Theology for a New Millennium.* New York: Doubleday, 1998.

_____. *Walter Wink: Collected Readings.* Edited by Henry French. Minneapolis: Fortress, 2013.

## SOCIAL SCIENCES, SYSTEMS, AND SYSTEM THINKING

Benefiel, Margaret. *Soul at Work: Spiritual Leadership in Organizations.* New York: Seabury, 2005.

Graves, Mark. *Mind, Brain and the Elusive Soul: Human Systems of Cognitive Science and Religion.* Burlington, VT: Ashgate Publishing, 2008.

Holland, Joe, and Peter Henriot. *Social Analysis: Linking Faith and Justice.* Rev. ed. Maryknoll, NY: Orbis Books, 1983.

Kahane, Adam. *Solving Tough Problems: An Open Way of Talking, Listening, and Creating New Realities.* San Francisco: Berrett-Koehler, 2004.

Meadows, Donella H. *Thinking in Systems: A Primer.* Edited by Diana Wright. White River Junction, VT: Chelsea Green Publishing, 2008.

Scharmer, C. Otto. *Theory U: Leading from the Future as It Emerges; The Social Technology of Presencing.* Cambridge, MA: Society for Organizational Learning, 2007.

Senge, Peter. *The Fifth Discipline: The Art and Practice of the Learning Organization.* New York: Doubleday/Currency, 1990.

Senge, Peter, C. Otto Scharmer, Joseph Jaworski, and Betty Sue Flowers. *Presence: Human Purpose and the Field of the Future.* Cambridge, MA: Society for Organizational Learning, 2004.

Watzlawick, Paul, John Weakland, and Richard Fisch. *Change: Principles of Problem Formation and Problem Resolution.* New York: W. W. Norton, 1974.

Wijsen, Frans, Peter Henriot, and Rodrigo Mejía, eds. *The Pastoral Circle Revisited: A Critical Quest for Truth and Transformation.* Maryknoll, NY: Orbis Books, 2005.

CPSIA information can be obtained
at www.ICGtesting.com
Printed in the USA
BVOW10s1137161217
502929BV00016B/288/P